Parliaments and Legislatures

Janet M. Box-Steffensmeier and David T. Canon, Series Editors

THE LOGIC OF PRE-ELECTORAL COALITION FORMATION

Sona Nadenichek Golder

The Ohio State University Press
Columbus

Library of Congress Cataloging-in-Publication Data

Golder, Sona Nadenichek.
The logic of pre-electoral coalition formation / Sona Nadenichek Golder.
    p. cm.—(Parliaments and legislatures)
Includes bibliographical references and index.
ISBN 0–8142–1029–5 (cloth : alk. paper)—ISBN 0–8142–9115–5 (cd-rom)
1. Electoral coalitions. I. Title. II. Series: Parliaments and legislatures series
JF2112.E44G65 2006
324.2'1—dc22
                    2006008849

Paper (ISBN: 978-0-8142-5721-0)

Type set in Adobe Garamond.

To my parents,

Jim and Nancy Nadenichek

CONTENTS

ILLUSTRATIONS

Figures

Tables

PREFACE

In this book, I investigate the conditions under which pre-electoral coalitions form. In most democracies, political parties who wish to exercise executive power are typically forced to enter some form of coalition. In effect, they can either form a pre-electoral coalition with another party (or parties) prior to election in the hopes of governing together afterward if successful at the polls, or they can compete independently and hope to form a government coalition after the election. The fact that coalition government is the norm rather than the exception across the world has encouraged a vast coalition literature to develop in political science. The overwhelming majority of this literature focuses purely on government coalitions. By contrast, electoral coalitions are virtually ignored. This lack of literature is surprising, given that pre-electoral coalitions are common, that they affect election outcomes, and that they have important policy and normative implications. I redress this imbalance in our knowledge of coalitions by focusing on pre-electoral coalitions in this book. I use a combination of methodological approaches (game theoretic, qualitative, and quantitative) to explain why pre-electoral coalitions form in some circumstances, but not in others.

I argue that there is a common underlying logic to the formation of pre-electoral coalitions that can be captured in a simple bargaining model between party leaders who care about office and policy. Using a two-stage bargaining game, I derive several hypotheses relating the likelihood of pre-electoral coalition formation to institutional and ideological features of the party system. I use in-depth qualitative analyses of electoral coalition history in France and in South Korea to provide support for the model's assumptions and hypotheses. I also subject the hypotheses to a more systematic statistical analysis using a new data set on pre-electoral coalitions in advanced industrialized democracies. I find that pre-electoral coalitions are more likely to form between ideologically compatible parties. They are also more likely to form when the expected coalition size is large (but not too large) and when the potential coalition partners are similar in size. They are also more likely to form if the party system is ideologically polarized and the electoral rules are disproportional.

Although party leaders often form electoral coalitions to win more votes and seats, the effects of pre-electoral coalitions do not end once the votes have been counted and legislative seats have been allocated. After presenting my explanation of pre-electoral coalition formation, I begin to link my analysis to the larger government coalition literature by showing how pre-electoral agreements affect several aspects of government coalitions in advanced industrialized democracies. I find that pre-electoral agreements increase the likelihood that a party will enter into government, they increase the ideological compatibility of governments, and they increase the speed with which governments take office.

In addition to these generally positive consequences, I argue throughout the book that pre-electoral coalitions provide an opportunity for combining the best elements of the majoritarian vision of democracy (increased accountability, transparency, government identifiability, and mandates) with the best elements of the proportional vision of democracy (wide choice, more accurate reflection of voter preferences in both the legislature and government). If this is a desirable goal, as I believe it should be, then the analyses conducted in this book show that political actors can encourage pre-electoral coalition formation by manipulating the electoral rules. As I clearly indicate, though, the actual effect of this manipulation will depend on the size of the party system and the ideological nature of political competition in each country.

I maintain a website for this book. On the website you will find a detailed codebook, as well as all the data and computer code necessary to replicate the results and figures in this book. The current URL is http://www.fsu.edu/~polisci/people/faculty/sgolder.htm. Please contact me if you have any comments, questions, or quibbles concerning the data or any of the analyses. It is my hope that other scholars will pursue the study of pre-electoral coalitions and improve our knowledge beyond what I have provided in this preliminary study—the study of electoral coalitions provides a fertile terrain for the opportunistic researcher.

ACKNOWLEDGMENTS

I am grateful to the many people who contributed time, energy, and constructive criticism to this book. The Politics Department at NYU provided a challenging and supportive graduate work environment and I cannot possibly speak highly enough of my experience there. If I had not been fortunate enough to work with Bill Clark, Mike Gilligan, Jonathan Nagler, Bing Powell, and Alastair Smith on the first stage of this project, I would have written an entirely different—and markedly inferior—book. Constant interactions over several years with Bill Clark made me a better social scientist, and the book reflects this in ways that are too numerous to itemize here. Jonathan Nagler's patience with questions and multiple drafts of every part of the book is also much appreciated; certainly the analysis, as well as its presentation, would be much less clear and informative without his countless suggestions on matters both large and small. I am lucky to have benefited as well from Bing Powell's enthusiasm, his knowledge of pre-electoral coalitions, and his willingness to serve on a dissertation committee outside his own university.

In addition to the members of my dissertation committee mentioned above, I owe a debt of gratitude to many scholars who provided feedback, data, or other useful information at various stages of this project. I thank John Aldrich, Neal Beck, Torbjörn Bergman, Steve Brams, Fred Boehmke, Jamie Druckman, Mark Hallerberg, Anna Harvey, Indriði Indriðason, Chris Kam, Marek Kaminski, Wonik Kim, Skip Lupia, Bernard Manin, Becky Morton, Adam Przeworski, Marty Schain, Chuck Shipan, Jeff Staton, and Paul Warwick. The anonymous reviewers of this book manuscript were unusually constructive in their criticisms and I thank them for the effort they put into improving the book. Malcolm Litchfield at The Ohio State University Press has been encouraging and enthusiastic throughout all of our interactions, including after finding out that I was expecting a baby a month before the final manuscript was due. I am grateful to Michael Lewis-Beck for providing me with a visiting position at the University of Iowa, which allowed me to spend the 2004–5 academic year revising this book and enjoying the collegial working environment in the Iowa political science department; I thank Fred Boehmke, Sara Mitchell, and Chuck Shipan for being especially welcoming. Parts of the analysis in chapter 3 are based on a similar study published in *Electoral Studies* (2005) under the title "Pre-Electoral Coalitions in Comparative Perspective: A Test of Existing Hypotheses." I thank Elsevier for permission to reprint the material here. Part of the analysis in chapter 6 was published in the *British Journal of Political Science* (2006) under the title "Pre-Electoral Coalition Formation in Parliamentary Democracies." I thank Cambridge University Press for permission to reprint this material.

The initial puzzle that sparked this entire project was based on my experiences as an intern in the French National Assembly during the 1995 presidential campaign. I was curious about the relationship between the two mainstream Right parties after seeing that both were internally divided over which of the two mainstream Right presidential candidates to support. The odd thing was that the two candidates proposed by the mainstream Right were from the same party, and the choice of which one to support seemed to be unrelated to party affiliation or policy. In fact, I was unable to find anyone at the National Assembly who could explain what the policy differences between the two parties were. Partway through graduate school I returned to this puzzle, wondering why the parties remained separate when their policy agendas were so similar and when their failures to coordinate could sometimes have disastrous electoral consequences. Around this time, I ran into my undergraduate thesis advisor, Daniel Verdier, at an APSA meeting. After I attempted to explain my inchoate dissertation idea to him, he immediately restated the question in terms of why parties form electoral coalitions. His reframing of my project was much more elegant than anything I was able to articulate at the time, and it gave me a clearer idea of how to proceed. It certainly wasn't the first time he had clarified my muddled ideas. Indeed, his willingness to provide round after round of criticisms of my undergraduate thesis—thereby improving it beyond all recognition—had an enormous influence on my decision to go to graduate school in political science.

I should mention two other teachers who played a significant role in my intellectual development. John Thompson was my biology teacher during my freshman year in high school and steered me toward the Illinois Mathematics and Science Academy, a new school then being set up by the state of Illinois. At IMSA I acquired a good background in math and science, which has been extremely important for my training as a political scientist. While at IMSA I also had the good fortune to meet Elia Lopez, who taught me French. The background in math, science, and foreign language that I received at IMSA set the stage for productive college and graduate studies. The influence of both John and Elia (whom I now consider to be family) goes beyond the disciplines they initially taught; both are outstanding teachers and I hope that some of their enthusiasm and technique is reflected in my own teaching.

I have saved my most important debts for last. I rely on the constant support and encouragement from my wonderful family: my parents, my brother Jon, my sister-in-law Rosanne, my 'new' English family, and my irresistibly adorable nephews Edward and Joseph. Of course, I owe the largest debt of gratitude to my best friend and husband Matt Golder, who has influenced every part of this book. He has always been willing to debate ideas and read multiple drafts of everything I write. I am especially grateful for his help with the final revisions of the book manuscript, completed under two rather pressing deadlines, one imposed by the editor and the other by the impending birth of our son Sean.

CHAPTER ONE

Introduction

Prior to the 2002 German legislative election, the Social Democrats and the Greens reached a pre-electoral agreement announcing that they intended to form a government together if they received sufficient votes at the polls and encouraged voters to support their coalition. In the French legislative elections a few months earlier, the major parties on both the left and right were largely successful in forming pre-electoral coalitions of their own. Doing so typically meant fielding single candidates from the left or right in each electoral district. Yet in the French presidential elections that same year, the absence of pre-electoral agreements on the left and on the right allowed an extreme-right candidate, Jean-Marie Le Pen, into the final round of the presidential elections, an event the world press described as "a political earthquake." Meanwhile, in the Dutch legislative elections, all of the political parties ran independent electoral campaigns, and there was a great deal of uncertainty as to the likely identity of the future coalition government up to and immediately following the legislative elections. These empirical observations raise the question as to why pre-electoral coalitions formed in Germany but not in the Netherlands, and why they formed in some French elections but not others. More generally, why do some parties coordinate their electoral strategies as part of a pre-electoral coalition, whereas others choose to compete independently at election time?

In most democracies, single parties are unable to command a majority of support in the legislature. Thus, political parties who wish to exercise executive power are typically forced to enter some form of coalition. In effect, they can either form an electoral coalition with another party (or parties) prior to an election, or they can compete independently at election time and form a government coalition afterwards. For the purposes of this study, 'electoral' or 'pre-electoral' coalitions are defined fairly broadly to include cases where party leaders announce to the electorate that they plan to form a government together if successful at the polls or if they agree to run under a single name with joint lists or nomination agreements.[1]

The common link between these situations is that parties or party leaders in a pre-electoral coalition never compete in elections as truly independent entities. The fact that coalition government is the norm rather than the exception across the world has encouraged a vast literature to develop in political science. The overwhelming majority of this theoretical and empirical literature focuses purely on government coalitions; electoral coalitions are virtually ignored. This book seeks to redress this imbalance in our knowledge of coalitions by focusing on pre-electoral coalitions; specifically, it aims to explain electoral coalition formation at the national level. Although parties may form pre-electoral coalitions for several reasons, the theoretical and empirical analyses conducted in this book focus primarily on electoral coalitions between parties whose goal is to enter government. By concentrating on national-level efforts to enter government, my analyses of pre-electoral coalition formation can be directly connected with the existing government coalition literature.

Understanding the formation of electoral coalitions is important because (i) they can have a considerable impact on election outcomes, government composition, and policies; (ii) they have important normative implications for the representative nature of government; and (iii) they are quite common. Consider the following simple example. Imagine a legislative election with single-member districts in which there are two blocs of parties, one on the left and one on the right. The right-wing bloc has more electoral support than the Left. Suppose the parties on the left form an electoral coalition and field a common candidate in each district, but the parties on the right compete independently. The Right would most likely lose in this situation. In this example, the possibility arises that a majority of voters could vote for a group of politicians who support similar policies and that these politicians might still lose the election by failing to coordinate sufficiently.[2] The result is that the left-wing party is elected to implement policies that a majority of the voters do not want. In other words, the absence of a pre-electoral coalition on the right can have a significant impact on the election outcome, on the government that forms, and on the policies that are likely to be implemented. Inasmuch as one places a normative value on the basic principle that the candidate with the most support among the electorate should be elected and should implement policy, it matters whether political elites choose electoral strategies and coalitions that make them more or less likely to win elections.

Coalition strategies employed by political parties also have important normative implications for the representative nature of governments. Powell (2000) distinguishes between majoritarian and proportional representation visions of democratic government. In the majoritarian vision, a party with a majority or plurality of the vote wins the election and governs the country until the next election. In this situation, members of the electorate know that their votes directly influence which party exerts executive power and implements policy. In the proportional representation vision, this is not necessarily the case, since coalition governments often form after the votes have been counted, beyond the scrutiny of the electorate. In effect, elections in proportional systems "serve primarily as devices for electing representative agents in postelection bargaining processes, rather than as devices for choosing a specific executive" (Huber 1996, 185). As a result, the lines of accountability are blurred, and it is unclear how well voter preferences are reflected in the government that is ultimately formed.

To some extent, pre-electoral coalitions can alleviate this problem by helping voters to identify government alternatives and to register their support for one of them. In fact, party leaders in the Netherlands, Ireland, and Germany have made this type of argument publicly in order to explain their participation in electoral coalitions and in an attempt to appeal to voters (Saalfeld 2000; Mitchell 1999; Klingemann, Hofferbert, & Budge 1994; De Jong & Pijnenburg 1986). Arguably, electoral coalitions increase democratic transparency and provide coalition governments with as much of a mandate as single parties in majoritarian systems. In fact, one might even say that pre-electoral coalitions provide an opportunity for combining the best elements of the majoritarian vision of democracy (increased accountability, transparency, government identifiability, strong mandates) with the best elements of the proportional representation vision of democracy (wide choice, more accurate reflection of voter preferences in the legislature). Given the important implications for the representative nature of government, one might want to know the conditions under which pre-electoral coalitions form.

Finally, electoral coalitions are not rare phenomena. There were 240 pre-electoral coalitions between 1946 and 2002 in the 23 advanced industrialized parliamentary democracies at the center of this book. Significantly, 70 (29.2%) of these 240 pre-electoral coalitions actually went on to form the government following the election. This number would be even higher if I also counted governments that contained electoral coalitions along with additional government partners. One hundred seventy-four (47.8%) of the 364 legislative elections between 1946 and 2002 had at least one pre-electoral coalition. Thus, about one-fifth (19.2%) of all the elections examined in this book produced a government that was based on a pre-electoral agreement. Again, this number would be even higher if I counted governments that comprised an electoral coalition along with other parties. A recent study of formal government coalition agreements in Western European parliamentary democracies concluded that when all coalition cabinets were considered, many had an "identifiable coalition agreement," and more than one-third were written *prior* to the election (Strøm & Müller 2000). Naturally, this study did not pick up all instances of electoral coalitions—it obviously omits all electoral coalitions that did not make it into government. However, it does serve to reinforce the point that coalition bargaining often occurs prior to elections in a wide range of countries and that a large proportion of government coalitions are based on pre-electoral agreements. The strong empirical link found between pre-electoral and government coalitions suggests that if we think that understanding government coalitions is important, which the vast literature on this subject suggests is the case, then it must logically follow that understanding pre-electoral coalitions is important, as well.

Despite these strong reasons for studying electoral coalitions, current research has almost nothing to say about them. Those quantitative analyses and formal models of coalition behavior that exist are typically used to predict which government coalition will form (Baron & Ferejohn 1989; Laver & Shepsle 1990; Austen-Smith & Banks 1990; Baron 1991; Strøm, Budge, & Laver 1994; Diermeier & Merlo 2004), who gets which portfolio (Warwick & Druckman 2001), how long the formation process takes (Diermeier & van Roozendaal 1998; Martin & Vanberg 2003), and how long the government coalition will last (King et al. 1990; Warwick 1994; Lupia & Strøm 1995; Merlo 1997; Warwick 1999; Diermeier & Stevenson 1999; Diermeier, Eraslan, & Merlo 2003). In other words, they focus almost entirely on government coalitions.[3] There are simply no formal models of government coalitions that incorporate the possibility of electoral coalitions. Pre-electoral coalitions are almost entirely absent in the quantitative literature, as well.[4] Only in the case study literature do references to pre-electoral coalitions crop up with any semblance of regularity. Even among those scholars who address electoral coalitions here, the primary interest is not in studying the pre-election stage of electoral competition as such; electoral coalitions are typically treated purely as an interesting aside (Strøm, Budge, & Laver 1994; Laver & Schofield 1998; Müller & Strøm 2000*b*; Strøm & Müller 2000). To this point, there has been no systematic, cross-national research focused on electoral coalitions.[5]

Given the prevalence of electoral coalitions and their potential normative and policy implications, I believe that this lack of focused research represents a serious omission in our knowledge of coalitions. In fact, this state of affairs has led G. Bingham Powell to claim in the conclusion to his highly influential book, *Elections as Instruments of Democracy*, that

> One area that cries out for more serious theoretical and empirical work is the appearance of announced preelectoral coalitions between political parties. We know too little about the origins of such coalitions and about the great variety of forms (shared manifestos, withdrawal of coalition partners, recommendations to voters) that they can take. But in a number of countries such coalitions unmistakably play a critical role at both electoral and legislative levels. (Powell 2000, 247)

My book begins to answer Powell's appeal by examining the conditions under which electoral coalitions form.

This research objective presupposes the existence of a common underlying logic to the formation of pre-electoral coalitions. To some extent, this objective represents a new approach to analyzing these coalitions. As I mentioned earlier, the limited research that already exists on electoral coalitions is often country or election specific. One consequence of this fact is the emphasis placed on factors that are idiosyncratic to particular countries, elections, or party leaders. For example, the inability of the moderate right in France to form electoral coalitions in certain elections has frequently been explained in terms of the personal animosities or plain "stupidity" of party leaders (Bell 2000; Goldey 1999; Knapp 1999; Nay 1994). While the country-specific research is both important and highly informative, it does not offer us a general theory for explaining why electoral coalitions form in some circumstances but not in others. I seek to provide such a theory here.

As with government coalition formation, the emergence of pre-electoral coalitions is the result of a bargaining process among party leaders. For example, party leaders who wish to form a pre-electoral coalition must reach agreement over a joint electoral strategy and the distribution of office benefits that might accrue to them. This process may involve outlining a common coalition platform; deciding which party gets to run the more powerful ministerial posts; choosing which party's candidates should step down in favor of candidates from their coalition partner(s) in particular districts; or determining which leader is to become prime minister. Clearly, any pre-electoral coalition bargaining process involves a thorny set of distributional and ideological issues. Ultimately, party leaders must weigh the incentives to form an electoral coalition against the incentives to run independently.

Before elaborating on these incentives, it is worth noting that the pre-electoral coalition formation process is not quite the same as the government coalition formation process. First, electoral advantages that come from competing together as a coalition, particularly in countries with disproportional electoral rules, will create incentives to form an electoral coalition that are no longer relevant in the post-election context. Put differently, forming a government coalition cannot influence the probability of electoral victory; electoral coalitions can. Second, the ideological compatibility constraint facing potential coalitions is likely to be stronger prior to the election than afterwards. This likelihood is because voters might be unwilling to vote for electoral coalitions comprising parties with incompatible policy preferences; after the election, parties have more leeway to enter into these types of government coalitions, because voters are no longer such an immediate constraint on politicians' actions. My point here is only that it would be a mistake to immediately assume that the factors that have been found to be important in the government coalition bargaining process will turn out to be the same factors that shape pre-electoral coalition formation.

The logic of electoral coalition formation that I present is based on the belief that party leaders care about winning office and policy (Müller & Strøm 1999). Party leaders must compare the utility that they expect to receive if they competed independently to the utility that they expect to receive if they competed as part of an electoral coalition. Consider first the case where party i decides to run independently. In this scenario, the party may be sufficiently successful at the polls that it gets to enter government. If the party wins more than 50% of the seats, it could form a government on its own. In this situation, the party would obtain all of the office benefits associated with being in power and could set policy at its own ideal point. Clearly, this would be the first choice for party i. However, party i will recognize that it is relatively rare for a single party to control a majority of the seats in most parliamentary systems. If party i is to enter government, then it is much more likely to do so as part of a government coalition. In this case, party i would receive some utility from its share of the office benefits and would suffer some utility loss from having government policy set at the ideal point of the coalition rather than at its own ideal point. Naturally, the utility loss suffered by each coalition partner would be lower the more ideologically compatible the government coalition. Finally, party i will know that there is some probability that it will not get to enter government if it runs independently. If this situation arises, then it will receive no office benefits and will suffer the utility loss associated with having the government set policy at the government ideal point and not at party i's ideal point. The lowest possible utility for party i from running independently would occur if it was in opposition and government policy was ideologically distant from its own ideal point.

The second case is when party i decides to run as part of an electoral coalition. Note that in order to form a pre-electoral coalition, it is likely that party i will need to make some concessions in terms of policy and office to its potential coalition partners. For example, it is highly unlikely that party i would get to set the coalition policy exactly at its own ideal point and/or obtain all of the office benefits if the electoral coalition entered government. These concessions are essentially the exact same concessions that parties that run independently would have to make when forming a government coalition after the election. Arguably, these concessions may be more costly to make prior to an election than afterwards. This possibility is because any concessions that must be made to other parties in terms of ministerial posts or coalition policies after an election can more easily be presented to party members as a consequence of the votes cast by the electorate; if the concessions occur before an election, they can only be blamed on the party leadership. Given this idea, one might reasonably wonder why parties do not simply wait until after the election to make these concessions. Indeed, in many elections, this is precisely what happens.

However, the key thing to note about pre-electoral coalitions is that they can affect the probability that a party gets to enter government. Recognizing this fact, party leaders will form a pre-electoral coalition if they think that doing so will increase their probability of entering government to such an extent that the expected utility from forming such a coalition is larger than the expected utility from running independently. There are several reasons why pre-electoral coalitions might be electorally advantageous.[6] First, it may be the case that an electoral coalition would attract a higher number of votes or seats than the coalition parties would jointly win running independently.[7] This situation might occur if voters are risk averse in regard to the policy positions of potential future governments; that is, they prefer being able to identify a government alternative to being faced with a lottery over possible government outcomes, even if the mean expected policy position in both cases is identical. The lottery over possible government outcomes is less desirable, because the variance in possible policy positions is greater (Enelow & Hinich 1981; Snyder & Ting 2002; Ashworth & Bueno de Mesquita 2006). By decreasing voter uncertainty over which government coalition might form and thus which policy would get implemented, the parties that form a pre-electoral coalition might attract more votes than would otherwise be the case.

Second, and probably more important, is the strong empirical evidence that disproportional electoral institutions provide an electoral bonus to large parties or coalitions through their mechanical effect on the translation of votes into seats (Duverger 1963 [1954]; Lijphart 1994; Cox 1997; Clark & Golder 2006). Since all electoral systems are disproportional to some extent, electoral coalitions may hold out significant advantages in terms of extra legislative seats. Although we do not yet have an entirely satisfactory model of how particular distributions of legislative seats get translated into government coalitions, it seems reasonable to think that these extra legislative seats will be positively correlated with an increased probability of being in government. If this is the case, then party leaders will have an incentive to form pre-electoral coalitions.

To sum up, I hope to generate a wider scholarly debate about the role played by electoral coalitions at election time. Pre-electoral coalitions are important. Not only are they commonplace, but they also have the ability to determine electoral and policy outcomes. They may even be preferable on normative grounds to government coalitions that are not based on an electoral agreement. As a result, they deserve more attention from researchers. In the chapters that follow, I develop a theoretical model of electoral coalition formation and expose the hypotheses that it generates to statistical and case study analyses. In an attempt to link these analyses with the existing coalition literature, I also begin to examine how the decision

to form an electoral coalition affects various characteristics of government coalitions. This research represents the first attempt to formally analyze those factors
that systematically influence the emergence of pre-electoral coalitions across elections and countries. The empirical analysis also represents the first time that data
on electoral coalitions across such a large number of countries have been collected
and analyzed.

The book proceeds in the following way. In the next chapter, I discuss in more
detail how I define and identify pre-electoral coalitions. In addition to stating my
coding rules and addressing several ambiguous cases, I also describe some of the
different forms that electoral coalitions take in various countries and briefly summarize the data used in the rest of the book. In chapter three, I examine two
hypotheses that are implicitly made in the existing coalition literature regarding
pre-electoral coalitions. The first states that pre-electoral coalitions should be more
common in disproportional electoral systems (Disproportionality Hypothesis).
The second hypothesis focuses on the electorate's desire to be able to identify
future governments (Signaling Hypothesis). I test these hypotheses using data on
pre-electoral coalitions in 23 advanced industrialized parliamentary democracies
between 1946 and 2002. The data support a modified version of the
Disproportionality Hypothesis—disproportional electoral rules do encourage pre-
electoral coalition formation, but only so long as the number of parties in the system is sufficiently large. There is no evidence for the Signaling Hypothesis.

While electoral institutions are clearly an important determinant of electoral
coalition formation, I argue in the conclusion to chapter three that the implication
in the coalition literature that pre-electoral coalitions are a simple function of electoral rules is probably too reductionist. I claim that a more nuanced understanding of pre-electoral coalition formation must take account of the distributional
costs in terms of policy and office benefits that arise during coalition bargaining,
as well as the potential electoral benefits. I develop a model of electoral coalition
formation that takes account of these distributional costs in chapter four. The
model is a bargaining game between two party leaders who must decide whether
to form an electoral alliance or not. I derive several implications that relate the
likelihood of pre-electoral coalition formation to various institutional and ideological features of the party system. Of the hypotheses that are generated, the most
important are that electoral coalitions are more likely when the potential coalition
partners share similar ideological preferences; when electoral institutions generate
an electoral bonus for competing as a coalition; when the party's expected share of
office benefits from running alone decreases; when the likelihood of entering government after running alone decreases; and when there is an extreme opposition
and the coalition is electorally beneficial.

In the following chapter, I use a detailed investigation of electoral coalitions in

Fifth Republic France and post-1987 South Korea to illustrate the causal process of pre-electoral coalition formation and the plausibility of my model's assumptions and implications. The unusual nature of the French semi-presidential regime offers an opportunity to examine the impact of different electoral institutions, namely legislative and presidential elections, on pre-electoral strategies while holding other country characteristics constant. Moreover, the French case provides a dramatic example of the impact that pre-electoral coalitions (or their absence) can have on election outcomes. The South Korean case supports the notion that there truly is an underlying general logic of electoral coalition formation. Although France is a country in Western Europe with a well-established democratic pedigree and South Korea is a relatively new democracy in East Asia, similar factors play an influential role in pre-electoral coalition formation in both countries. For example, evidence from both South Korea and France indicate that distributional issues play a significant role in determining the ease with which electoral coalitions form. If these issues can be resolved, then even the most strident and long-held personal animosities among party leaders can be overcome. The South Korean case also provides evidence that my model of electoral coalition formation can be usefully applied to presidential democracies.

In chapter six, I conduct a cross-national statistical analysis of the hypotheses generated by my bargaining model using a data set containing information on potential coalition dyads in 292 legislative elections in 20 advanced industrialized parliamentary democracies between 1946 and 1998. The results provide strong support for all of my hypotheses. Pre-electoral coalitions are more likely to form when parties are ideologically compatible, when the expected coalition size is large (but not too large), and when the potential coalition partners are of similar size. They are also more likely to form if the party system is ideologically polarized and the electoral rules are disproportional.

In the seventh chapter, I begin to link my study of pre-electoral coalition formation more directly with the existing government coalition literature by examining several aspects of the relationship between electoral and government coalitions. I find that electoral coalitions significantly increase the likelihood that member parties enter government; in other words, they affect the identity of government coalitions. I also find that governments that are based on pre-electoral agreements are not only more ideologically compatible than those that are not, but that they also get to take office more quickly. While there are several reasons to think that electoral coalitions might also improve government stability, I find no evidence to support this idea. Overall, the evidence presented in this chapter indicates that the effect of pre-electoral coalitions does not end with the counting of votes and the allocation of legislative seats; electoral coalitions continue to affect important aspects of the government formation process even after elections are over.

In the conclusion, I summarize the theoretical, empirical, and methodological contributions that my study makes to our understanding of electoral coalitions, and I address its normative implications. I also suggest that, although this book represents the first systematic, cross-national analysis to focus on pre-electoral coalitions, a fruitful area of future research would be to develop a more unified approach to government formation that simultaneously incorporates both pre-electoral and government coalitions.

CHAPTER TWO

Identifying Electoral Coalitions

The empirical study of electoral coalitions poses a particular challenge for the researcher. While the identity of government coalitions is typically well documented, the same cannot be said for pre-electoral coalitions. Put simply, it is often quite difficult to determine which, if any, parties actually formed an electoral coalition in a particular election, what the terms of each electoral alliance were, and how successful electoral coalitions were at the polls. The basic problem is that electoral coalitions are not always listed in official election results or on electoral ballots; where they are, they are rarely disaggregated to list their constituent parties. This situation leaves the interested researcher scouring through the vast case study literature that analyzes elections and party competition. The problem is magnified once one realizes that pre-electoral coalitions have rarely been the focus of scholarly attention in these studies. These practical issues may explain why I have failed to locate a detailed database on these coalitions and why there have been no cross-national statistical analyses examining pre-electoral coalition formation prior to this study.[1]

In the appendix at the end of this book, I provide a country-by-country description of the pre-electoral coalitions that I found in the case study literature and the sources used to identify them. The countries include Australia, Austria, Belgium, Canada, Denmark, Finland, France, Germany, Greece, Iceland, Ireland, Israel, Italy, Japan, Luxembourg, Malta, the Netherlands, New Zealand, Norway, Portugal, Spain, Sweden, and the United Kingdom from 1946 to 2002. These countries correspond to the 23 parliamentary democracies most commonly included in government coalition data sets (Mershon 2002). In this chapter, I discuss how I define pre-electoral coalitions and address ambiguous cases, I describe the various forms that electoral coalitions take in different countries, and I provide a brief overview of the data employed in the upcoming analyses.

2.1 Defining Pre-Electoral Coalitions

How do you know a pre-electoral coalition when you see one? There is as yet no accepted definition of electoral coalitions in the existing literature. For the purposes of this book, I define a pre-electoral coalition in the following way:

Definition: A pre-electoral coalition is a collection of parties that do not compete independently in an election, either because they publicly agree to coordinate their campaigns, run joint candidates or joint lists, or enter government together following the election.

There are, of course, finer distinctions that can be made among the various types of electoral coalition. For example, one might argue that coalitions composed of parties with different geographic bases of support are qualitatively different from those composed of parties that typically compete in the same districts. Given the limited research on pre-electoral coalitions to date, though, I prefer to focus in this book on the defining characteristic of a pre-electoral coalition—that parties do not compete independently at election time—rather than on the various ways in which these coalitions can be further disaggregated. The definition shown above employs two objective and observable criteria for identifying pre-electoral coalitions.

Criterion I: An electoral coalition must be publicly stated.

This criterion is important because one of the primary reasons for forming a coalition prior to an election rather than afterwards is to affect voter behavior. While the requirement that electoral coalitions be publicly stated does not necessarily entail that there is an explicit written agreement between the member parties, it does rule out what might be considered 'implicit' coalitions. For example, an outgoing coalition government that is expected to reconstitute itself if given the opportunity might be considered an implicit electoral coalition. The principal problem with including such implicit coalitions in a systematic analysis is that it relies on the subjective evaluation of the analyst as to whether the relevant parties really are coordinating their campaign strategies or not. Moreover, there is no way of knowing if these implicit coalitions would actually have formed the expected government coalitions if they were unsuccessful at the polls. By ruling out these implicit coalitions, I minimize the probability of committing a Type II error when classifying pre-electoral coalitions.

Criterion II: Member parties in an electoral coalition cannot compete in elections as truly independent entities.

This second criterion is fairly inclusive and recognizes that parties can coordinate their electoral strategies in a variety of ways. For example, a coalition strategy might entail merely announcing an intention to govern together if the coalition is successful at the polls, as is sometimes the case in the Netherlands, or it might involve choosing a single coalition candidate to run in each district, as is often the case in France.

While these two criteria help identify pre-electoral coalitions in general, the focus of this book is on national-level electoral coalitions. As a result, I also employed the following criterion when identifying pre-electoral coalitions.

Criterion III: The electoral coalition must be at the national level.

This third criterion means excluding electoral coalitions that compete only in a particular region of a country. In the Spanish case, this definition means that electoral coalitions such as Convergencia i Unió (Convergence and Union), Unidade Galega, the Galician National Popular Block, the Basque Left, and Herri Batasuna (United People) are all omitted from the upcoming analyses (Newton 1997).[2] The third criterion also means excluding several sub-national electoral coalitions in Japan and Finland that were negotiated by local party leaders. Although parties regularly form electoral coalitions to contest mayoral or gubernatorial elections in Japan (Christensen 2000; Johnson 2000), I found evidence for only two national-level electoral coalitions.[3] Local party leaders do sometimes negotiate electoral alliances in various constituencies in Finland, as well. However, "for the most part electoral alliances have been understood simply as technical arrangements which do not structure the bargaining situation. In Finnish elections the parties strive to maximize their parliamentary strength, with government participation in mind; but pre-electoral executive agreements are practically non-existent, and coalition alternatives are not presented to the electorate" (Nousiainen 2000, 270). I found evidence for only three national-level electoral coalitions in Finland.[4] While national-level electoral coalitions did not become commonplace until the Fifth Republic in France, I did find evidence of sub-national coalitions in the Fourth Republic. These sub-national coalitions are not included in the forthcoming analyses, either.

On the whole, it was relatively easy to identify pre-electoral coalitions at the national level using these three criteria. There were only two ambiguous cases of electoral coalition formation in the sample of countries employed in this book.[5] In virtually every pre-electoral coalition that I found, all of the member parties explicitly endorsed the coalition. However, there were two Austrian elections (1986, 1995) in which the Socialist Party announced an intention to govern together with the People's Party. The ambiguity arises because although the People's Party did not publicly reciprocate this announcement, it did not actually reject the proposed coalition, either. I took the absence of a rejection on the part of the People's Party as a tacit endorsement of the proposed pre-electoral coalition. A similar situation occurred in Ireland in 1992, when the Fine Gael leader publicly proposed a pre-electoral coalition with Labour and the Progressive Democrats. However, in this instance, the leader of the Labour Party immediately and publicly rejected the proposed pre-electoral coalition (Mair 1999, 146). Naturally, I do not code this Irish case as an electoral coalition. Although I code the two Austrian cases as pre-electoral coalitions, I should note that my inferences in the following chapters do not depend on this coding decision.

Using the coding rules outlined above, I found evidence of 240 pre-electoral coalitions in the 23 parliamentary democracies studied in this book. While I have done my best to identify all national-level electoral coalitions that formed between 1946 and 2002, I recognize that my data collection efforts are only as good as the sources that I consulted. Given that some country experts address pre-electoral coalitions in more detail than others, one must conclude that I may have missed one or two electoral alliances.

2.2 Data Overview

Table 2.1 presents some basic information about the pre-electoral coalitions examined in this book. The 240 electoral coalitions that I found competed in 364 legislative elections between 1946 and 2002. Only Canada and Malta have had no experience with pre-electoral coalitions at the national level. While some countries such as Japan, the United Kingdom, New Zealand, and Luxembourg have had few electoral coalitions, others such as Australia, France, Germany, Greece, Israel, and Portugal have had many. In fact, pre-electoral coalitions have competed in all Australian elections, 93.3% of Germany's elections, and 90% of Portugal's elections. The electoral success of pre-electoral coalitions shows considerable variation across countries, too. For example, roughly two-thirds of the governments in Australia and France, and one-half of German governments, have been based on pre-electoral alliances. In contrast, none of the pre-electoral coalitions in Iceland, Japan, Luxembourg, and the United Kingdom have ever made it into government. Pre-electoral coalitions have consistently won a large percentage of the vote in countries such as Australia, Austria, France, and Germany. On average, pre-electoral coalitions comprised 2.8 parties. Although most electoral coalitions (62.5%) formed between two parties, some coalitions have been quite large. For example, the Union of the Democratic Center comprised fourteen parties in the 1977 Spanish elections, and the United Camp of the Nationally Minded contained nine parties in the 1946 Greek elections.

Table 2.1
Descriptive Data about Pre-Electoral Coalitions (PECs) by Country

Country	Election Years	# of Elections	# of PECs	% Elections with PECs	% Votes for PECs	Govts. Based on PECs #	Govts. Based on PECs %	Size of PECs
Australia	1946–2001	23	25	100	46.5	15	65.2	2.0
Austria	1949–2002	17	12	58.8	44.7	9	52.9	2.0
Belgium	1946–1999	18	14	61.1	8.1	1	5.6	2.2
Canada	1949–2000	17	—	—	—	—	—	—
Denmark	1947–2001	22	8	36.4	3.6	1	4.5	2.1
Finland	1948–1999	15	3	20.0	6.9	1	6.7	3.3
France	1946–2002	15	23	73.3	59.7	10	66.7	3.0
Germany	1949–2002	15	19	93.3	57.9	8	53.3	2.3
Greece*	1946–2000	19	25	73.7	26.4	4	21.1	3.2
Iceland	1946–1999	17	8	47.1	6.7	0	0	2.4
Ireland	1948–2002	17	9	47.1	24.4	5	29.4	2.4
Israel	1949–1999	15	26	86.7	35.5	0	0	3.5
Italy	1948–2001	14	9	35.7	23.5	2	14.3	4.5
Japan	1947–2000	20	2	5.0	2.4	0	0	3.5
Luxembourg	1954–1999	10	3	30.0	8.5	0	0	2.0
Malta	1966–1998	8	—	—	—	—	—	—
Netherlands	1946–2002	17	8	35.3	19.0	3	17.6	2.6
New Zealand	1946–2002	20	2	10.0	2.6	1	5.0	2.0
Norway	1949–2001	14	9	64.3	23.8	5	35.7	3.2
Portugal	1976–2002	10	14	90.0	24.6	2	20.0	2.6
Spain	1977–2000	8	11	87.5	3.1	1	12.5	4.4
Sweden	1948–2002	18	8	38.9	17.0	2	11.1	2.5
UK	1950–2001	15	2	13.3	3.2	0	0	2.0
TOTAL		364	240			70		2.8

Sources: Listed in the Appendix to this book.
Notes: Table lists (i) the election years included; (ii) the number of legislative elections; (iii) the number of pre-electoral coalitions; (iv) the percentage of elections with pre-electoral coalitions; (v) the average percentage of votes going to pre-electoral coalitions in all elections; (vi) the number and percentage of governments based purely on pre-electoral coalitions (no additional parties); and (vii) the average number of parties in each pre-electoral coalition by country.
* indicates that the years 1968–1973 are not included; — indicates that there were no pre-electoral coalitions.

I should note at this point that there is a difference between the number of pre-electoral coalitions listed in table 2.1 and the number of pre-electoral coalitions that I am able to include in some of my upcoming analyses. This is not an issue in the next chapter, where my empirical analysis includes all of the national-level pre-electoral coalitions in my sample. However, it does become an issue in chapters six and seven, where some of my empirical analyses require information on the ideological position of various parties. The problem arises because my source for information on each party's position in the ideological space—the Campaign Manifesto Research Group (MRG)—occasionally treats electoral coalitions as if they were single parties (Budge et al. 2001). Since all of the pre-electoral coalitions in Greece and Israel are coded as single parties, I am forced to omit Greece and Israel from my analyses in chapters six and seven. I am also forced to drop Malta, because no Maltese party is included in the MRG data set. While a few electoral coalitions between *very small* parties in other countries are also coded as single parties, this particular data constraint may actually be appropriate for my purposes. In practical terms, the very small size of the parties in these few cases suggests that the goal of these pre-electoral coalitions is probably to overcome some threshold of representation, rather than to enter government. Although my theory itself does not require the primary goal of parties that form pre-electoral coalitions to be entry into government, the basic theory, as I present it throughout much of the book, is couched in terms of parties in parliamentary democracies that have an interest in entering government. Thus, it is arguably appropriate that the pre-electoral coalitions included in the empirical analyses conducted in chapters six and seven are formed primarily between parties that are large enough to realistically have an eye toward entering government. In any case, this situation is forced upon me by the constraints of the MRG data set.

2.3 Types of Electoral Coalitions

For the purposes of this book, I distinguish between parties that compete independently at election time (no pre-electoral coalition) and parties that do not compete independently (pre-electoral coalition). As I have already stated, this seems a useful starting point, given the limited nature of the research concerning electoral coalitions that exists at present. However, future research might want to move beyond this simple dichotomy and think more along the lines of a continuum of electoral coordination, with completely separate and independent parties competing in elections at one end of the spectrum, and party mergers at the other end. Different points on this continuum would represent different degrees of electoral coordination. For example, parties that agree to present only one candidate per district in a single-member district electoral system or run candidates on a joint list under a coalition name would represent a relatively high degree of electoral coordination. Parties that ask their electorates to vote for more than one member of an electoral coalition in countries where individuals have multiple votes, or where votes can be transferred to other parties, would represent a middling degree of electoral coordination. Parties that simply announce to the electorate that they hope to form a government coalition after the election would represent a relatively low degree of electoral coordination. The specific form that electoral coordination takes in a particular country is likely to depend on the electoral rules, the regional distribution of the party system, and other factors relating to the relative strengths and ideological positions of different parties. Although I do not distinguish between these different types of electoral coalitions or different degrees of electoral coordination in the upcoming analyses, let me briefly describe some of the more common forms that these coalitions take in the 23 parliamentary democracies at the center of this book.

2.3.1 Nomination Agreements

Nomination agreements between parties represent a relatively high level of electoral coordination on my hypothetical continuum, since they involve parties agreeing to present a coalition candidate in each district rather than each party putting up its own candidate. Such nomination agreements are a typical form of electoral coordination in countries with single-member districts. In France, parties often choose to nominate a single coalition candidate in each district before the first round of elections, or they agree to withdraw their respective candidates in favor of a coalition candidate prior to the second round of voting. For example, the two mainstream right parties (UDF and RPR) in France agreed to put up a single candidate in 385 districts in the first round of the 1981 legislative elections (Bell 2000). In contrast, electoral coalitions between the Socialist and Communist Parties in France do not typically occur in the first round of voting; instead, the parties nearly always agree to compete independently in the first round and then give the best-placed candidate on the left a free-run in the second round. The two national-level pre-electoral coalitions that have occurred in the United Kingdom since 1946 have also involved the use of nomination agreements. In the 1980s, the Liberal Party and the newly-formed Social Democratic Party "recognized that competition between them would be mutually destructive . . . [As a result], they quickly worked out an electoral pact in which constituencies were allocated between the two parties, so that nowhere would they oppose each other. Furthermore, they ran a joint electoral campaign, which, in turn, required some degree of joint policy-making" (Rasmussen 1991, 168).[6]

Nomination agreements have also been employed at various times in Germany, Italy, and New Zealand. During the 1950s in Germany, the Christian Democratic Union (CDU) formed an electoral alliance with the German Party (DP), in which it agreed not to nominate candidates in certain constituencies held by the DP in return for the DP's continued support of Konrad Adenauer as Chancellor. This electoral alliance was crucial to the DP's 'survival' in the 1953 and 1957 legislative elections (Saalfeld 2000, 39). Following the introduction of a new, mixed electoral system, the major Italian parties grouped together into four competing electoral cartels (Progressives, the Pact for Italy, the Freedom Pole, the Pole of Good Government) for the 1994 legislative elections, with the goal of fielding common candidates in each of the single-member constituencies; these same parties ran separate (or joint) lists in the more proportional upper tier (Daniels 1999, 82–84). The only electoral coalition that formed in New Zealand prior to the adoption of a mixed electoral system in 1996 also consisted of a nomination agreement—the New Labour Party agreed to stand in the general seats and allow Mana Motuhake to stand in the Maori seats for the 1990 elections.

2.3.2 Joint Lists

Joint party lists also represent a relatively high level of electoral coordination since they involve parties agreeing to a single list of coalition candidates. Joint party lists are quite common in Israel, where parties typically run under a new coalition name. For example, Maki and Rakah ran as Moked (Focus) in the 1973 Israeli legislative elections, and Labor and Mapam formed an electoral alliance known as Maarach (Alignment) for the 1969 elections. Since Israeli parties tend to run under joint lists when they form electoral alliances, it is often difficult to determine how many votes come from each member's electorate. As a result, Israeli electoral results are often reported as though the electoral coalitions were single parties. Indeed, there are instances where scholars may describe a particular coalition as "a parliamentary bloc, a combination of single parties rather than a single party," yet they later refer to the same coalition as if it were a single party (Akzin 1979). This confusion obviously makes it difficult for any analyst who is trying to identify the existence of electoral coalitions in Israel.[7] Somewhat interestingly, Israeli electoral coalitions are actually treated as single parties for the purposes of determining who is eligible to become the formateur—customarily, the 'party' that wins the largest number of seats in the Knesset [Israeli parliament] becomes the formateur (Elazar 1979). For instance, the Likud coalition of the Liberals and Herut won more votes than did the Alignment coalition of Mapam and Labor in 1977; as a result, Likud took the lead in forming the government.

Electoral coalitions based on joint lists also occur in other countries such as the Netherlands, Portugal, and Greece. For example, the three Christian Democratic parties in the Netherlands—the Catholic People's Party, the Christian Historical Union, and the Anti-Revolutionary Party—formed a joint list under the heading of Christian Democratic Appeal for the 1977 legislative elections. These three parties later merged in 1980 into a single party, the Christian Democratic Accord (Koole 1994; De Swaan 1982). In Portugal, the Portuguese Communist Party formed a joint list with the small Green Party, under the heading of the Unitarian Democratic Alliance, for the 1987 legislative elections, and the Center Social Democrats, the Social Democrats, and the Popular Monarchist Party ran under the single banner of the Democratic Alliance in 1979 (Cunha 1997, 36–37). In Greece, the Christian Democrats, Communist Party-Interior, Socialist Initiative, Socialist March, and U.D. Left formed a joint list under the heading of the Alliance of Progress and Left-Wing Forces for the three legislative elections in 1989 and 1990.

2.3.3 Dual Ballot Instructions

A slightly lower level of electoral coordination often occurs in countries where individuals get to cast two votes in different electoral tiers.[8] In these countries, electoral coalitions often take the form of party leaders telling their supporters to cast one vote for their party, and the second vote for their coalition partner. This type of electoral coalition occurs quite frequently in Germany, where individuals cast one vote for a constituency candidate elected by plurality rule and a second vote for a party list in a multi-member (regional) district. It is usually understood in the German case that the district vote will go to the candidate from the larger coalition member, and the list vote will go to the smaller partner to ensure that the small party passes the 5% electoral threshold. For example, almost two-thirds of the Free Democrats' (FDP) list vote for the 1994 elections came from supporters of its larger coalition partner, the Christian Democratic Union. "With a core support of approximately 3% of the electorate, the FDP has often relied on a substantial share of so-called 'borrowed votes' (*Leihstimmen*) to straddle the 5 per cent threshold and secure its representation in the Bundestag" (Saalfeld 2000, 40). Given that neither of the two largest parties in Germany seems capable of winning an overall majority of seats on its own, the FDP has been courted as an electoral coalition partner by both the Christian and the Social Democrats; indeed, the FDP has formed electoral alliances with both parties over the years.

2.3.4 Vote Transfer Instructions

In countries where voters get to rank their preferences over candidates and preferences are transferable, electoral coalitions often take the form of party leaders telling their supporters to rank their own party first, and a coalition member second. This is a relatively easy request to make of voters compared to asking them to support a single coalition candidate, as party leaders in non-transferable single-ballot systems are forced to do. These vote transfer instructions are similar in many ways to the dual ballot instructions discussed above. For example, parties in Australia often give individuals 'how-to-vote' cards outside polling stations, with clear instructions on how to rank candidates so that the flow of preferences will benefit the party if the party is running separately, or the coalition if a pre-electoral agreement is in place. The National Party and the Liberals in Australia have formed a "nearly permanent" electoral coalition that competes against the Labour Party in every election, with the long-term understanding that if the former gains a majority, they will form a government together (Klingemann, Hofferbert, & Budge 1994).[9] Australia's alternative-vote electoral system "gives much scope to the political parties to control the re-direction of preferences, and it is arguable that preferences [have] controlled the last five federal elections" (McAllister 2003, 382).

The existence of preferential voting in Ireland's more proportional single transferable vote system produces electoral coalitions similar to those in Australia. For example, the electorates of Fine Gael and Labour were instructed to list their preferred party's candidate first and their coalition partner's candidate second when these parties reached a pre-electoral arrangement for several elections during the 1970s and early 1980s. Irish voters pay attention to these instructions, and "[h]igh transfer rates among parties can make all the difference to the distribution of a fairly small number of seats . . . [G]iven that the Dáil [the Irish parliament] is often delicately balanced and governments rarely enjoy sizable majorities (if they have one at all), transfers can make or break a prospective coalition" (Mitchell 1999, 246). Perhaps because vote transfers can play such an important role in determining electoral outcomes in Ireland, the country experts who analyze Irish elections often explicitly address whether or not parties choose to form electoral coalitions.

2.3.5 Public Commitment to Govern Together

Electoral coalitions that simply involve parties publicly announcing their intention to govern together if successful at the polls represent a relatively low level of electoral coordination in comparison to nomination agreements, joint lists, dual ballot instructions, and vote transfer instructions. This type of electoral coalition occurs in many countries such as New Zealand, the Netherlands, and Germany. For example, the Alliance and Labour Party in New Zealand formed a loose electoral coalition stating that they would govern together if they won the elections in 1999 (Vowles 2002). In the Netherlands, the Labor Party (PvdA), Liberal Democrats (D66), and the Radical Party (PPR) formed a pre-electoral coalition for the 1971 and 1973 Dutch elections. These three parties announced that they would govern together if successful at the polls, even though they did not compete under a joint coalition list (Timmermans & Andeweg 2000). In Germany, it is generally understood that the Christian Democratic Union (CDU) and the Christian Social Union (CSU) will work together in parliament and govern together if successful at the polls. Voters never actually get a chance to vote for both parties, since the two parties run in different geographic regions—the CSU in Bavaria, the CDU in the rest of the country. Although the CDU and CSU are often seen as a single party, they should rightfully be considered a two-party electoral coalition, because they have separate party organizations and leadership; they also formally organize themselves as a common parliamentary bloc after each election (Norpoth 1982; Mackie & Rose 1991; Laver & Schofield 1998; Saalfeld 2000).

Interestingly, some parties also make public commitments to *not* govern with certain parties (Strøm, Budge, & Laver 1994; Hillebrand & Irwin 1999; Müller 2000; Müller & Strøm 2000*b*; Narud & Strøm 2000). For example, party leaders in Germany, Austria, Norway, and the Netherlands sometimes announce the parties they will refuse to govern alongside under any circumstances, effectively ruling out certain government cabinet configurations. For example, prior to the 1949 German election, the CSU stated that it would not participate in any government with the Social Democrats or the Bavarian Party. More recently, all parties rejected the possibility of forming a government with the Party of Democratic Socialism (the former Communist party in East Germany) prior to the 1990, 1994, and 1998 elections (Saalfeld 2000, 39). A recent empirical study shows that 'anti-coalition pacts' such as these make it more unlikely that a potential government including these parties will form (Martin & Stevenson 2001).

2.4 Conclusion

While I have tried to make my coding rules as clear as possible, I recognize that other scholars may prefer different coding criteria. Depending on the question being addressed, I can imagine scholars wanting to distinguish between different types of pre-electoral coalitions, such as those based on nomination agreements or joint lists and those based simply on a publicly stated intention to govern together. For the purposes of this book, I employ a fairly inclusive definition of pre-electoral coalitions that ignores, to some extent, the variety of forms that electoral coordination can take. I simply distinguish between parties that publicly coordinate their campaign strategies at the national level (pre-electoral coalitions) and those that do not (no pre-electoral coalitions). I believe that this is a useful starting point for research on electoral alliances. I have no doubt that some country experts will disagree with my reading of the case study literature as it relates to electoral coalitions in their country of expertise. Partly for this reason, my data and codebook are publicly available on my homepage. Analysts should feel free to use these data to further examine the robustness of my results and to begin analyzing the differences between the various types of electoral coalitions. Indeed, as scholars begin to ask different questions about electoral coalitions, such distinctions will be required.

CHAPTER THREE

Existing Theories

3.1 Existing Theories of Pre-Electoral Coalitions

While there has been little systematic investigation of pre-electoral coalitions to this point, it would be misleading to imply that electoral coalitions are never mentioned in the coalition literature. In fact, if one looks carefully enough in the coalition literature one can see that two implicit hypotheses are made regarding pre-electoral coalition formation. The Disproportionality Hypothesis states that pre-electoral coalitions should be more common in disproportional electoral systems. In this case, electoral coalitions are formed as a means of overcoming some barrier of representation. The Signaling Hypothesis focuses on the electorate's desire to be able to identify the nature of future governments. In this case, electoral coalitions act as a signaling device, indicating the likely shape of the post-election government coalition. While the Disproportionality Hypothesis is predominant in the literature, the Signaling Hypothesis tends to be called upon to explain why pre-electoral coalitions sometimes form in highly proportional electoral systems. To date, neither of these hypotheses has been carefully analyzed or tested. In this chapter I examine the theoretical underpinning of each argument in turn, I generate testable hypotheses, and I subject them to statistical analysis using a data set comprising all of the legislative elections between 1946 and 2002 in the 23 parliamentary democracies listed in table 2.1.

3.1.1 Disproportional Electoral Rules

By far the predominant argument in the literature is that disproportional electoral systems encourage pre-electoral coalition formation (Shepsle & Bonchek 1997, 190–91). Strøm, Budge, & Laver (1994, 316) state, "Systems not based on PR [proportional representation] lists tend to force parties to coalesce before elections in order to exploit electoral economies of scale. The more disproportional the electoral system, the greater the incentives for preelectoral alliances." The argument is fairly straightforward. Electoral rules that consistently benefit larger parties should encourage party leaders to forge pre-electoral alliances. While the implicit goal of pre-electoral coalition formation in this argument appears to be to gain more seats, this need not be the main objective of party leaders. If the size of a party in terms of legislative seats is highly correlated with being part of a government coalition or being chosen as formateur, then party leaders in parliamentary systems could increase their chances of being in government by joining an electoral coalition (Laver & Schofield 1998).

This book opened with an empirical puzzle: Why did pre-electoral coalitions form prior to the 2002 legislative elections in Germany and France, but not in the Netherlands? The disproportionality argument outlined here implies that pre-electoral coalitions are a simple function of electoral rules. Thus, the claim would be that pre-electoral agreements were reached in France because of the majoritarian nature of French electoral institutions, and that they were not reached in the Netherlands owing to the highly proportional nature of Dutch electoral institutions. Of course, the German case is slightly ambiguous, given the way its electoral system combines majoritarian and proportional elements.

While the disproportionality argument has a great deal of intuitive appeal, it needs to be qualified. Imagine a country with a highly disproportional electoral system in which there is only one seat being contested (or one seat per district, the extreme case being a presidential election). The argument as stated above, and in the literature, suggests that pre-electoral coalitions should be quite common in this country. However, if there were only two parties, then there would clearly be no reason to form an electoral coalition. Except for periods of war or political crisis, when political elites may want to form a government of national unity, one would not expect to see electoral alliances in a two-party system. In other words, the incentives to form a pre-electoral coalition only really exist when there are more than two parties. The intuition from this example can be stated more generally: disproportionality encourages pre-electoral coalition formation, *but only when the number of parties is sufficiently large.* In fact, Duverger (1963 [1954], 328) made a similar point when he said in the 1950s that "[t]he action of the simple-majority single-ballot system is totally different according to whether it coincides with a dualist or a multi-party system. In the first case the idea of electoral alliances is logically unthinkable: if the two parties were to unite there would be only one candidate and the election would take on a plebiscitary character that would completely change the nature of the regime." It is unclear why the conditional part of this hypothesis has been dropped or forgotten in the contemporary coalition literature.

Disproportional electoral rules should only encourage electoral coalition formation when the party system is sufficiently large. A vast literature exists investigating the factors that determine the size of the national party system in various countries (Duverger 1963 [1954]; Lijphart 1994; Amorim Neto & Cox 1997; Clark & Golder 2006). There is strong theoretical and empirical evidence that more disproportional electoral systems are associated with fewer political parties. It is the existence of a 'mechanical effect' in favor of large parties that creates incentives for strategic voting on the part of voters and for strategic withdrawal on the part of political entrepreneurs. The end result is that parties typically merge and coalesce so as to exploit electoral economies of scale in disproportional systems. This is precisely the same argument presented in the coalition literature for why pre-electoral coalitions form in disproportional systems. Note that this argument raises an interesting puzzle. If the incentives to coalesce are so great in disproportional systems, then one should not actually observe pre-electoral coalitions in these countries; there simply will not be a sufficiently large number of independent parties. It is only when there are 'surplus' or 'excess' parties that choose to retain their party identity in spite of the incentives created by disproportional systems that one would expect to observe electoral coalitions.

Determining when and why some political parties will retain their separate identities rather than merge or coalesce into a larger party is a complex question that goes beyond the scope of this book. However, several institutions are already known to influence how likely parties are to retain their separate identities. One such institution is the use of fusion candidacies, where multiple parties can nominate the same candidate. Fusion candidacies were employed in many US states in the nineteenth century, and it is interesting to note that electoral alliances were quite common between the Democratic Party and various other parties (depending on the state) at this time. Although this practice continues in New York State, it was stopped in most other states more than a century ago. The end of fusion candidacies contributed quite markedly to the evolution of a party system in which the Democratic and Republican parties were the only viable parties outside New York State (Argersinger 1980). Majority requirements are also thought to encourage parties to retain their separate identities (Duverger 1963 [1954]). Certain characteristics of presidential elections, such as the use of runoff procedures, their temporal proximity to legislative elections, and the number of presidential candidates, have also been found to influence the number of parties (Golder 2006).

The size of the party system is also likely to be determined by the extent to which the party system is nationalized. The Duvergerian logic outlined above applies primarily to the district level. Although a country with single-member districts may well be expected to have two main parties in any given district, there is nothing to say that these parties will necessarily be the same across different districts. Chhibber & Kollman (2004) have shown that the extent to which this local two-party system is mirrored at the national level will depend on the relative importance of national and sub-national governments. If the most salient political issues are at the national level, and the national government controls most of the economic power, the party system is likely to be highly nationalized, with strong linkages across districts. In this case, disproportional electoral rules should lead to few parties. However, if there are no strong linkages across districts, then the number of parties in the national legislature may be larger than what one would expect from simply looking at the electoral rules. This idea may help to explain some 'non-Duvergerian' outcomes in party system size at the national level.

Although various institutions obviously influence whether there will be a 'surplus' or 'excess' number of parties, these institutions themselves are not the focus of the analysis here. They are relevant only to the extent that they create a party system of sufficient size that parties are able to take advantage of joining a preelectoral coalition in order to gain office and policy benefits. Thus, the principal point that I want to emphasize is simply that the disproportionality hypothesis regarding pre-electoral coalitions must be conditional in nature:

Disproportionality Hypothesis: Disproportionality increases the likelihood of pre-electoral coalition formation only when there are a sufficiently large number of parties

3.1.2 Signaling Devices

While the Disproportionality Hypothesis is predominant, a second explanation for pre-electoral coalition formation can be discerned in the literature. In this alternative argument, pre-electoral coalitions are treated as signaling devices with respect to voters. There appear to be at least three separate motives behind forming an electoral coalition as a signaling device: (i) to signal that member parties can form an effective government coalition; (ii) to signal the identity of a potential future government as clearly as possible; and (iii) to signal the desire of political parties to give voters a more direct role in choosing government coalitions. These variants of the signaling argument are typically found in the case study literature dealing with coalitions. They are often used to explain what appear to be anomalous cases of electoral coalition formation in highly proportional electoral systems. As such, they tend to be case-specific and rather ad hoc.

The argument that electoral coalitions send a signal to voters that member parties can form an effective government coalition has been made in the case of Ireland, Sweden, and India. Each of these countries has experienced long periods in which a single party has dominated the executive (Fianna Fáil in Ireland, the Social Democrats in Sweden, the Congress Party in India). Those voters who preferred one of the smaller, opposition parties in these countries risked 'wasting' their vote if they voted for this party. Opposition parties formed electoral coalitions in these countries to signal their ability to compete effectively with the ruling party and encourage the electorate to vote for them. In Sweden, the Social Democrats were dominant for decades because the various opposition parties were so ideologically distant from one another that they were not seen as a credible government alternative. Eventually, the three 'bourgeois' parties formed electoral coalitions in the 1970s as a signal to voters that their policy positions had sufficiently converged that they could offer a viable governing alternative (Hancock 1998, 231–32). Similarly, opposition parties in Ireland formed pre-electoral coalitions as a way of signaling to voters that they were a viable alternative to Fianna Fáil (Farrell 1987, 137–38). In India, opposition parties formed an electoral coalition based on a common anti-corruption platform to bring down the long-dominant Congress Party (Andersen 1990, 528–30).

The argument that electoral coalitions are a device to signal the identity of potential future government coalitions is perhaps more common. Pre-electoral coalitions can be used to signal with whom member parties will try to form a government if elected. As a result, pre-electoral coalitions can be expected to offer benefits to risk-averse voters who would rather know the identity of the post-election coalition for sure, rather than wait for the lottery that occurs during a government coalition bargaining process. These benefits are likely to be quite significant in those countries where the post-election bargaining process is very uncertain. Some of the parties in Germany are quite explicit in their campaign messages about the coalition government that they will form if elected. They often tell voters to support a particular coalition by splitting their votes in the constituency and party-list portions of the ballot, precisely because doing so can affect the identity of the post-election government coalition (Roberts 1988, 317–37). Pappi and Thurner (2002, 213) note that in "the German system, voters recognize the realistic options for a new coalition government and the German two-vote system offers voters an opportunity to support not only their party, but also the specific coalition advocated by their party."

The final variant of the signaling argument is that party leaders form electoral coalitions to signal their desire to have voters play a larger role in determining government coalitions. At least, this was the public justification behind the electoral coalitions that formed in the Netherlands in the early 1970s (De Jong & Pijnenburg 1986; Andeweg 1989; Hillebrand & Irwin 1999; Rochan 1999). Coalition parties claimed that voters would feel that the future government coalition was more legitimate if they knew ahead of time what they were voting for.[2] Some analysts have argued that this motivation has been important in Germany, as well. For example, Klingemann, Hofferbert, and Budge (1994) state that the Free Democrats (FDP) and whichever of the major parties was its partner at the time benefited from forming an electoral alliance, since they could claim to have a direct popular mandate once in office.

If pre-electoral coalitions are to be useful as signaling devices, it must be the case that they translate fairly accurately into the government coalitions that eventually form after elections. If this is not the case, then the electorate is unlikely to continue voting for them in the future. In other words, public commitments to form a government with another party if successful at the polls should actually be implemented. On the whole, there seems to be strong empirical evidence to support this idea (Laver & Schofield 1998; Strøm, Budge, & Laver 1994; Martin & Stevenson 2001). In fact, cases where members of a successful pre-electoral coalition do not enter government together appear to be so unusual that they warrant particular comment in the case study literature. Two cases that are mentioned involve pre-electoral coalitions in Luxembourg and Norway. In Luxembourg, the Socialist Party and the Christian Democrats formed an electoral coalition for the 1968 elections and together won 68% of the vote. Following the election, though, the trade union affiliated with the Socialist Party prevented the party from entering government (Dumont & Winter 2000, 405). In Norway, the three 'bourgeois' parties (the Conservative Party, the Christian People's Party, and the Center Party) formed a pre-electoral coalition for the 1981 elections and did well enough that they were expected to form the government. However, while forming the government, the parties had a disagreement over the issue of abortion, and both the Christian People's Party and the Center Party refused to enter government with the Conservatives. After supporting the minority Conservative government for a couple of years, the Christian People's Party and the Center Party did eventually join the government in 1983 (Narud & Strøm 2000, 177). I do not consider the government that formed after the election in these two cases to be based on a pre-electoral coalition.[3] Despite these two cases, it does appear that parties that form pre-electoral coalitions do enter government together if given the opportunity.

The three variants of the signaling story have often been developed in a case-specific and ad hoc manner. As a result, it is difficult to delineate shared features and generate testable claims that can easily be evaluated across different cases. The variant of the signaling story that can most easily be generalized is the one that focuses on the identifiability of potential future governments. The basic claim is that pre-electoral coalitions are more likely to form when the identifiability of future governments is uncertain. One only needs a measure of identifiability to be able to test this idea. Although measures of 'identifiability' do exist in the literature, the creators themselves acknowledge that the measurement criteria are very 'impressionistic' (Strøm 1990; Powell 2000; Shugart 2001). One alternative to these impressionistic measures is to assume that uncertainty about the identity of future governments is correlated with the number of potential governments that could form. The number of potential governments is obviously an increasing function of the number of parties. This statement means that those countries with a large number of parties should also have a high level of uncertainty as to who will be in the next government. This line of reasoning generates the following testable hypothesis:

Signaling Hypothesis: Pre-electoral coalitions are more likely to form when there are a large number of parties.

3.2 Data and Model

Before specifying the model to test the Disproportionality and Signaling Hypotheses, it is useful to first examine the *unconditional* disproportionality hypothesis that is predominant in the contemporary coalition literature. Remember that this hypothesis states that electoral coalitions will be common and successful in disproportional systems such as those that employ a majoritarian electoral formula; they should be absent or uncommon in systems that employ a proportional formula (Laver & Schofield 1998; Strøm, Budge, & Laver 1994). In table 3.1, I present information on the number of electoral coalitions that have formed in elections using majoritarian formulas, as opposed to those that have formed in elections using some form of proportional representation (M. Golder 2005). Majoritarian systems—plurality rule, absolute majority rule, alternative vote, single non-transferable vote—all require the winning candidate to obtain a plurality or majority of the vote. Although it is possible to distinguish between proportional, multi-tier, and mixed electoral systems in my sample of countries, I do not do so here—they are all classified as proportional systems because they employ a proportional formula in at least one electoral tier. Table 3.1 also provides information on the average number of pre-electoral coalitions, the average percentage of the vote received by these coalitions, and the average effective number of electoral parties by electoral formula. The effective number of electoral parties is calculated as $1 / \Sigma v_i^2$, where v_i is the percentage of votes won by the ith party (Laakso & Taagepera 1979). If the unconditional hypothesis is correct, then pre-electoral coalitions should be both significantly more frequent and more successful in countries that employ majoritarian systems than in those using proportional systems.

The evidence in table 3.1 is quite clear. Pre-electoral coalitions are just as likely to form in proportional systems as in majoritarian ones. Indeed, the percentage

Table 3.1

PECs by Electoral Formula

Electoral Formula	# of Elections with PECs	without PECs	% of Elections with PECs	% of Vote for PECs	Effective # of Electoral Parties
Majoritarian	37	64	37	19.8	3.2
Proportional	137	126	52	20.7	4.2

Notes: Data are based on 364 legislative elections from 1946 to 2002 in the 23 countries listed in table 2.1. Majoritarian electoral formulas include plurality rule, absolute majority rule, the alternative vote, and the single non-transferable vote. Proportional electoral formulas include proportional, multi-tier, and mixed electoral systems (M. Golder 2005).

of elections with pre-electoral coalitions is higher in proportional systems than in majoritarian systems. Moreover, the average percentage of the vote won by pre-electoral coalitions is also slightly higher in proportional systems than in majoritarian systems. In sum, there is very little evidence thus far in favor of the unconditional disproportionality hypothesis found in the existing coalition literature. This outcome is exactly as I predicted earlier. Note that the average number of electoral parties is significantly lower in majoritarian systems than in proportional ones. By encouraging political parties to coalesce and merge, disproportional systems have fewer parties and, hence, fewer opportunities for electoral coalitions to form. Making the disproportionality hypothesis conditional on the number of parties was motivated precisely by the need to take account of the opportunity structure facing individual parties. The question now is whether there is evidence in favor of the *conditional* Disproportionality Hypothesis.

Up to this point, I have expressed the Disproportionality and Signaling Hypotheses in terms of the likelihood of pre-electoral coalition formation—whether an electoral coalition forms or not. However, the literature is slightly ambiguous on this point, referring at different times to the likelihood that pre-electoral coalitions will form, to the electoral success of these coalitions, and to the relative importance of electoral coalitions. In this chapter, I test the Disproportionality and Signaling Hypotheses using (i) the percentage of the vote received by pre-electoral coalitions and (ii) the percentage of parties involved in a pre-electoral coalition as dependent variables. In chapter six, I examine how the disproportionality of the electoral system and the number of parties affect the actual likelihood of electoral coalition formation. The results from that analysis are qualitatively similar to those presented in this chapter, using the different dependent variables just mentioned.[4]

The Disproportionality and Signaling Hypotheses can be tested using the following multiplicative interaction model:

$$\text{PEC} = \beta_0 + \beta_1 \text{Effective Threshold} + \beta_2 \text{Electoral Parties}$$
$$+ \beta_3 \text{Effective Threshold} \times \text{Electoral Parties} + \varepsilon \qquad (3.1)$$

where PEC is one of the two dependent variables already mentioned. *Effective Threshold* captures electoral system disproportionality and is measured using Lijphart's effective threshold.[5] The higher the effective threshold, the more disproportional the electoral system. An alternative measure of electoral system disproportionality is the district magnitude. While district magnitude has long been considered the decisive factor in determining the proportionality of an electoral system (Rae 1967; Taagepera & Shugart 1989; Cox 1997), it captures only one element of it. In contrast, the effective threshold takes account of several aspects of the electoral system—the district magnitude, legal thresholds, and upper-tier seats. It is for this reason that I prefer to use the effective threshold. I should note, though, that qualitatively similar results to those presented here are found if the log of average district magnitude is used instead of effective thresholds. *Electoral Parties* is the effective number of electoral parties. The interaction term is required to test the conditional nature of the Disproportionality Hypothesis.

The marginal effect of *Electoral Parties* is

$$\frac{\partial PEC}{\partial Electoral\ Parties} = \beta_2 + \beta_3 \textit{Effective Threshold}$$

According to the Signaling Hypothesis, this quantity should always be positive, since an increase in the number of electoral parties is expected to increase both dependent variables irrespective of the effective threshold. It follows from this idea that β_2 should be positive. The Signaling Hypothesis does not make a precise prediction about β_3, because it says nothing about the modifying effect of electoral system disproportionality.

The marginal effect of *Effective Threshold* is

$$\frac{\partial PEC}{\partial Effective\ Threshold} = \beta_1 + \beta_3 \textit{Electoral Parties}$$

The Disproportionality Hypothesis predicts that this quantity should only be positive when the number of electoral parties is sufficiently large. Since β_1 indicates the marginal effect of effective thresholds when there are no electoral parties, this coefficient should be zero (or negative). Given that the marginal effect of effective thresholds should be increasing as the number of parties grows, β_3 should be positive. While this theory does not provide us with a clear expectation as to when the marginal effect of effective thresholds will become positive and significant, the Disproportionality Hypothesis will have found little support if this never occurs across the observed range for the number of electoral parties. The flip side of the Disproportionality Hypothesis is that the marginal effect of electoral parties should only increase the two dependent variables when the electoral system is sufficiently disproportional. Thus, β_2 should be zero (or negative), since this coefficient indicates the marginal effect of electoral parties in highly proportional systems (*Effective Threshold* = 0). This prediction is in direct contrast to the Signaling Hypothesis, where β_2 was expected to be positive.

I use the data described in chapter 2 to test the Disproportionality and Signaling Hypotheses. Thus, I analyze all 364 legislative elections that took place in Australia, Austria, Belgium, Canada, Denmark, Finland, France, Germany, Greece, Iceland, Ireland, Israel, Italy, Japan, Luxembourg, Malta, the Netherlands, New Zealand, Norway, Portugal, Spain, Sweden, and the United Kingdom from 1946 to 2002. The data set contains evidence of 240 pre-electoral coalitions competing in 174 elections. Unfortunately, my analysis omits parties that won less than 1% of the national vote, because official electoral statistics typically do not list them. Descriptive statistics for the data are shown in table 3.2. The percentage of the vote for pre-electoral coalitions ranges from zero, in elections where there were no coalitions, to 99.12% in the 1976 German election. The 1976 German election also had the highest percentage of parties in a pre-electoral coalition (100%). Effective thresholds range from a low of 0.6% in Israel in 1949 to a high of 35% in countries such as the United Kingdom with single-member districts. The lowest effective number of electoral parties was 1.99 in the 1971 New Zealand elections, and the highest was 10.29 in the 1999 Belgian elections.

I tested the Disproportionality and Signaling Hypotheses using a pooled analysis. The reader might be concerned that the data are censored, since it is not possible to observe the electoral support for pre-electoral coalitions if no coalition actually forms. After all, there were 190 elections with no pre-electoral coalitions. One might be tempted to omit countries and elections where there were no pre-electoral coalitions to avoid this censoring issue. However, doing so leads to biased and inconsistent estimates, since those countries that have factors discouraging the formation of pre-electoral coalitions would be systematically under-represented. The second temptation is to include countries and elections that do not have pre-electoral coalitions but code electoral coalition support as zero. Including these countries and elections is wrong, since doing so also results in inconsistent estimates (Wooldridge 2002, 524–25). The correct procedure would be to include all observations, but to use a tobit model to take account of the censored nature of the data. However, it turns out that using a tobit model in this particular case

Table 3.2
Descriptive Statistics for PECs

Variable	N	Mean	Standard Deviation	Min	Max
Percentage Vote for PECs	364	20.42	28.46	0	99.12
Percentage of Parties in PECs	364	22.86	27.85	0	100
Electoral Parties	364	3.90	1.42	1.99	10.29
Effective Threshold *	349	13.43	12.86	0.6	35

*Data on effective thresholds are missing for Austria (1994–2002), Belgium (1995–2002), and Greece (1946–64).

yields almost exactly the same inferences as using straightforward ordinary least squares (OLS). Given that interpreting the results from tobit models can be quite complicated (Sigelman & Zeng 1999) and that my inferences are unaffected, I prefer to report OLS results. I employed the Beck and Katz (1995) procedure for panel-corrected standard errors to take account of panel heteroskedasticity and contemporaneously correlated errors—this procedure would not have been possible with the tobit model.

3.3 Results and Interpretation

The results from my analysis are shown in table 3.3. Models 1 and 2 refer to the two dependent variables that I use. Model 1 refers to the percentage of the vote won by pre-electoral coalitions, and Model 2 refers to the percentage of parties in a pre-electoral coalition. The first column provides a direct test of the Signaling Hypothesis, because the effective number of electoral parties is the only variable included. I do not show the equivalent results for the case where the dependent variable is the percentage of parties in a pre-electoral coalition, because they are qualitatively similar to those already shown. By including *Electoral Threshold* without an interaction term, the second column provides yet another test of the unconditional disproportionality hypothesis. Finally, the last two columns provide a test of the conditional Disproportionality Hypothesis by presenting results from the full model outlined in equation (3.1).

The first column provides no support for the Signaling Hypothesis. The number of parties in a country seems to have no significant impact on pre-electoral coalitions. Nor is there any evidence that an increase in the number of parties will have any effect on the vote for pre-electoral coalitions when we control for electoral sys-

Table 3.3

Regression Results: Disproportionality vs. Signaling Hypotheses

Model 1: Dependent variable is the percentage of the vote won by pre-electoral coalitions.
Model 2: Dependent variable is the percentage of parties in a pre-electoral coalition.

Regressor	Signaling (Model 1)	Unconditional Disproportionality (Model 1)	Conditional Disproportionality (Model 1)	(Model 2)
Electoral Parties	-0.05	0.86	-3.22*	-1.98
	(1.04)	(1.40)	(1.76)	(1.48)
Effective Threshold		0.17	-1.27***	-0.99***
		(0.12)	(0.47)	(0.43)
Effective Threshold × Electoral Parties			0.42***	0.35***
			(0.14)	(0.12)
Constant	20.68***	14.42**	30.71***	27.21***
	(4.04)	(6.71)	(7.89)	(6.73)
Observations	359	344	344	344
R^2	0.000	0.005	0.051	0.043

Note: Data are based on 364 legislative elections from 1946 to 2002 in 23 parliamentary democracies. $*p < 0.10$; $**p < 0.05$; $***p < 0.01$ (two-tailed). Panel-corrected standard errors appear in parentheses.

tem disproportionality (column 2). The results from the full model outlined in equation (3.1) also provide no support for the Signaling Hypothesis (columns 3 and 4). The marginal effect of electoral parties on both the percentage of votes won by pre-electoral coalitions and the percentage of parties in a pre-electoral coalition is negative in highly proportional systems, that is, when *Effective Threshold* = 0. This result is in direct contrast to the Signaling Hypothesis, which predicts that this effect should always be positive. The positive sign on the interaction coefficient does indicate that this reductive effect declines as the effective threshold increases, though.

As expected, there is no evidence in support of the unconditional disproportionality hypothesis (column 2). An increase in the effective threshold appears to have no significant effect on pre-electoral coalitions. However, there is considerable support for the conditional Disproportionality Hypothesis (columns 3 and 4). As predicted, the interaction term *Effective Threshold × Electoral Parties* is positive and significant in both Model 1 and Model 2. While this finding is supportive of the Disproportionality Hypothesis, it should also be the case that the marginal effect of effective thresholds is positive when the number of electoral parties is sufficiently high. Although the coefficient on *Effective Threshold* is negative in both models, it is important to remember that this coefficient only captures the marginal effect of effective thresholds when there are no electoral parties

Figure 3.1
The Marginal Effect of Effective Thresholds on:

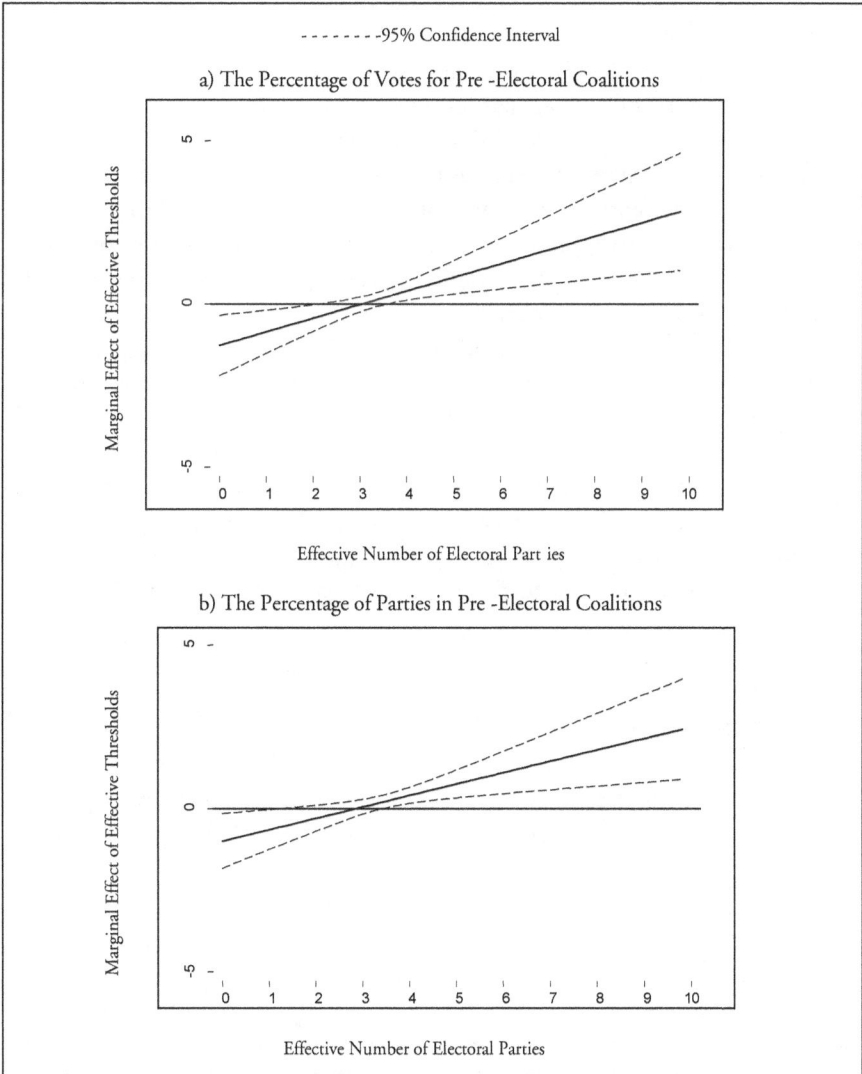

- - - - - - -95% Confidence Interval

a) The Percentage of Votes for Pre-Electoral Coalitions

Effective Number of Electoral Part ies

b) The Percentage of Parties in Pre-Electoral Coalitions

Effective Number of Electoral Parties

(Brambor, Clark, & Golder 2006). As should be obvious, this coefficient is substantively meaningless, and it is necessary to evaluate the marginal effect of effective thresholds at more realistic values for the number of electoral parties. This is exactly what I do in figure 3.1.

Figure 3.1 graphically illustrates the marginal effect of effective thresholds on the percentage of the vote won by pre-electoral coalitions (the top figure) and on the percentage of parties in a pre-electoral coalition (the bottom figure) as the effective number of electoral parties changes. The solid, sloping lines indicate how the marginal effect of effective thresholds ($\beta_1 + \beta_3$ *Electoral Parties*) changes with the effective number of electoral parties. The two-tailed 95% confidence intervals around the lines indicate the conditions under which effective thresholds have a significant effect—they exert a significant effect whenever the upper and lower bounds of the confidence intervals are both above (or below) the zero line.

As predicted, effective thresholds have a positive effect on pre-electoral coalitions only when the number of parties is sufficiently large. Specifically, the marginal effect of effective thresholds will increase the percentage of votes for pre-electoral coalitions when the effective number of electoral parties is greater than 3.5. It will increase the percentage of parties in a pre-electoral coalition when the number of parties is greater than 3.4. These results are substantively meaningful, since 48% and 56% of the sample have an effective number of electoral parties higher than 3.5 and 3.4, respectively. Thus, the evidence clearly supports the *conditional* Disproportionality Hypothesis that parties are more likely to be in a pre-electoral coalition and that these coalitions are more likely to be electorally successful in disproportional electoral systems so long as the party system is sufficiently large.

3.4 Conclusion

This brief analysis represents the first attempt to formulate and test hypotheses relating to pre-electoral coalitions using cross-national data. Specifically, it tests the two hypotheses most commonly made (often implicitly) about pre-electoral coalitions in the literature—the Disproportionality and Signaling Hypotheses. The results from a pooled analysis of pre-electoral coalitions in 23 parliamentary democracies from 1946 to 2002 clearly support the Disproportionality Hypothesis—parties are more likely to be in pre-electoral coalitions, and these coalitions are more likely to be successful in countries that have a disproportional electoral system and a large number of parties. Although the number of parties in a country was taken as given in this analysis, I did indicate several institutions that might encourage political parties to retain their separate identities in disproportional systems despite electoral incentives to merge or coalesce.

In contrast, there was little evidence that electoral coalitions are more likely to form when there are many parties, so as to signal the identity of future governments to voters (Signaling Hypothesis). While the evidence in support of the

Disproportionality Hypothesis seems clear, I believe that one should be cautious in rejecting the Signaling Hypothesis on the basis of this analysis alone. As my earlier discussion indicated, there are several versions of the Signaling Hypothesis, and only one variant was tested here. Moreover, the proxy for the identifiability of future governments used in this analysis was the effective number of electoral parties. It may simply be the case that this is not a particularly good proxy. The fact that countries such as the Netherlands and Israel do have a number of successful pre-electoral coalitions despite their highly proportional electoral institutions should make one wary of rejecting the Signaling Hypothesis too hastily.

The evidence presented in this chapter shows that electoral institutions play an important role in explaining pre-electoral coalition formation. Though the link between electoral rules and pre-electoral coalitions has long been suspected, this chapter is the first to systematically analyze and find evidence for such a relationship. Although this is an important step, the implication common in the coalition literature that pre-electoral coalitions are a simple function of electoral rules is probably too reductionist. After all, there are costs to forming pre-electoral coalitions. Just as government coalitions emerge out of a bargaining process between party leaders, so do pre-electoral coalitions. Party leaders who are thinking about forming a coalition must reach an agreement as to how they would distribute office benefits if they come to power. For example, party leaders have to decide which party will get to run the more powerful ministries and who is to become prime minister or president. They may also have to decide which party should step down in favor of the other at the district level. It is likely that these distributional issues will be hard to resolve in some circumstances. Political parties also have to reach agreement on a coalition policy that they would implement if successful at the polls. The fact that parties must make concessions on office and policy may explain why pre-electoral coalitions often fail to form, even when there appear to be clear electoral incentives to do so. A more nuanced understanding of pre-electoral coalition formation must take account of the distributional costs that arise during coalition bargaining, as well as the potential electoral benefits. The following chapter provides a formal model in which the electoral benefits of coalition formation are clearly weighed against the associated distributional costs. The analysis will show that it is only under particular conditions that pre-electoral coalitions actually form.

CHAPTER FOUR

A Theoretical Model

In this chapter, I present a theoretical model of pre-electoral coalition formation. The analysis emphasizes that party leaders must carefully weigh the costs and benefits associated with coordinating their pre-electoral strategies when deciding whether to form an electoral coalition. The model provides clear predictions about the conditions under which electoral coalitions are likely to form. The chapter is divided into two sections. In the first, I outline the basic intuition behind the model. In the second, I formalize this intuition and examine how particular variables affect the likelihood of electoral coalition formation.

4.1 The Intuition

Given that it is often infeasible for a single party to govern alone in most democracies, party leaders are faced with a strategic choice. They can form an electoral coalition either prior to the election or compete independently at election time and possibly participate in government coalition bargaining afterwards. As I have already stated, the vast majority of the coalition literature in political science ignores the first possibility. However, the fact that one regularly observes electoral coalitions across a broad range of countries suggests that they must offer some form of political advantage—at least some of the time. Since electoral coalitions do not always emerge, it must equally be true that there are costs associated with party leaders coordinating their pre-electoral strategies. It seems natural, then, to seek an explanation of electoral coalition formation in terms of its associated costs and benefits. I argue that party leaders can be expected to care about policy, office, and votes when they make decisions about whether to participate in electoral coalitions (Müller & Strøm 1999).

4.1.1 Office

Just as with government coalition formation, the emergence of pre-electoral coalitions is the result of a bargaining process among party leaders. Thus, I use a bargaining model to analyze the formation of electoral coalitions (Morrow 1994; Osborne & Rubinstein 1990). Some of the issues that concern party leaders prior to an election are likely to be very similar to those involved in any post-election bargaining process. In particular, party elites must decide how office benefits are to be distributed if they win the election. It seems an obvious assumption to make that politicians care about winning office both for its own sake and for the ability to affect policy. Winning office allows them to enjoy the perquisites of power and to influence policy (Downs 1957; Mayhew 1974). It follows, though, that they also care about their place in the party or coalition hierarchy. After all, only a limited number of party members can hope to win highly visible and important national posts. Any electoral coalition agreement must be able to overcome what can be a complex set of distributional issues both among elites from the same party and across elites from different parties.

These distributional issues are particularly stark if there are few offices available to satisfy the party elites. For example, only one party leader can be the official presidential candidate of an electoral coalition. Legislative elections might offer party elites an easier opportunity to reach an agreement on distributional issues, since there are multiple legislative seats and ministerial portfolios to hand out. In other words, one might expect that the divisibility of office benefits would affect the ease with which pre-electoral coalition agreements are reached. As will be shown in the next chapter, it seems to be the case in French elections that parties on both the right and the left find it easier to organize nomination agreements prior to the first round of voting in legislative elections rather than in presidential ones. However, even pre-electoral agreements in legislative elections can be problematic, since they raise the possibility that some candidates will be forced to step down in favor of candidates from another party. Evidence from South Korea also suggests that the divisibility of office benefits may be a crucial determinant of how easy it is to reach presidential electoral coalition agreements. For example, the presence of term limits in South Korea seems to make electoral coalitions for presidential elections more attractive than they might otherwise be, because the leader of one party can throw his support behind a candidate of another party in exchange for a promise of similar support in future elections. This promise is deemed more credible because of the presence of term limits.

Questions of credibility and commitment become an issue in pre-electoral coalition bargaining when nomination agreements are not being used. For example, party elites in a proportional representation system might be able to reach an agreement on how to divide the spoils of office before an election occurs. However, there is no concrete guarantee that one of the parties will not renege on this agreement afterwards. A strong electoral performance by one of the coalition parties might cause it to want to renegotiate, or even cancel, the deal. There are no third-party enforcers for these types of agreements unless one considers the threat of future voter sanctions to be great enough to deter parties from reneging. When nomination agreements are employed, though, there is no obvious way for parties to renege on their commitments after the election, since the constituencies have already been divided up and the electoral campaign has already been fought. As a result, questions of commitment are less pertinent when party leaders are discussing nomination agreements. As I indicated in a previous chapter, though, it turns out that questions of credibility and commitment are rarely a problem in practice, even when discussions of electoral coordination do not involve nomination agreements (Strøm, Budge, & Laver 1994). Laver and Schofield (1998, 28) note that when

> the coalition formation strategies of electoral coalitions are publicly announced—as they must be, since a more powerful legislative bargaining bloc is precisely what electoral alliances set out to offer the electorate—then the extent to which the alliance can subsequently be abandoned is a significant empirical matter. Certainly, when two or more parties promise to go into government together if they are able, such promises tend only rarely to be broken.

It is also important to realize that political parties are engaged in repeated interactions. If a coalition partner refuses to honor the terms of an electoral agreement, then that party may find itself unable to gain electoral coalition partners in the future. Mitchell (1999) argues that, though parties could change partners between the pre-electoral and post-electoral stages, "they may risk credibility costs if they do so. In practice parties that have formed electoral coalitions and offered themselves as a government-in-waiting do tend to govern together if the numbers allow it."[1]

4.1.2 Policy

While party leaders care about office benefits, it seems clear that they also bring policy concerns to the table during any electoral coalition bargaining process. In those models of government coalition formation that include policy as a component of the players' utility function (Austen-Smith & Banks 1988), party leaders bargain over the policy that they will introduce as the government coalition. Typically, the bargaining process results in a 'coalition policy' that is some weighted average of the policy ideal points of the parties in the government coalition. Obviously, such a bargaining process must occur when pre-electoral agreements are made as well.

However, policy concerns take on more significance during electoral coalition bargaining than during government coalition bargaining, since the party leaders do not know if they will actually get to form the government. They face the possibility that an opposition party or coalition might win the election and implement its ideal policy. This 'opposition government' might implement moderate or extreme policies. I believe that the ideological position of the opposition may be taken into account during pre-electoral coalition bargaining. In particular, I expect that party leaders are more willing to compromise on office and policy issues if they face an ideologically extreme opposition party with a credible expectation of electoral success. Imagine two countries in which moderate right-wing parties are considering whether to form an electoral coalition. In one country, the principal opposition party is on the extreme left, and in the other it is on the center left. Holding everything else constant, the parties on the right are likely to feel a greater urgency to overcome bargaining conflicts in the first country compared to the second, because they risk increasing the possibility that policy far from their ideal point will be implemented if they fail to form an electoral coalition. Right-wing parties faced by the center-left party may feel less obliged to compromise, since policy will be fairly moderate regardless of the election outcome.

4.1.3 Votes

Of course, these distributional and ideological issues are moot if the pre-electoral coalition is expected to be disadvantageous from an electoral standpoint. Party leaders are unlikely to engage in electoral coalition bargaining if they can expect to do as well or better by running separately at election time. There is no guarantee that participation in an electoral alliance is going to increase the likelihood of participating parties entering government or increasing their seat or vote shares. Potential coalitions can either be super-additive, additive, or sub-additive. A super-additive coalition is one in which the coalition wins more votes or seats than the coalition members can expect to win running separately. A coalition that wins the same number of seats is additive, whereas a coalition that wins fewer seats is sub-additive (Kaminski 2001). Coalitions between parties with extremely disparate policy platforms may well be sub-additive. Even if the party leaders were willing to form a coalition, voters might reject it because one of the members supported objectionable policies. For instance, a coalition that consisted of a small party on the far right and a small party on the far left would have difficulty in winning the support of either electorate if the main policy issues of the election fell along a standard left-right issue dimension.[2] I would argue that it is a fairly safe assumption that party leaders will not wish to participate in electoral coalitions if they think that such a coalition offers no significant electoral gains.[3]

The extent to which a pre-electoral coalition offers gains is likely to be a function of the electoral institutions in a given country. As the discussion in chapter three suggested, disproportional electoral systems should provide larger incentives for party leaders to reach pre-electoral agreements than proportional ones. One would expect the electoral bonus associated with electoral coalition formation to be higher the more disproportional the system. This line of reasoning also holds for presidential and legislative elections. Since only one party can win the presidency, size matters. As a result, the electoral bonus associated with forming a pre-electoral coalition in presidential systems is likely to be larger than that associated with forming a similar coalition in legislative elections. It is interesting to note that it is precisely where the electoral incentives to form a coalition are highest (presidential elections) that the distributional issues that need to be overcome are the most problematic.

Party elites often invest considerable resources in various methods to measure the size of the electoral benefits associated with possible coalitions (Kaminski 2002). For example, party leaders sometimes employ private polling companies to carry out surveys asking voters whether they would support particular coalition arrangements (Kaminski 2001). Other party leaders engage in coalition experiments at the regional level to evaluate the performance of particular combinations of parties (Downs 1998). Based on these local experiences, party leaders then decide whether these coalitions should be implemented at the national level. In many cases, politicians often go to great lengths to determine whether an electoral coalition is likely to offer significant electoral benefits or not.[4]

It is clear that party leaders' concerns with office, policy, and votes should be incorporated into models of pre-electoral coalition formation. The first thing to note is that party leaders will be unwilling to form a coalition if it offers no electoral advantage or if the coalition's policy would be incompatible with their party's preferences. The second is that a coalition may not see the light of day even if it offers electoral benefits; party elites still have to overcome a whole host of distributional and policy differences. Finally, the extent to which these elites are faced with a moderate or extreme opposition party may influence how willing they are to compromise on these differences. To give this intuitive argument precise meaning, I now turn to a more formal description of its structure and underlying assumptions.

4.2 The Model

The model is based on a standard, two-person sequential bargaining game. There are two possible coalition partners (Party Leader A, Party Leader B) and an opposition party. In order to keep the model as simple as possible, the opposition party is not treated as a strategic actor in this game. The two party leaders must decide whether to run separately or form an electoral coalition. To form an electoral coalition, they must reach agreement on a coalition policy and a post-election distribution of offices. The two party leaders will only decide to form a pre-electoral coalition if the expected utility from this agreement is greater than the expected utility from running separately (the reservation price).

4.2.1 Structure and Payoffs

Figure 4.1 depicts the timeline of the bargaining model. The game takes place in two periods $t = \{1, 2\}$ because the substantive question that motivates this analysis suggests that the bargaining process is most accurately modeled as a finite period game. Once elections have been called, the election date is fixed, and any bargaining process must necessarily come to an end at this point in time. The choice of two periods is arbitrary, but as the game has finite duration, the addition of more periods would not change the conclusions with regard to whether or not a pre-electoral coalition forms. In figure 4.1, the beginning of the second period is indicated by a horizontal line. Each decision node is illustrated by a box containing the name of the player whose turn it is to move there and the decision that must be made.

The game begins in period 1 at the topmost decision node, where Party A either makes an offer or does nothing. If an offer is made, Party B accepts or rejects it. If Party B accepts it, the bargaining game ends, and a pre-electoral coalition (PEC) forms. If Party B rejects it, the game enters a second period, in which Party B can make a counter-offer. If no counter-offer is made, the game ends without the formation of a pre-electoral coalition (No PEC). If a counter-offer is made, Party A must decide whether to accept or reject it, and the game ends with PEC or No PEC. If Party A made no offer in period 1, Party B decides whether to make an offer in the second period. If no offer is made, the game ends with No PEC. If an offer is made, Party A accepts or rejects it, and the game ends with PEC or No PEC. Each time a player has the opportunity to make an offer, he picks from a continuum of choices that corresponds to the potential electoral coalition agreements that each player can propose. The continuum arises because each electoral coalition offer is a particular division of an overall 'pie.'[5]

As I mentioned earlier, party leaders will decide to form an electoral coalition only if the expected utility from forming a coalition is larger than the expected utility from running separately (the reservation price). Let me begin by outlining how the reservation price is calculated. The reservation price for each party is simply the sum of (i) what they expect to get if they win the election after competing separately, weighted by the probability that they win; and (ii) what they expect to receive if they do not win the election, weighted by the probability that they do not win. It is important to remember that 'winning' the election may mean different

Figure 4.1
Timeline of PEC Formation Game

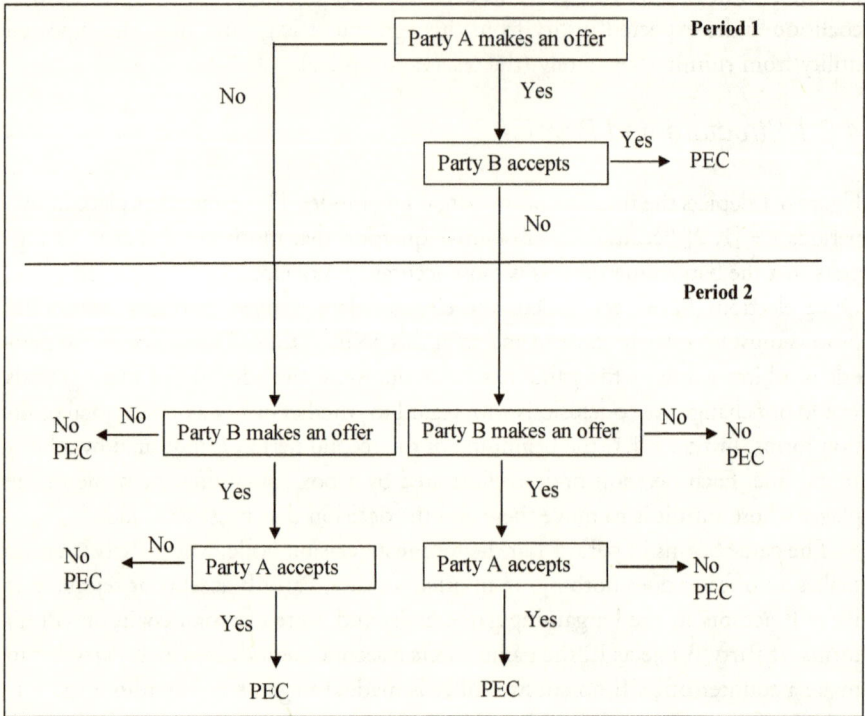

things in parliamentary and presidential regimes. For the purposes of this study, 'winning' in a parliamentary system means entering the government, and 'winning' in a presidential system means gaining control of the presidency.

The probability that party leaders 'win' after running separately (or divided) is P_{i_d}, and the probability that they 'lose' is $1 - P_{i\_d}$. If they lose, they do not receive any office benefits and must suffer the utility loss associated with having the opposition set policy. Party leaders suffer a utility loss whenever policy is not implemented at their own ideal point. I capture this utility loss with a standard quadratic loss function, $-(p_i - p_{opp})^2$, where p_i refers to the policy ideal point of party i and p_{opp} refers to the policy of the non-strategic opposition party. This loss function means that as the policy of the opposition moves further away from party i's ideal point, then party i's utility decreases at a faster and faster rate.[6] To simplify the notation, I call this utility loss λ_{i_opp}.

If they win after running separately, then they receive utility from office benefits (s_i) and policy (λ_{i_gov}). The total amount of office benefits available is large S. Without loss of generality, this value is normalized to 1. In a presidential regime, S refers to the office benefits associated with the presidency. Naturally, the expected share of office benefits will either be $s_i = S$ or $s_i = 0$ in a presidential system. In other words, if you win the presidency, you gain all of the office benefits; if you lose the presidential election, you gain nothing.[7] In a parliamentary regime, one can think of S as the collection of ministerial portfolios available to the governing coalition and s_i as the share of these portfolios going to party i. It seems reasonable to think that the share of ministerial portfolios going to party leaders who enter government will be equal to their share of the government-controlled legislative seats, i.e.,

$$s_i = \frac{seats_i}{seats_{gov}}$$

where $seats_i$ is the number of seats won by party i and $seats_{gov}$ is the number of legislative seats won by the government coalition. This assumption seems particularly reasonable given that one of the most consistent empirical regularities in comparative politics is that the share of ministerial portfolios in government coalitions is predicted quite well by the relative share of seats that the coalition partners control in the legislature (Laver 1998; Warwick & Druckman 2001). As before, the utility loss suffered by party i in terms of policy (λ_{i_gov}) is determined by a quadratic loss function capturing the ideological distance between party i's ideal point (p_i) and the policy actually implemented by the government coalition (p_{gov}).

Party leaders must compare the reservation price that I have just outlined with the expected utility that they would receive from forming an electoral coalition. This expected utility is simply the sum of (i) what they expect to get if they win as a coalition, weighted by the probability that the coalition wins; and (ii) what they expect to receive if they lose as a coalition, weighted by the probability that they lose. The probability that they win as an electoral coalition (or as united parties) is $P_u{}^t$, where t refers to the period in the game in which the coalition forms; the probability that they lose as a coalition is $1 - P_u{}^t$. I assume that $P_u{}^1 > P_u{}^2$ in order to incorporate a cost of delay and capture the notion that forming a coalition three months before an election is preferable to forming one a few days before it (Smith 2004). More time to plan and execute a coherent and coordinated campaign strategy is presumably an asset in electoral competition. If the pre-electoral coalition offers an electoral advantage, then $P_u{}^1 > P_{i\_d}$ or $P_u{}^2 > P_{i\_d}$. Note that I make no assumption as to whether the electoral coalition will be advantageous or not.

If the coalition does not win, the parties receive no office benefits, and each must suffer a utility loss from having the opposition set policy (λ_{i_opp}). If the coalition wins, though, the parties receive a share of the office benefits $(o_i^t$ or $1 - o_i^t)$ and experience a utility loss associated with implementing coalition policy (λ_{i_pec}). By necessity, $o_i^t \geq 0$ and $1 - o_i^t \geq 0$. When parties form an electoral coalition, they have to agree to a particular division of the office benefits. Since this division of the office benefits is determined prior to the election, I make no assumption that this division will be proportional to the post-electoral share of government-controlled legislative seats controlled by each party. This is why I refer to the share of office benefits going to party i when it runs as an electoral coalition as o_i but refer to the share of office benefits going to party i when it runs separately as s_i.

The utility loss associated with having the electoral coalition policy rather than one's own ideal point is calculated as follows. The coalition policy (p_{pec}) is first calculated by weighting the ideological distance between the potential coalition partners $(|p_A - p_B|)$ by the relative legislative strength of the coalition members $(s_{uA}$ or s_{uB}, where $s_{uA} + s_{uB} = 1$). If party A is to the left of party B, then p_{pec} can be calculated as either $p_A + s_{uB}|p_A - p_B|$ or $p_B - s_{uA}|p_A - p_B|$. A simple numerical example might better illustrate how p_{pec} is calculated. Take a policy space from 0 to 100, where Player A is located at 50 and Player B is located at 60. The coalition policy would be somewhere between the two parties, and the larger of the two should exercise a stronger influence over the coalition's policy. To determine the weighted average for the coalition, use the expected seats or votes to be won by each player, s_{uA} and s_{uB}. Imagine that $s_{uA} = 0.8$ and $s_{uB} = 0.2$. Thus, Player A has to cede 20% of the policy distance to Player B, and Player B in turn will yield 80% of the policy distance to Player A. The coalition policy (p_{pec}) would be set at 52. I let $\lambda_{i\_pec} = -(p_i - p_{pec})^2$. I do not assume that $s_{uA} = s_A$ or that $s_{uB} = s_B$, since a party may win more seats (or fewer) as part of an electoral coalition compared to running alone.

The payoffs associated with each of the potential outcomes of the timeline outlined in figure 4.1 are listed in table 4.1. Player A's payoffs are listed first, followed by a semicolon and then Player B's payoffs.

4.2.2 Equilibrium Behavior and Comparative Statics

Having outlined the structure of the bargaining game and the payoffs, it is now possible to examine the equilibrium behavior of the party leaders. I follow common practice and solve the game through backward induction for sub-game perfect Nash equilibria. There are three sub-game perfect Nash equilibria, depending on the specific values of the model's parameters.[8] In two of the equilibria, an electoral coalition forms in the first round, while in the other, the parties run separately.

Table 4.1

Actors, Actions, and Payoffs in Bargaining Game

Period	Actors	Possible Action	Expected Payoffs
1	A	(i) offer electoral coalition	
		(ii) make no offer	
		(if Party A makes offer)	
		(i) accept offer	$P_u^1(o_A^1 - \lambda_{Apec}) - \lambda_{Aopp}(1 - P_u^1);$ $P_u^1((1 - o_A^1) - \lambda_{Bpec}) - \lambda_{Bopp}(1 - P_u^1)$
		(ii) reject offer	
2		*(if Party A makes offer, B rejects)*	
	B	(i) offer electoral coalition	
		(ii) make no offer	$P_{A\_d}(s_A - \lambda_{Agov}) - \lambda_{Aopp}(1 - P_{A\_d});$ $P_{B\_d}(s_B - \lambda_{Bgov}) - \lambda_{Bopp}(1 - P_{B\_d})$
		(if Party A makes offer, B rejects, B makes counter-offer)	
	A	(i) accept offer	$P_u^2(o_B^2 - \lambda_{Apec}) - \lambda_{Aopp}(1 - P_u^2);$ $P_u^2((1 - o_B^2) - \lambda_{Bpec}) - \lambda_{Bopp}(1 - P_u^2)$
		(ii) reject offer	$P_{A\_d}(s_A - \lambda_{Agov}) - \lambda_{Aopp}(1 - P_{A\_d});$ $P_{B\_d}(s_B - \lambda_{Bgov}) - \lambda_{Bopp}(1 - P_{B\_d})$
2		*(if Party A makes no offer)*	
	B	(i) offer electoral coalition	$P_{A\_d}(s_A - \lambda_{Agov}) - \lambda_{Aopp}(1 - P_{A\_d});$ $P_{B\_d}(s_B - \lambda_{Bgov}) - \lambda_{Bopp}(1 - P_{B\_d})$
		(if Party A makes no offer, Party B makes offer)	
	A	(i) accept offer	$P_u^2(o_B^2 - \lambda_{Apec}) - \lambda_{Aopp}(1 - P_u^2);$ $P_u^2((1 - o_B^2) - \lambda_{Bpec}) - \lambda_{Bopp}(1 - P_u^2)$
		(ii) reject offer	$P_{A\_d}(s_A - \lambda_{Agov}) - \lambda_{Aopp}(1 - P_{A\_d});$ $P_{B\_d}(s_B - \lambda_{Bgov}) - \lambda_{Bopp}(1 - P_{B\_d})$

In order to ease the presentation of the equilibria, I first simplify the presentation of the payoffs somewhat. Let

- $R_A \equiv P_{A\_d}(s_A - \lambda_{Agov}) - (1 - P_{A\_d})\lambda_{Aopp}$

This expression represents Player A's expected payoff from running independently.

- $R_B \equiv P_{B\_d}(s_B - \lambda_{Bgov}) - (1 - P_{B\_d})\lambda_{Bopp}$

  This expression represents Player B's expected payoff from running independently.

- $\Omega^1 \equiv P_u^1(1 - \lambda_{Apec} - \lambda_{Bpec}) - (1 - P_u^1)(\lambda_{Aopp} + \lambda_{Bopp})$

  This expression represents the total expected 'electoral coalition pie' in round 1.

- $\Omega^2 \equiv P_u^2(1 - \lambda_{Apec} - \lambda_{Bpec}) - (1 - P_u^2)(\lambda_{Aopp} + \lambda_{Bopp})$

  This expression represents the total expected 'electoral coalition pie' in round 2.

One can think of R_A and R_B as representing the 'reservation' prices for each player, respectively. In other words, these are the payoffs that each player will receive if no electoral coalition agreement is reached by the end of the second period. The terms Ω^1 and Ω^2 represent the total 'pie' available in the game to an electoral coalition formed in round 1 and round 2, respectively.

Let $(X_t, 1 - X_t)$ be the offer made by Player A in period t, where X_t is Player A's share of the electoral coalition pie and $1 - X_t$ is Player B's share. Let $(W_t, 1 - W_t)$ be the offer made by Player B in period t, where W_t is Player A's share of the electoral coalition pie and $1 - W_t$ is Player B's share. I make the assumption that if a player is indifferent between making an offer and not making an offer, he will choose to not make an offer. This assumption has a substantive justification if one believes that there are costs associated with making an electoral coalition offer. This assumption does not affect the comparative statics or the model's implications.[9] As I have already mentioned, there are three possible sub-game perfect Nash equilibria, given the payoffs and assumptions outlined above:

1. If $R_B < \Omega^2 - R_A$, then Player A offers ($X_1 = \Omega^1 - \Omega^2 + R_A$, $1 - X_1 = \Omega^2 - R_A$) in the first round and Player B accepts; if the game were to reach the second round, Player B offers ($W_2 = R_A$, $1 - W_2 = \Omega^2 - R_A$) and Player A accepts.

2. If $\Omega^2 - R_A \leq R_B \leq \Omega^1 - R_A$, then Player A offers ($X_1 = \Omega^1 - R_B$, $1 - X_1 = R_B$) in Round 1 and Player B accepts; if the game were to reach the second round, Player B does not make an offer.

3. If $R_B > \Omega^1 - R_A$, then neither player makes an offer in either round.

The proof for each equilibrium is provided in the appendix to this chapter. An electoral coalition forms in the first round in equilibria 1 and 2 but never forms in equilibrium 3.

The equilibria of the model allow a certain number of insights into electoral coalition formation. However, before moving on to an analysis of the comparative statics, it is worth taking a moment to better understand the intuition and distributional consequences associated with each of these equilibria. Although the first two equilibria result in the formation of an electoral coalition, the nature of the bargain itself is very different. In the first equilibrium, the player who moves last (in this case Player B) is able to determine the nature of the bargain that is ultimately reached. This is the result of having a two-period model in which Player B can make a credible threat to reject an initial offer from Player A that is insufficiently attractive. Player B knows that if the game enters a second period, he can always make a take-it-or-leave-it offer that will be accepted by Player A. This, in turn, is the result of having a large enough 'electoral coalition pie' (Ω^2) to bargain over relative to the disagreement payoffs (R_A and R_B) available from running separately. Both parties clearly benefit from forming an electoral coalition in this equilibrium. The bargain reached in the second equilibrium is very different. In this case, Party A is able to obtain all of the gains from reaching a pre-electoral agreement; Party B only ever receives his disagreement payoff. The reason that the distributional consequences of forming an electoral coalition are different in the second equilibrium is that Party B can no longer credibly threaten to reject an offer made by Party A in the first round. In contrast to the first two equilibria, no electoral coalition forms in the third equilibrium, because there are no gains to be made from reaching a pre-electoral agreement. Both parties would have to give up so much in the bargaining process to get the other to accept that each would be better off running alone.

How do the variables in the model affect whether or not an electoral coalition forms? Remember that there are two possible states of the world: one in which an electoral coalition forms (equilibria 1 or 2), and one in which it does not (equilibrium 3). The comparative statics generated by the model are shown in table 4.2.

The model provides clear implications. First, electoral coalitions are more likely to form as the probability that the coalition wins increases (P_u^1 and P_u^2). In practice, the probability that a coalition is successful will be a function of the electoral rules in a given country. For example, disproportional electoral institutions such as low district magnitude or high electoral thresholds provide an electoral bonus for pre-electoral coalitions through their mechanical effect on the translation of votes into seats (Duverger 1963 [1954]). The corollary of this implication is that pre-electoral coalitions are less likely to form the greater the probability that a party wins after running independently (P_{i_d}). Second, the probability of electoral coalition formation should increase when the ideological distance between the potential coalition partners decreases, because λ_{i_pec} will fall. Third, pre-electoral coalition formation should also be more likely when the ideological distance between a

Table 4.2

Comparative Statics from Bargaining Game

Increase in Variable	Probability of Electoral Coalition Formation
Probability first -period PEC wins (p_u^1)	Increasing
Probability second -period PEC wins (P_u^2)	Increasing
Probability i wins given no PEC (P_{i_d})	Decreasing
Distance between i and PEC positi on (λ_{i_pec})	Decreasing
Distance between i and opposition (λ_{i_opp})	Increasing if $p_u^t > p_{i\_d}$
	Decreasing if $p_u^t < p_{i\_d}$
Party i's share of office benefits given no PEC (s)	Decreasing

Note: "Increasing" means non-decreasing.

party's policy and that of the opposition increases (λ_{i_opp} increases). However, this inference holds only if the coalition is electorally advantageous ($P_u^t > P_{i\_d}$). In other words, having an extreme opposition will make electoral coalition formation more likely only if the probability of winning as a coalition is greater than the probability of winning running separately. Finally, electoral coalitions are more likely as a party's expected share of office benefits from running alone (s_i) decreases relative to its expected share of office benefits as part of a coalition.

4.3 Conclusion

The theoretical model presented in this chapter sought to explain why, and under what circumstances, electoral coalitions form. The answer, I argue, lies in a careful analysis of the costs and benefits associated with forming a coalition prior to the election. In order to fully understand this cost-benefit analysis, I presented a game-theoretic model in which two party leaders are involved in a sequential bargaining process where they must decide whether or not to coordinate their pre-electoral strategies. Both party leaders get to propose an electoral coalition agreement if they wish. Any coalition offer that is proposed by either party leader can be rejected or accepted. At the end of the game, the payoffs are distributed as a function of the decisions reached in the game. I find that there are two types of equilibrium outcomes—either an electoral coalition forms in the first period of the game, or no coalition forms at all.

The model generates several testable implications that will be evaluated in the next two chapters using qualitative and quantitative analyses. These implications are that coalitions should be more likely to form if the chance of winning as a coalition increases. On the other hand, if a party's chance of winning when running alone increases, it will be less likely to join a coalition. If an opposition victory would mean that extremely unsatisfactory policies will be implemented, a party's likelihood of joining a coalition goes up, but *only if* joining such a coalition makes it more likely that the opposition would not win. Of course, greater ideological compatibility between the potential coalition partners makes pre-electoral coalition formation more likely.

The implications generated by the model should seem reasonable. However, it would be a mistake for the apparent plausibility of these results to cause the reader to question the usefulness of formalizing the process through which party leaders bargain over electoral coalition formation and the insights that it generates. For example, an informal analysis may well have reached the conclusion that electoral coalitions are more likely when there is a large ideological distance between the party's ideal policy and the policy of the likely opposition. On the face of it, this situation seems quite plausible. However, the model clearly illustrates that this is the case only if the pre-electoral coalition is expected to be electorally beneficial. Without formalization, it would have been easy to overlook the conditional nature of this hypothesis.

The fact that the model incorporates the ideological positions of other potential governments is an important insight that has not been taken into account to any great extent in the existing formal or empirical coalition literature. For example, although government coalition analysts have suggested for years that coalitions are more likely to form between parties with similar policy preferences, one does not find similar references in the coalition literature regarding the ideological position of the likely opposition. This situation is odd, since one would think that party leaders who are deciding whether to form a coalition and contemplating the possibility of being in opposition should take account of the ideological position of other potential governments, irrespective of whether this coalition bargaining process occurs prior to the election or afterward.

I now turn to a qualitative analysis of pre-electoral coalitions in France and South Korea to show that the assumptions underlying my bargaining model, as well as the predictions that it generates, are plausible and generate useful intuitions for thinking about the electoral strategies chosen by party elites.

Appendix: Proofs for Equilibria

The bargaining model presented in this chapter has three sub-game perfect Nash equilibria. Here I provide a proof for each equilibrium.

Equilibrium 1: If $R_B < \Omega^2 - R_A$, then Player A offers $(X_1 = \Omega^1 - \Omega^2 + R_A, 1 - X_1 = \Omega^2 - R_A)$ in the first round and Player B accepts; if the game were to reach the second round, Player B offers $(W_2 = R_A, 1 - W_2 = \Omega^2 - R_A)$ and Player A accepts.

Proof: There are two diverging paths in the timeline outlined in figure 4.1. I focus first on the one in which Player A makes an initial offer. At the last decision node on the right-hand side of the timeline, Player A must decide whether to accept or reject a coalition offer made by Player B. He will accept this offer only if he receives at least as much utility as he would get from rejecting it. In other words, he accepts if he receives at least R_A. If Player B makes an offer, he will want to maximize his payoff. Thus, he will offer exactly R_A to Player A and keep the rest of the 'electoral coalition pie' for himself. Player B would propose the agreement pair $(R_A; \Omega^2 - R_A)$ in the second period. It is important to note that Player B will only make this counter offer if $\Omega^2 - R_A > R_B$. If this condition does not hold, then Player B will prefer to make no offer in the second period. A little substitution and algebra indicate that this is precisely the condition associated with the first sub-game perfect Nash equilibrium outcome.

Continuing with the proof and assuming that this condition holds, Player A knows that he must give at least $\Omega^2 - R_A$ to Player B in order for him to accept a first period offer. Since Player A wants to maximize his payoffs, as well, this is all he will offer Player B. He will keep the rest, namely $\Omega^1 - \Omega^2 + R_A$, for himself. Player A will want Player B to accept the initial offer, since the associated payoff is larger than if the game continued into the second period. This situation is immediately obvious, since $\Omega^1 > \Omega^2$. Thus, if Player A does make an initial offer, then the agreement pair will be $(\Omega^1 - \Omega^2 + R_A; \Omega^2 - R_A)$, and an electoral coalition will form in the first period.

The question is whether Player A will actually make this initial offer. The result will depend on the payoffs he expects to receive if he does not make an offer in period 1. Finding the answer requires examining the left-hand side of the timeline, which has so far been overlooked. The important thing to note is that the second period on this side of the timeline is identical to the one already examined. Thus, we know that if the second period is reached, then Player B will make an electoral coalition offer of $(R_A; \Omega^2 - R_A)$. This offer will be accepted by Player A. Since we already know that Player A can guarantee himself a payoff of $\Omega^1 - \Omega^2 + R_A$ if he makes an electoral coalition offer in period 1 (which is larger than R_A), we know that he will always make an offer in the first period. Thus, the sub-game perfect Nash equilibrium outcome is one in which Player A makes an initial offer that is accepted by Player B. The game never enters a second period. This equilibrium outcome assumes that the condition $R_B < \Omega^2 - R_A$ holds.

Q.E.D.

Equilibrium 2: If $\Omega^2 - R_A \leq R_B \leq \Omega^1 - R_A$, then Player A offers ($X_1 = \Omega^1 - R_B$, $1 - X_1 = R_B$) in Round 1, and Player B accepts; if the game were to reach the second round, Player B does not make an offer.

Proof: Given that there are two diverging paths in the timeline, I again focus first on the one in which Player A makes an initial offer (the right-hand side). I have already shown in the previous proof that if Player B makes an offer in the second period, then it will be the agreement pair (R_A; $\Omega^2 - R_A$). However, it may be the case that Player B prefers not to make a counter offer in the second period. This case will be true if $R_B \geq \Omega^2 - R_A$.

If this condition holds, then Player A knows that he only has to give R_B to Player B for him to accept an offer in the first period. Since Player A wants to maximize his payoff, he will propose the agreement pair ($\Omega^1 - R_B$; R_B) if he wants his offer to be accepted. However, it may be the case that Player A prefers his initial offer to be rejected if his expected payoff in the second period is larger. This will be the case if $R_A > \Omega^1 - R_B$. The second sub-game perfect Nash equilibrium relies on the fact that this condition does not hold. In other words, it must be the case that if Player A makes an offer in the first period, he does not want it to be rejected.

The only remaining question at this point is whether Player A prefers to make an offer that is accepted in the first period or make no offer at all. Finding the answer requires examining the left-hand side of the timeline. Again, the second period in this half of the timeline is identical to the one already examined. Thus, Player A expects that Player B will make no offer in the second period. Given the assumption that $R_A < \Omega^1 - R_B$, we know that Player A will always make an offer in the first period. Thus, the sub-game perfect Nash equilibrium outcome is one in which Player A makes an initial offer that is accepted by Player B. The game never enters a second period. This equilibrium assumes that $R_B \geq \Omega^2 - R_A$ and $R_A < \Omega^1 - R_B$ both hold. With a little algebra, it is clear that these conditions can be rewritten as $\Omega^2 - R_A \leq R_B \leq \Omega^1 - R_A$, which is the condition associated with equilibrium 2.

Q.E.D.

Equilibrium 3: If $R_B > \Omega^1 - R_A$, then neither player makes an offer in either round.

Proof: To a large extent, this proof is identical to the previous one. Again I focus first on the right-hand side of the timeline, in which Player A makes an offer. I have already shown that if Player B makes an offer in period 2, then Player A will accept it. As in the previous proof, I now assume that Player B prefers not to make a counter-offer in period 2. This case will be true if $R_B \geq \Omega^2 - R_A$. I have also shown that if Player A wants his initial offer to be accepted, then he will propose the agreement pair $(\Omega^1 - R_B; R_B)$. In the previous proof, I then assumed that Player A would only make an initial offer if it was going to be accepted. In other words, his payoff from having his offer accepted was larger than that from having his offer rejected and Player B making no counter-offer. The precise condition was that $R_A < \Omega^1 - R_B$. I now assume that this condition does not hold. This assumption is the only thing that distinguishes equilibrium 3 from equilibrium 2.

The question that needs to be resolved is whether Player A would prefer to make an offer that he knows is going to be rejected or make no offer at all. Finding the answer requires examining the left-hand side of the timeline. Again, the second period in this half of the timeline is identical to the one already examined. Thus, Player A expects that Player B will make no offer in the second period. It is clear that Player A will receive R_A whether he makes no initial offer in the first period or he makes an offer that gets rejected. Player A is, therefore, indifferent between these actions. As I stated earlier, I assume that if a player is indifferent between making an offer and not making an offer, then he will choose to do the latter.[10] Thus, the sub-game perfect Nash equilibrium is one in which both players fail to make an offer. This equilibrium assumes that $R_B \geq \Omega^2 - R_A$ and $R_A > \Omega^1 - R_B$ both hold. With a minor bit of algebraic manipulation, it is easy to see that if the second condition holds, the first automatically does, as well. The second condition can be expressed as $R_B > \Omega^1 - R_A$, which is the condition associated with the third equilibrium.

Q.E.D.

CHAPTER FIVE

France and South Korea

In this chapter, I use a detailed investigation of electoral coalitions in Fifth Republic France and post-1987 South Korea to begin evaluating the plausibility and usefulness of the implications generated by the theoretical model presented in the previous chapter. To a large extent, the selection of these specific countries is somewhat arbitrary, since I believe that there is a general underlying logic of pre-electoral coalition formation that is not country specific. However, an analysis of electoral coalition history in France and South Korea is particularly informative for a number of reasons. First, the two countries are very distinct in terms of their geography, democratic history, and party systems. France is a well-established democracy in Western Europe whose party system is characterized by a well-entrenched left-right cleavage. In contrast, South Korea is a newly democratic country in East Asia whose party system is characterized by an almost total absence of ideological division. If similar factors are found to influence electoral coordination in such different contexts, then this would provide strong evidence that there truly is a general underlying logic to pre-electoral coalition formation.

Second, the unusual nature of France's semi-presidential regime offers an almost unique opportunity to evaluate the impact of different institutions on pre-electoral strategies while holding other country characteristics constant. For example, the ability to observe legislative and presidential elections in the same country allows us to explicitly examine whether the divisibility of office benefits affects the likelihood of electoral coalition formation in a manner consistent with the theory presented in the previous chapter. France is also particularly informative because it offers so many clear examples of electoral coalition success and failure on both the left and right of the political spectrum. Moreover, the ability (or inability) of political parties to form electoral coalitions has often had a large impact on election outcomes in France. The result of the 2002 presidential election, in which the extreme right candidate, Jean-Marie Le Pen, made it through to the second round because the left-wing parties failed to coordinate their electoral strategies, is perhaps the clearest example of this situation.

Third, the short overview of electoral coalitions in South Korea is useful for illustrating the danger of putting too much stock in personal feuds as an explanation for the inability of party leaders to reach pre-electoral agreements. Descriptive accounts of electoral campaigns and elections in countries such as France often emphasize the significant role that personal feuds and long-standing rivalries play in the electoral coalition formation process (Bell 2000; Knapp 1999). Although the absence of ideological divisions in Korean politics has meant that politics is largely driven by personal enmity and disdain, the history of electoral coalitions in South Korea clearly indicates that the most strident and long-held personal animosities threatening electoral coordination can be overcome if only party leaders can resolve the distributional issues associated with electoral coalition formation.

Finally, the investigation of electoral coalitions in France and South Korea illustrate that my theory can be usefully employed to explain pre-electoral agreements in semi-presidential and presidential regimes. Throughout the presentation of my theoretical model in the previous chapter, I was careful to indicate how it applied to both parliamentary and presidential regimes. However, as with the vast majority of the government coalition literature, the statistical analyses conducted in chapters three and six focus primarily on parliamentary democracies. Studying France and South Korea in this chapter helps to show that my theory can also provide insights into the electoral coalition formation process in non-parliamentary democracies.

5.1 French Fifth Republic

Pre-electoral coalitions have played an important and often dramatic role in determining electoral outcomes in France. Consider the surprising outcome of the first round of the 2002 French presidential elections. It had been widely expected that Jacques Chirac, the president and leader of the mainstream Right, would make it through to the second round, along with Lionel Jospin, the Socialist prime minister and leader of the mainstream Left. The real question for months had been which of the two men would win the second round. Then, unexpectedly, the left vote was split among so many candidates that the Socialist leader came in third behind the extreme-right politician Jean-Marie Le Pen. The French press described the event as an earthquake, and the French elections were, for a couple of weeks, the subject of world-wide speculation. Most analyses of this particular election will no doubt focus on the disturbing success of the extreme Right. However, it is worth emphasizing that this political 'earthquake' had as much to do with the inability of the French Left to form a coherent pre-electoral coalition as it did with an increase in the strength of the extreme Right. After all, Le Pen enjoyed only a rather modest increase in his vote share compared to what he had received in the previous presidential elections of 1995.[1]

The outcome of the first round in 2002, though admittedly a surprise, is not unprecedented. The Left had approached the 1969 presidential elections in such "total disarray" that none of the left-wing candidates made it to the second round (Pierce 1980). This situation enabled a little-known centrist candidate, Alain Poher, to compete in the second round against Georges Pompidou. In 1981, the unwillingness of Jacques Chirac to publicly encourage his electorate to support the remaining mainstream right candidate (Valéry Giscard d'Estaing) after Chirac had been eliminated in the first round of the presidential elections clearly contributed to François Mitterrand's electoral victory (Wright 1995; Ysmal 1989). The inability of the moderate Right to form a cohesive electoral alliance in these elections and at the subsequent legislative elections a few weeks later enabled the first left-wing government to come to power since the Popular Front in 1936.

These examples raise the question as to why party leaders were willing and able to form pre-electoral coalitions in some French elections, but not in others. The bargaining model presented in the previous chapter suggests that it should be possible to explain the observed variation in terms of the changing concerns of party elites with votes, office, and policy.

5.1.1 Votes

The first question to ask is whether parties in France have an electoral incentive to form pre-electoral coalitions. As my analysis in chapter three indicates, party elites are more likely to form pre-electoral coalitions when there are many parties and the electoral system is disproportional. Since France is well known both for its plethora of parties and its highly disproportional electoral institutions used to elect its president and legislature, French party leaders nearly always have incentives to form pre-electoral coalitions.

The French party system consists of numerous parties spread all across the political spectrum. At the moment, the mainstream Left consists of the Socialist Party (PS), the Communist Party (PCF), the Left Radical Party (PRG), and various environmental parties such as the Green Party (Greens), the Independent Ecological Movement (MEI), and Ecological Generation (GE-Les Bleus). On the extreme left are several other parties such as Workers' Struggle (LO), the Communist Revolutionary League (LCR), and the Workers' Party (PT). On the mainstream right there are the Gaullists (UMP), the Union for French Democracy (UDF), and an environmental party called Citizen Action and Participation (CAP21). On the extreme right there is the National Front (FN) and the break-away National Republican Movement (MNR). There are also a number of per-sonalistic parties such as Pasqua (Charles Pasqua) and Movement for France (Philippe de Villiers), as well as several rural parties such as the Hunting, Fishing, Nature and Tradition party (CPNT) and the Right to Hunt party (DC). Many of these parties win a significant number of votes and legislative seats. Fully 16 parties managed to win more than 1% each of the national vote in the 2002 leg-islative elections and at least 10 of these parties won legislative representation, according to the *Election Politique* website.

The French electoral system is highly disproportional. Presidential and legisla-tive elections both have two rounds of voting, in which a limited number of can-didates progress to the second round. If a presidential candidate wins an absolute majority of the national vote in the first round, then he or she is automatically elected president. If this is not the case, then the top two candidates go through to the second round, which is held two weeks later; since the introduction of direct presidential elections in 1962, all presidential elections have gone to a second round. Whoever wins the most votes in the second round becomes president. Legislative elections are very similar. Each electoral district is a single-seat district, and any candidate who passes a threshold of electoral support in the first round of voting is eligible to enter a second round one week later.[2] The particular threshold that must be overcome has changed twice since the foundation of the Fifth Republic. It was originally set at a relatively low 5% of the vote in 1958. This per-centage was subsequently increased to 10% for the 1967 election and 12.5% for the 1978 election.[3] The plurality winner in the second round of voting becomes the elected deputy. The first-past-the-post nature of legislative and presidential elections, along with the fact that only a limited number of candidates can progress to the second round, clearly provides incentives for electoral coalitions to form. In fact, the right-wing president Giscard d'Estaing specifically increased the thresh-old that needed to be overcome to enter the second round of legislative elections to 12.5% in 1978 in order to force centrist and center-right parties to merge or form alliances with his own party. This move was motivated by the growing suc-cess of the Socialists and the Communists at local elections in the mid-1970s (Duhamel 1999).

Given the nature of the electoral system in France, party leaders have a range of pre-electoral choices for legislative and presidential elections. One option is for parties to compete independently at election time and refuse to form an electoral coalition in either round of voting. This is what happened on the left prior to 1965, and it is what typically occurs now between the National Front and the moderate right-wing parties.[4] A second option for party leaders is to compete against each other in the first round and then form an electoral coalition for the second round. This has been a common occurrence in legislative elections among the mainstream parties on both the left and the right. A third option is for parties to form an electoral coalition prior to the first round. This option requires choosing a single candidate to run in each district. Although this option is not as common as the previous one, it does occur with some frequency on both the left and the right. The last option is for parties to move beyond electoral coalitions and simply merge into a single party. The center-left parties chose this option when they merged to form the Socialist Party in 1969. The non-Gaullist parties on the right also chose this option when they formed the UDF in 1978 (Massart 1999; Portelli 1994; Bell & Criddle 1984). Something similar seems to have occurred after the 2002 legislative elections, following the success of the UMP pre-electoral coalition between the Gaullists, the Liberal Democrats (DL), and part of the UDF.

5.1.2 Office

The fact that the disproportional electoral institutions employed to elect presidents and legislators are very similar might lead one to expect that pre-electoral coalitions are equally common in presidential and legislative elections. One might even argue that pre-electoral coalitions should be slightly more common in presidential elections, given that only two candidates can actually enter the second round. However, the information provided in table 5.1 illustrates that this is not the case. While electoral coalitions are relatively frequent in legislative elections, they are quite rare in presidential contests. In fact, pre-electoral coalitions have only formed twice in presidential elections.

What explains this variation across legislative and presidential elections? The bargaining model from the previous chapter notes that while party leaders should react to the potential electoral gains that might accrue from forming an electoral coalition, they are just as likely to be concerned with the expected office benefits associated with the coalition. The salient point about presidential elections is that only one party leader can win the presidency. The fact that the presidential office is not divisible means that the other coalition partner essentially receives no office benefits. As a result, the expected utility of joining a presidential electoral coalition is likely to be quite low for at least one of the coalition parties. In contrast, distributional issues are likely to be resolved more easily in legislative elections, because ministerial portfolios and National Assembly seats are more divisible—both coalition partners receive office benefits. Thus, one explanation for why electoral coalitions form more often in legislative elections than in presidential ones has to do with the relative divisibility of office benefits across these elections.

Table 5.1

Electoral Coalitions in French Legislative and Presidential Elections

Election Year	Presidential Elections	Legislative Elections	
		Round 1	Round 2
1958		None	None
1962		None	UNR+UDT+RI
			PCF+SFIO+PRG
1965	PCF+FGDS		
	(FGDS:SFIO+PRG+CIR)		
1967		UNR+UDT+RI	UNR+UDT+RI+CD
		FGDS:SFIO+PRG+CIR	FGDS+PCF+PSU
		UNR+RI	UNR+RI+PDM
			FGDS+PCF
1969	None		
1973		UDR+RI+UC	UDR+RI+UC+REF
		UGDS:PS+PRG	UGDS+PCF+PSU
1974	PCF+PS		
1978		UDF:CDS+PR+RI	UDF+RPR
		PS+PRG	PS+PRG+PCF
1981	None	RPR+UDF	
		PS+PRG	PS+PRG+PCF
1986*		RPR+UDF	—
		PS+PRG	
1988	None	RPR+UDF	
		PS+PRG	PS+PRG+PCF
1993		RPR+UDF	
		PS+PRG	PS+PRG+PCF
		Greens+GE	
1995	None		
1997		RPR+UDF	
		PS+Greens+PRG	PS+Greens+PRG+PCF
2002	None	UMP:RPR+UDF+DL	
		PS+Greens+PRG	PS+Greens+PRG+PCF

* indicates that the legislative elections employed proportional representation; there was no second round. All coalitions that formed in the first round also formed in the second round; only additional coalitions are listed as forming in the second round. If the parties ran under a common coalition name, this is shown first followed by a colon and the names of the member parties.

Left-Wing Parties: Socialist Party (**PS:** 1969–, SFIO: 1905–69); Communist Party (**PCF**); Left Radical Party (**PRG:** 1998–, PRS: 1996–98, MRG: 1973–96, MGRS: 1972–73, Radicals: 1901–72); Generation Ecology (**GE**); Green Party **Greens**); Unified Socialist Party (**PSU**); Convention of Republican Institutions (**CIR**).

Right-Wing Parties: Union for French Democracy (**UDF**); Gaullists (**UMP:** 2002–, **RPR:** 1976–2002, UDR: 1968–76, UDVe: 1967–68, UNR-UDT: 1962–67, UNR: 1958–62); Liberal Democrats (**DL**); Democratic Union of Labor (**UDT**). Democratic Center (**CD**); Social Democratic Center (**CDS**); Independent Republicans (**RI**); Progress & Modern Democracy (**PDM**); Republicans (**PR**); Reform Movement (**REF**); Center Union (**UC**).

Electoral Coalition Names: Federation of the Democratic & Socialist Left (**FGDS**); Union for a Presidential (Popular) Majority (**UMP**); Democratic & Socialist Union (**UGDS**); Union for French Democracy (**UDF**). Several of these coalitions became single parties.

This explanation is exactly as suggested by the theoretical model in the previous chapter. I now illustrate the importance of distributional conflict in more detail with a description of coalition formation in French presidential and legislative elections.

Presidential Elections   The fact that only two candidates can go through to the second round of French presidential elections would suggest that party elites should have considerable electoral incentives to form pre-electoral coalitions. Presumably, party leaders on the left would like to avoid the outcomes of the 1969 and 2002 elections, where the left-wing vote was split among so many candidates that none of them made it into the second round. The electoral incentives for parties to coordinate their pre-electoral strategies would not be so great if the presidency held little power. However, the presidency is considered to be an extremely important political prize. Indeed, when the president enjoys a legislative majority, he holds the most powerful position in the country (Duhamel 1999; Keeler & Schain 1996; Charlot 1994; Hayward 1993). It is only when the president lacks a majority that the system behaves as if it were a parliamentary regime dominated by the prime minister. The presidency has been the dominant political position throughout the Fifth Republic, with the exception of the three periods of 'cohabitation' between 1986–88, 1993–95 and 1997–2002.[5] The nature of the semi-presidential regime in France means that party leaders care a great deal about controlling both the legislature and the presidency.

Despite the obvious importance of the presidential position and the incentives created by the electoral system, there have only ever been two examples where parties on the left or the right actually coordinated their strategies so as to present a single presidential candidate for election. In both cases, the Communist Party (PCF) accepted a non-communist candidate as the main standard bearer for the Left. Both times, the electoral coalition quickly collapsed under the strain of distributional conflicts, as the PCF came to realize that the chief beneficiary of these pre-electoral agreements was the Socialist Party (Johnson 1981).

The willingness of the Communist Party to accept a Socialist candidate in 1965 and 1974 stems from the widely held belief that a Communist could never be elected president during the Cold War period. It is important to remember that the rise of the Socialist Party (PS) as the dominant party on the left was almost unthinkable in the 1960s and early 1970s. The PCF had been the largest party in 1945 and was still the dominant party on the left by a considerable margin during the early years of the Fifth Republic. To a large extent, the PCF could only expect to benefit from supporting François Mitterrand as the single candidate of the left in the 1965 presidential elections. The PCF hoped to gain from a show of left-wing unity without ceding any authority to the Socialists. In fact, the PCF probably did not expect Mitterrand to even make it into the second round, let alone make the election competitive—Mitterrand won 44.8% of the vote in the second round compared to Charles de Gaulle's 55.2% (Johnson 1981). It was only because a centrist candidate, Jean Lecanuet, managed to win 15.6% of the vote in the first round that a second ballot involving Mitterrand and de Gaulle was actually required. It was this unforeseen occurrence that indirectly began to establish Mitterrand's reputation as the leader of the Left.

It was the Socialists who were the most reluctant to consider an electoral coalition with the Communists in the early years of the Fifth Republic. To some extent, this reluctance can be traced to the traditional and deep-seated hostility on the non-Communist left toward the PCF (Jackson 1990; Judt 1986). However, more important were the relative positions of the two parties among the electorate. The PCF was by far the dominant party on the left, and any alliance with the Communists would automatically position the Socialists as minority partners. Many feared that the emerging left-right polarization of the political system threatened the very existence of the Socialist Party, given its small size relative to the PCF. This situation helps to explain why one-third of Socialist voters refused to support the PCF in the second ballot of the 1962 legislative elections (Williams, Goldey, & Harrison 1970). A national electoral coalition with the Communists also threatened the Socialists' ability to conclude alliances with both the Center and the Left. For example, it threatened the Socialist policy of allying with the center-Right in Marseilles but with the PCF in certain regions of Paris. Moreover, an alliance with the PCF was expected to cause problems in winning over those center-Left and center-Right voters who had not thrown in their lot with de Gaulle in 1962. These voters were influential, since they represented the swing vote throughout the 1960s (Portelli 1994; Ysmal 1989).

The Socialists ultimately accepted an electoral coalition in 1965 only after having unsuccessfully attempted to build a federation of the center-Left around the presidential candidate of Gaston Deferre.[6] Deferre had wanted to build a 'grande fédération' of progressive forces reaching rightward to the Christian democratic movement (MRP) (Jenson 1991). However, center-Right voters seemed more likely to vote for the Gaullists than for the center-Left (Hanley 2002). This center-Left federation eventually fell apart at the end of 1964 because of reluctance on the part of the MRP to participate in it. It also collapsed under the pressure exerted by the Communists in municipal elections, from parts of the Socialist Party that refused the centrist discourse, and from the reappearance of the Catholic school question (Jenson 1991).[7] The failure of the center-Left federation left the way open for Mitterrand to run against de Gaulle in 1965. Mitterrand had organized the non-Communist Left under the banner of the Fédération de la Gauche Démocrate et Socialiste (FGDS) and allied it with the Communists. The relative success enjoyed by his candidacy helped to cement the idea of a Left-Left alliance.

The events of May 1968 and the presidential elections of 1969 provided further evidence that a Left-Left alliance was capable of providing realistic opposition to the Gaullists. In February 1968, the Socialists and the Communists reached an agreement on a common electoral 'platform,' thereby consolidating the initiative that had begun in the 1965 presidential elections. However, the left-wing alliance soon began to disintegrate in May 1968, after several weeks of widespread strikes and rioting by students and workers. Without consulting the leadership of the PCF or the FGDS, Mitterrand announced that he was willing to lead the Left in taking up its responsibilities for transition after the defeat of de Gaulle, which he argued was imminent. This announcement appeared as a coup d'état to the FGDS and "reeked . . . of Fourth Republic centrism" to the Communists (Jenson 1991). The alliance between the FGDS and the PCF collapsed; the FGDS itself fell apart. As a result, each party on the left put up its own candidate and refused to form electoral pacts in the 1969 presidential elections. This situation meant that two right-wing candidates, Poher and de Gaulle, contested the second ballot run-off. The disastrous outcome of these elections for the Left provided further evidence that a change in electoral strategy was needed.

> With the Left balkanized as never before during the Fifth Republic, a number of lessons cried out to be learnt from the disasters of 1969. First, [Socialist candidate Gaston] Deferre's exclusively Centre-Left version of Socialism had been routed at the polls, securing indeed the lowest Socialist vote ever. Second, the Communist go-it-alone strategy was shown to be no way for that party to get a candidate through to the second round, despite a remarkably avuncular performance by Jacques Duclos. It had been amply demonstrated how not to play the presidential game, and the most certain long-term beneficiary of the Left's fragmentation of 1969 was François Mitterrand, who had shown four years earlier how far a united Left could go. (Bell & Criddle 1984)

Thus, by the end of the 1960s, it had become apparent to the Left that there were no electorally viable alternatives to a left-wing alliance. The total number of votes cast for the Left as a whole had not dramatically declined in 1969. However, the failure to coordinate meant that the Left lost a huge number of seats. This result suggested that if the Left could only reach agreement, then they might achieve electoral success. In 1972, the Communists, the Socialists, and the small left-radical MRG successfully negotiated a 'Common Program,' in which they agreed upon a platform for an eventual left-wing government, as well as cooperation in future elections (Bell 2000; Frears & Parodi 1979; Johnson 1981). The Left as a whole advanced in the 1973 legislative elections, drawing higher than usual vote shares. The PCF was still the leader by a small margin, with 21.3% of the vote to the Socialists' 20.4%. The PCF leadership, not yet worried about the increasing strength of the Socialist Party, backed the Left's most viable presidential candidate (Mitterrand) in the 1974 presidential elections. Mitterrand led the vote in the first round of balloting before narrowly losing to the mainstream-Right candidate, Giscard d'Estaing; Mitterrand won 49.2% compared to Giscard d'Estaing's 50.8%. Shortly thereafter, the Communist-Socialist alliance hit rocky ground because of shifts in the electoral support for the two parties.

Even though opinion polls in 1977 foreshadowed an almost certain victory for a united Left in the parliamentary elections of 1978, most analysts agree that the electoral coalition collapsed under the weight of strong distributional conflicts between the Communists and the Socialists. The Communist Party had agreed to the Common Program at a time when it was the largest party on the left and could expect to dominate a coalition government. However, the Socialist Party had been the chief beneficiary of the Common Program and had displaced the PCF as the dominant party on the left. The 1977 polls indicated that the Socialists could expect to win 35% of the vote compared to 20% for the Communists (Wright 1995, 425). From this perspective, Mitterrand's claim in the early 1970s that his fundamental objective was to build a great Socialist Party on the terrain occupied by the Communists in order to demonstrate that "out of five million communist voters, three million can vote socialist" turned out to be remarkably prescient (Portelli 1994; Bergounioux & Grunberg 1992). The Socialists could now expect to call the shots in any left-wing coalition government. As Wright (1995, 426) states, "To the Communist leadership, such a prospect must have seemed a worse threat than a continuation of conservative rule." Once the Communist leadership realized that the Socialist Party was getting nearly as much support as the PCF, they withdrew from the electoral alliance agreements in an attempt to arrest the Socialist Party's growing momentum (Melchior 1993; Johnson 1981; Frears & Parodi 1979).

Ever since the late 1970s, the PCF has been fighting against Socialist hegemony on the left. This fight has meant refusing to form electoral coalitions with the Socialist Party prior to the first round of both presidential and legislative elections. Indeed, the PCF has sometimes taken steps to directly undermine the electoral advance of the Socialists. For example, the candidacy of the Communist Party leader Georges Marchais prior to the 1981 presidential elections "was an act of pure defiance. It was motivated by the desire to build up, as in the elections of 1978 and 1979, a Communist resistance to Socialist advance, and by a particular concern to establish a strong base from which to defend Communist positions in the municipal elections due in March 1983" (Bell & Criddle 1984).

Unlike the Left, the parties on the right have never formed an electoral coalition in presidential elections. Until the mid-1970s, the dominance of the Gaullist party meant that there was never a need to form a coalition. In the early years of the Fifth Republic, de Gaulle had managed to sweep through the floating electorate on the right and in the center that had not been tied down by party allegiances under the Fourth Republic.[8] He picked up 50% of the vote from the National Center of Independents and Peasants (CNIP), 30% from the People's Republican Movement (MRP), and 30% from the Radical Party in the 1962 legislative elections, thereby wiping out most of the political center (Charlot 1971). The dominant role played by the Gaullist party only came to an end in 1974, when the party split following the death of the incumbent Gaullist president, Georges Pompidou. The majority of the party supported Jacques Chaban-Delmas in the 1974 presidential elections, while a minority followed the rising politician Jacques Chirac in supporting Valéry Giscard d'Estaing and his new party (UDF). This split initiated a long-standing power struggle between the Gaullists and the UDF for supremacy on the mainstream right.

Although Giscard won the 1974 presidential elections, the Gaullists remained the largest party in the legislature. As a result, Giscard relied on Gaullist support to implement his policy and was forced to appoint a Gaullist prime minister, Jacques Chirac. Although Chirac was a loyal prime minister at first, he soon began to assert himself as the real leader of the mainstream Right and as the only candidate capable of arresting the electoral rise of the Left. By 1976, the tension between the two men had become so great that Chirac resigned and positioned himself to challenge Giscard in future presidential elections (Portelli 1994). Following an acrimonious presidential campaign in 1981, first-round loser Chirac conspicuously failed to encourage his supporters to vote for Giscard in the second round (Bell 2000; Becker 1994; Ysmal 1989). The leaders of the two parties were fighting for supremacy of the Right more than they were fighting against their left-wing opponents (Bell 2000; Martin 1993). When Chirac was unable to advance to the second round, he may well have calculated that a second presidential mandate for the UDF leader would give the UDF too much of an advantage over his own party. Ultimately, Giscard lost the election, even though the aggregate score for the Right had been higher than that for the Left in the first round (Du Roy & Schneider 1982; Bréchon 1995).

Ongoing coordination failures on the right have had significant consequences in terms of its ability to enter government and control policy (Bréchon 1995; Ysmal 1989, 76–77). In fact, the Right was only able to control the government for six years in the period from mid-1981 to mid-2002. The Socialist Party was the primary beneficiary of this internal fighting. The most egregious example of conflicts on the right helping the Left was perhaps the 1981 presidential election, in which the Right lost control of the presidency for the first time in the history of the Fifth Republic. Since then, voters have not coordinated on a single preferred mainstream right party, and party elites have been largely unwilling to compromise. As a result, the Left was able to dominate French government for a couple of decades.

Given the high political cost and the incentives generated by the electoral system, it is hard to explain the unwillingness and inability among right-wing leaders to coordinate their pre-electoral strategies without emphasizing the distributional issues that separated them. After all, there were very few ideological differences between the two mainstream parties in this period (Golder 2000). Some scholars have pointed to the personal animosities or plain 'stupidity' of party leaders to explain the dearth of right-wing presidential coalitions (Bell 2000; Knapp 1999). However, these accounts are unconvincing for several reasons. For example, they cannot explain why the non-Communist Left managed to merge into the Socialist Party in 1969 and why the Left managed to form two presidential coalitions in 1965 and 1974 despite party leaders sharing personal animosities at least as large as those on the right (Alexandre 1977). Nor do they explain why the Right has been able to form successful coalitions for legislative elections.

Legislative Elections   Table 5.1 illustrates that electoral coalitions on both the left and right have been much more common in legislative elections than in presidential elections. Although some pre-electoral agreements are concluded in particular districts in the first round of voting in legislative elections, most occur prior to the second round. Pre-electoral coalitions for legislative elections have become increasingly comprehensive over time on the mainstream left and right, and this fact has resulted in a sharp decrease in the number of second-round contests with more than two candidates. This case is shown quite clearly in table 5.2.

The catalyst for these increasingly comprehensive agreements was the conclusion of the 1972 Common Program committing the Socialists and the Communists to a policy of withdrawal in favor of the best-placed candidate on the left after the first round. The goal of this agreement was to avoid splitting the left-wing vote in the second round. It was remarkably successful, given that only one of the 81 second-round presidential contests with three or more candidates in 1973 involved multiple left-wing candidates. Seventy-eight of these second-round contests involved multiple mainstream-right candidates. Moreover, a left-wing candidate managed to win the seat in four of these 78 contests, even though the right-wing candidates won a majority of the votes. It was in response to the Left's success in 1973 that the Gaullists and the UDF signed a 'Majority Pact' in June 1977 with a similar withdrawal policy (Jaffré 1980; Frears & Parodi 1979). As with the Left, the effect on the number of mainstream-right candidates competing in the second round was quite dramatic. Table 5.2 illustrates that there was only one second-round contest in 1978 with more than two candidates. While there

Table 5.2

Electoral Thresholds and Second-Round Candidates in France

Election Year	Threshold (% of Registered Voters)	Average Number of Candidates Eligible for 2nd Round	Number of 2nd Round Contests with More than Two Candidates
1958	5*	5.02	351
1962	5*	4.33	140
1967	10	3.08	74
1968	10	2.76	48
1973	10	3.32	81
1978	12.5	2.93	1
1981	12.5	2.33	1
1988	12.5	2.14	9
1993	12.5	1.96	15
1997	12.5	2.19	79
2002	12.5	2.04	10

* indicates that the threshold is based on the number of actual votes cast rather than on the number of registered voters. Figures in columns three and four are calculated based on the official election results from the Ministry of the Interior.

were 79 second-round contests with more than two candidates in 1997, all but three of these contests were the result of an extreme-right (FN) candidate maintaining his candidacy and not the result of multiple candidates from the mainstream left or right maintaining their candidacies.[9]

In order to further match the success of the Left's withdrawal agreements, the mainstream-right parties have made efforts to nominate a single right-wing candidate for the first round in each of the legislative elections since 1978.[10] For instance, the Gaullists and the UDF agreed on 385 unique candidates for the first round of the 1981 elections (Bell 2000). The fact that nearly all of these 'unique' candidates were incumbents suggests that agreeing to allow sitting deputies to run unopposed from fellow moderate-Right politicians is one way that party elites on the right have been able to resolve distributional issues associated with electoral coalition formation. Of course, making such agreements is likely to work only in those districts where a reasonably popular deputy is seeking reelection. Despite attempts by party leaders to coordinate their electoral strategies through nomination agreements such as these, some politicians refuse to step down. Electoral contests where this situation occurs are referred to as unapproved primaries (*primaires sauvages*). For example, although the mainstream-Right parties designated over 450 unique candidates for the 1993 elections, many politicians who were not selected decided to run anyway (Backman & Birenbaum 1993). On the whole, though, the pre-electoral coalitions (withdrawal and nomination agreements) between parties on the mainstream left and right have been successfully implemented and have been instrumental in reducing the number of candidates who compete in the second round of legislative elections. Indeed, the nomination agreement reached by the mainstream Right prior to the first round of the legislative elections in 2002 was the most comprehensive and successful electoral coalition in the history of the French Fifth Republic.[11]

One might argue that the sharp reduction in the number of second-round contests with more than two candidates after 1973 was caused by the introduction of a larger electoral threshold (12.5%) for the 1978 elections and not the increasing use of pre-electoral withdrawal agreements on the left and right. While it is fairly obvious that rising electoral thresholds have reduced the average number of candidates qualifying for the second round, table 5.2 suggests that the higher thresholds do not fully explain the drop-off in the number of second-round contests with more than two candidates. For example, the number of second-round contests with more than two candidates in 1997 (79) was similar to that in the 1960s, despite the use of the higher (12.5%) electoral threshold. As I have already stated, all but three of these 79 contests in 1997 involved an extreme-Right (FN) candidate maintaining his candidacy in the second round. The important point here is that these FN candidates were precisely those candidates who were not participants in any pre-electoral pact. Thus, it seems safe to say that both electoral thresholds *and* pre-electoral agreements have clearly helped the reduction in the number of second-round contests with more than two candidates.

Empirically, table 5.1 indicates that electoral coalitions are much more common in the second round of legislative elections than in the first. Why might this be the case? Traditional explanations have claimed that the French two-round majority system does not provide any incentives to form a coalition in the first round, because parties are free to compete in the first round and coordinate in the second (Massart 1999). This notion of how the electoral system works fits with the popular refrain that "in the first round, you choose; in the second round, you eliminate" (Cayrol 1971; Mény 1996). I believe that these traditional explanations are wrong.

The presence of electoral thresholds creates incentives for parties to form electoral coalitions in the first round rather than waiting until the second round. The most obvious reason is that a pre-electoral pact might be the only way for a party to make it into the second round. However, it is worth noting that there may be benefits to forming an electoral coalition in the first round even if a party already knows for sure that it is going to make it into the second round. Unlike American elections, in which there are often several months between party primaries and legislative elections, there is only one week between the two in French elections. As Tsebelis (1990, 191) argues, this short delay means that if "the two partners of a coalition go too far in criticizing each other in the first round, they will not have time to change their strategies in the second round and heal the wounds (even if they wish to)." Parties could avoid these difficulties if they formed an electoral coalition in the first round. It must also be remembered that the transfer of votes between rounds from one candidate to another is often far from perfect. Thus, waiting until the second round before forming an electoral coalition can be a dangerous strategy (Cole & Campbell 1989). For example, Jaffré (1986) notes that right-wing losers in the first round do not necessarily offer their full support to the right-wing politician who continues on to the second round, even when this politician is facing a left-wing opponent. The fact that the number of parties competing in the first dual-ballot election in 1958 was half that typically found in the proportional representation elections of the Fourth Republic provides tentative evidence to suggest that party elites were already aware of these strategic incentives at this early date (Bourcek 1998, 119). It is for these reasons that the traditional explanation as to why electoral coalitions are more common in the second round is not entirely convincing.

A more plausible explanation for the observed variation in the timing of electoral coalitions in French legislative elections has to do with the distributional issues at stake in coalition formation. Though party leaders may have an incentive to coordinate their pre-electoral strategies in the first round and have a single candidate representing their camp, it is not always possible to find an agreement that suits everyone. Hanley (1999) makes this point when he states:

> If proximate parties can agree on a single candidacy on the *first* ballot, their chances are maximized even more. Voters' attention is focused on the sole real choice (assuming that not too many are put off by the withdrawal of their traditional champion), and the possibility of winning more seats at the first round increases. If *désistement* [withdrawal agreement] is one way of restricting competition, then first-ballot agreements are, potentially, an even better one. The main problem is to strike an agreement among the competitors that suits everyone.

Striking an agreement that suits everyone is the problem. Even if it is easier to reach pre-electoral agreements in legislative elections than in presidential ones, this does not mean that there are no distributional issues to overcome. For example, such agreements still require some candidates to step down in favor of candidates from other parties. To some extent, these distributional problems can be overcome in those districts in which one party has a clear competitive advantage over its potential coalition partner. Anecdotal evidence suggests that this is precisely what happens in those districts where electoral coalitions are formed in the first round (Hecht & Mandonnet 1987; Spoon 2004). However, it is not immediately obvious how party leaders can reach agreement in those districts where both candidates are competitive. After all, why would a candidate be willing to step down if he or she has a distinct possibility of progressing to the second round and winning? Waiting until the second round to form a coalition allows these divisive choices to be made by the electorate. All the party elites have to agree to is to abide by the decision made by the voters and support whichever candidate from their camp receives the most votes. It is arguable, then, that electoral coalitions are less common in the first round of legislative elections, because party leaders prefer to let the electorate solve distributional disputes for them.

5.1.3 Policy

Distributional disputes that lie at the heart of the coalition formation process help to explain why pre-electoral coalitions in France are more common in legislative elections than in presidential elections. However, they do not explain why the Left did not consistently engage in electoral coalition building prior to the 1970s or why the Right was more divided in the 1980s than it had been in the early years of the Fifth Republic. Distributional issues cannot explain this temporal variation. It is only by focusing on the policy differences among potential coalition partners and between opposing electoral coalitions that one can explain this observed variation. The bargaining model that I presented in the previous chapter suggests that potential coalition members with widely divergent ideologies will find it difficult to reach pre-electoral agreements. It also predicts that electoral coalitions are more likely to form when the opposition party or coalition is more extreme in its policy preferences. The history of electoral coalitions in France provides significant support for these predictions.

Differences *within* Electoral Coalitions   One explanation for why left-wing electoral coalitions were relatively rare prior to the 1970s is that the Socialist Party was vehemently opposed to the Communist Party's dogmatic allegiance to Stalinism. Many Socialists believed Guy Mollet's famous remark that the French Communist Party was "not on the left, but in the East" (Du Roy & Schneider 1982, 25). During the height of the Cold War, the close ties between the PCF and the Soviet Union were a distinct electoral liability (Hanley 2002). Although the PCF was the largest party on the left, a majority of the French electorate opposed its ideology. This situation probably contributed to common perceptions of it as an undesirable coalition partner. The fact that the other parties on the left were small and fragmented meant that these parties could not credibly offer the electorate a moderate policy if they were to govern with the Communists (Bell & Criddle 1984). As a result, the PCF found few willing electoral partners.

The Communists did begin to seek out some limited withdrawal arrangements for the second round of legislative elections following the disastrous results of the 1958 election. The PCF leaders had little choice but to reach some kind of electoral agreement with the other parties on the left if they were to avoid being marginalized. Although these withdrawal agreements were far from perfect, they were sufficiently effective to increase the number of seats received by the Communists from 10 in 1958 to 41 in 1962.[12] The non-Communist parties on the left also benefited, increasing their number of seats from 65 to 106 (Williams, Goldey, & Harrison 1970).

Although the PCF abandoned its strategy of militant autonomy in favor of limited left-wing alliances for the 1962 elections, it was not until the reorganization of the Socialist Party and the Communist Party's sustained policy of 'destalinization' and democratization in the late 1960s that pre-electoral agreements on the left became common. The revision of the PCF's Stalinist policies derived from its desire to reenter mainstream politics, prevent the Socialists from drifting into an alliance with the centrist parties, and regain some of the popularity it had lost owing to its 'betrayal' of the student and worker uprising in Paris in 1968 and its timid reaction to the Soviet invasion of Czechoslovakia. Besides making a commitment to party pluralism, negotiated programs, and internal democratization, the Central Committee's manifesto of Champigny-sur-Marne in December 1968 acknowledged that while the revolution remained an end, it was no longer a means (Gildea 1997). This revision of PCF ideology showed that the Communists had adopted a more conventional interpretation of electoral democracy and were willing to play by a set of coalitional rules that were more acceptable to its potential left-wing allies (Jenson 1991).

The reorganization of the Socialist Party also made electoral coalition formation on the left easier. In 1969, various non-Communist parties merged into the Socialist Party (PS). This move was seen as part of a larger plan to eventually contain the PCF within a wider left-wing alliance (Melchior 1993; Bell & Criddle 1984; Johnson 1981; Frears & Parodi 1979). By this stage, the leaders of the moderate left-wing parties had accepted the conclusion that a broad electoral coalition encompassing the entire Left was a necessary prerequisite to winning national elections.[13] To some extent, this reorganization of the Socialist Party created a greater ideological affinity between the PS and the PCF. The new Socialist Party united three currents of the non-Communist Left that each had some sort of ideological affinity with the 'reformed' Communist party. The PS accepted the dogma of the necessary 'break with Capitalism,' and the PCF accepted that democracy would not be replaced by a dictatorship of the proletariat if the Left won. This acceptance made it much easier for the party elites to form a programmatic alliance in 1972.

Despite these ideological changes, it would be wrong to overstate the extent to which the PCF and the PS shared similar policy objectives. Moderate voters on the left were never entirely willing to vote for the Communists (Frears & Parodi 1979; Williams, Goldey, & Harrison 1970). Since Communist voters *were* typically willing to support Socialist candidates, the shifting of the electoral fortunes of the two parties is not entirely surprising. By the mid-1970s, the PS attracted more votes than the PCF did. Leaders on the right still played on the electorate's fear of Communist rule, as this had always proven to be an effective campaign tactic. The rupture of the left-wing coalition prior to the 1978 legislative elections was particularly advantageous for the Right (Hanley 2002; Du Roy & Schneider 1982; Fabre 1978). The PCF actually campaigned against the Socialists, and many moderate voters seemed hesitant to support a potentially unstable PS-PCF government (Jaffré 1980). The day after the first round of the legislative elections, the Socialists and the Communists tried to reestablish their electoral alliance (Lavau & Mossuz-Lavau 1980). However, by then it was too late. By not agreeing to the electoral coalition publicly and further ahead of time, the transfer of votes was not sufficiently effective to obtain the left-wing victory that had been expected (Bell 2000). Jaffré (1980) argues that "the incessant quarrels between the Communist party and the Socialists . . . destroyed the Left's credibility as an alternative governing coalition [in 1978]. An important segment of public opinion felt that Communist participation in a Government would have a negative effect in many areas." The election results confirmed the Socialist Party's new dominance on the left—the PS received 24.4% of the vote, compared to 20.5% for the PCF. From this point on, there was little the PCF could do to prevent increasing levels of support for the Socialists. In the end, being the smaller partner of a victorious Left coalition may have seemed better than continuing with the Right's conservative policies (Johnson 1981). This idea helps to explain the PCF's willingness to form cohesive second-round (though still not first-round) electoral coalitions with the Socialists through the 1980s and 1990s.

While ideological differences have often made the formation of left-wing electoral coalitions difficult, this has never really been the case on the right. Among the elites of the moderate Right, there are "very few real differences of policy" (Frears & Parodi 1979, 23–24). There is also strong evidence that the electorates of the Gaullist party (RPR) and the UDF share similar policy preferences and are willing to support candidates from either party. At least one poll asked RPR and UDF voters in 1986 whom they would vote for in the upcoming legislative election according to two different hypotheses: (i) if the UDF and RPR ran separate lists, and (ii) if the UDF and RPR ran a single list. Using voter intentions and simulations, pollsters concluded that the unified list would receive 15 more seats than the two parties could expect to receive running separately. Given that the Right only had a majority of two seats in the 1986 elections, an extra 15 seats would have been a significant gain (Bourlanges 1986).[14] Other survey data have consistently shown that most voters on the mainstream right were in favor of a union of the two parties (Jaffré 1986; Charlot 1993; Wilson 1998; Duhamel 2000). These survey data were echoed by a growing number of French political scientists and commentators (Duhamel 1995, 319–20; Donegani & Sadoun 1992; Duverger 1996, 473; Jaffré 1986, 66; Wilson 1998, 40; Cole & Campbell 1990, 133).

The 1995 presidential election provided further evidence that the mainstream Right cannot be separated into two parties with substantive policy differences. The UDF failed to present its own candidate and simply divided its support between two RPR candidates, Jacques Chirac and Edouard Balladur. Although the UDF split its support between these two candidates, there were no real policy differences between them (Mazey 1996, 13; Fysh 1996, 74; Goldey 1997, 56; Gaffney 1997, 78). The weight of the evidence suggests that there was little division between the 'Orleanist' UDF and the 'Bonapartist' RPR in these elections.[15] Instead, it seemed that the divisions in the UDF were related to what they expected each RPR candidate to offer them if he won.

If ideological divisions among potential coalition partners were the only determinant of how easy it is to reach pre-electoral agreements, then the Right should have found it easier to form electoral coalitions than the Left. The fact that the Right was much more divided in the 1980s and 1990s than earlier, even though the UDF and RPR remained ideologically similar, therefore suggests that other factors are also important. The bargaining model in the previous chapter suggests that the ideological position of the likely opposition party or coalition might be able to explain this temporal variation in electoral coalition formation on the right.

Differences *between* **Electoral Coalitions**   The French case offers considerable evidence that electoral coalitions are easier to form when parties face a more extreme opposition party. For example, one explanation for why the Right was more divided in the 1980s and 1990s than it had been previously focuses on the collapse of the PCF as the dominant left-wing party in the 1970s. The threat posed by the Communists was largely responsible for the rise of the Gaullist hegemony on the right and the electoral collapse of the centrist parties (CNIP, MRP, and Radicals) between 1958 and 1962. Moderate voters were simply unwilling to support center parties if doing so risked increasing the likelihood of a Communist government. Moreover, vote transfers on the right in the second round of legislative elections were more effective when the Left candidate was a Communist rather than a Socialist (Frears & Parodi 1979; Williams, Goldey, & Harrison 1970). In sum, electoral coordination on the right was strong when there was a realistic threat of a Communist-led government. It was only when the Socialists had obviously become the dominant party on the left that the non-Gaullist parties on the mainstream right broke away from the Gaullists to form their own united party (UDF) in 1978. Right-wing parties no longer had to worry about a Communist-led opposition coming to power if they failed to sufficiently coordinate their electoral strategies. The moderate nature of Socialist policies in the 1980s and 1990s has not created overwhelming incentives for the Right to overcome its internal distributional conflicts. Mitterrand's experiment with nationalization, state subsidies, and minimum wage increases between 1981 and 1983 was relatively short-lived. Since then, the Socialists have consistently implemented moderate neoliberal economic and social policies (Schmidt 1996).

To some extent, the fact that the mainstream parties on the left and right are now so similar has increased the relative importance of distributional conflicts in French politics. Individual party leaders seem to be less willing to make compromises under these circumstances. In the 2002 presidential elections, there were nine candidates representing the Left.[16] The parties on the left no longer felt obliged to support a single left-wing candidate. In fact, many of the extremist parties on the left justified presenting their own candidates by saying that this was the only way to give the electorate a meaningful choice. Although extreme-left candidates have typically been inconsequential, they gathered so much support in the 2002 presidential elections that the Left lost its realistic chance to regain control of the presidency. Prior to the election, it was not clear whether the Left or Right would win the presidency. Thus, it was all the more devastating a blow to the Left that their candidate was unable to advance to the second round because so many Left voters turned to parties on the extreme left.

The reaction of mainstream parties to the rise of the extremist National Front (FN) also underscores the importance of policy differences to coalition formation. Parties on the extreme right in France have typically failed to enjoy electoral success or political longevity. For example, while the Poujadists managed to win 11.7% of the national vote in 1956, their support had diminished to 1.2% by 1958, and they did not compete in any other elections. Jean-Marie Le Pen's National Front represents an exception. Since its breakthrough in the early 1980s, it has managed to consistently win over 10% of the vote in legislative elections. Although the FN's electorate does come from both the traditional left and right, most FN voters place themselves on the right of the ideological spectrum. This situation has put pressure on the UDF and the RPR, since they have been losing voters to the moderate Left and the extreme Right. The RPR and the UDF have also been deeply aware that the electorate is unlikely to judge them favorably if their ongoing electoral divisions allow the National Front to win seats in the National

Assembly.[17] This situation explains why the leaders of the moderate Right have consistently made public statements denouncing local alliances with the extreme Right.

As time has passed, these developments have increasingly forced the leaders of the mainstream Right to overcome their remaining coordination problems. As I mentioned in the previous section, the leaderships of the two mainstream-Right parties have attempted to coordinate on a single candidate in the first round of legislative elections. Recently, this is less a reaction to the Left as it might have been in the early days of the republic than a reaction to the threat of the extreme-Right opposition gaining national power. For example, it was in response to Le Pen's strong showing in the 2002 presidential elections that the Right formed the most comprehensive and cohesive pre-electoral coalition to have emerged during the Fifth Republic. Partly as a result, the FN candidates were unable to win any seats in the 2002 legislative elections despite the party's strong showing in the presidential elections a few weeks earlier.

The rise of the extreme Right has even led to pre-electoral agreements between the Left and the Right. If the National Front appears to have a realistic chance of winning a legislative seat, then the Left and Right occasionally form a 'Republican Front,' in which the best-placed candidate from either camp is given a free run to compete against the FN candidate in the second round.[18] The increasingly similar position of the mainstream parties on the left and the right has led to a situation in which the moderate Right is arguably closer to the moderate Left in ideological terms than to the anti-system FN. In sum, there is strong evidence that the ideological position of opposition parties influences the ease with which electoral coalitions form.

5.1.4 Summary

The French analysis is replete with instances where pre-electoral strategies on the left and right have had a significant impact on who becomes president, which party wins a legislative majority, and who gets to implement policy. It is impossible to deny that electoral coalitions matter in important substantive ways to French voters. Although electoral coalition failure is often blamed on the personal animosities or plain stupidity of party leaders, the evidence presented here suggests that there are some underlying systematic factors that influence electoral coalition formation.

While the electoral systems employed in presidential and legislative elections create incentives for party leaders to coordinate pre-electoral strategies, it seems that difficulties overcoming distributional issues have meant that electoral coalitions are much rarer in presidential elections than in legislative ones. As I indicated in the previous chapter, party leaders pay close attention to the electoral viability of pre-electoral coalitions when making their decisions whether to coordinate their electoral strategies. If a potential electoral coalition is unlikely to attract significant votes, then distributional conflicts become a moot point. The early reluctance on the part of the Socialists to join forces with the Communists illustrates this point, since the Socialists feared that the coalition might end up losing votes, with disgruntled voters moving toward the Center and the moderate Right. When pre-electoral coalitions look like they are going to be electoral failures, they soon collapse. For example, Deferre's attempt to create a coalition between the Left and the Center in the early 1960s failed because it did not attract a sufficiently large number of voters.

As my theoretical model predicts, ideological differences within coalitions can influence the ease with which pre-electoral agreements are reached. For example, the history of the Left in France suggests that the growing ideological affinity between the Socialists and the Communists was important for reaching an agreement on the Common Program in the early 1970s. Note, though, that the history of the Right shows that ideological affinity between potential coalition partners is not sufficient to guarantee that an electorally beneficial coalition will form. Also, as predicted, electoral coalitions form more easily if opposition parties are ideologically extreme. This finding was illustrated by the fact that the French mainstream Right was more willing to overcome their divisions in the 1960s and 1970s, when they faced a powerful Communist Party, than in the 1980s and 1990s, when they faced a powerful Socialist Party.

The French analysis indicates that the timing of electoral coalition formation matters. For example, the failure of the Socialists and the Communists to form a pre-electoral coalition until late in the game in 1978 clearly benefited the Right. In contrast, the Right's early and very public announcement that they would form a coalition in the legislative elections of 2002 bore fruit with a large legislative majority. These examples provide some support for my decision to add a cost of delay into the two-stage bargaining model in the previous chapter.

Finally, when French party leaders choose unique candidates prior to the first round of legislative elections, the number of districts given to a particular party is largely in proportion to that party's overall level of national support. Thus, when the small Left Radical Party forms first-round coalitions with the larger Socialist Party, the Socialists get to put up candidates in the lion's share of the districts. Similar patterns have emerged, with first-round coalitions between the Socialists and the Greens in the elections of 1997 (Boy & Villalba 1999) and 2002 (Spoon 2004). The fact that the bargains reached between party leaders in France seem to reflect the relative electoral strength of parties provides some support for my assumption in the bargaining model that office benefits and coalition policy are determined by the proportional size of the players.

5.2 South Korea (Sixth Republic)

The history of pre-electoral coalitions in France suggests that the assumptions and implications of the theoretical model presented earlier are plausible. But are they generalizable? In this section, I briefly evaluate the extent to which the model can also help explain the history of electoral coalitions in South Korea. There has been enormous variation in electoral coalition formation in South Korea since the first democratic elections in 1987. At some points in time, pre-electoral agreements have been reached between feuding party leaders, despite striking personal animosities. Yet it has also been the case that ideologically similar, pro-democracy presidential candidates preferred to compete against each other rather than form a winning coalition against the official candidate of the former military dictatorship. As in the French case, conflict over the distribution of office benefits plays a central role in explaining the variation in coalition formation. Unlike France, though, electoral coalitions have been relatively common in presidential elections. I argue that the use of constitutional term limits in the South Korean case reduces the distributional conflict that plagues party leaders who are deciding whether to form a coalition in presidential elections.

5.2.1 Office

South Korea has not been a democracy in much of the postwar period. It was arguably under authoritarian rule, even in the 'democratic' period of Syngman Rhee between 1948–60 (Henderson 1988). After a brief flirtation with democracy following Rhee's downfall, military rule was imposed. It was not until 16 years later, in 1987, that the first direct presidential elections were held in South Korea. The intense coalition negotiations that have preceded every presidential election since then have centered on the distribution of office benefits.

Consider the transitional elections of 1987. As one might expect, the only important cleavage in this election was between the supporters of the authoritarian regime and those of the democratic opposition. The presidential election was to be held under simple plurality rule, and it was clear that a majority of the electorate preferred the democratic opposition to General Roh Tae Woo, the official candidate of the military regime. General Roh was the hand-picked successor of the military dictator, President Chun Doo Hwan. The wide gap between the pro-democracy policies that the opposition camp wanted to implement and the policies that the military incumbent preferred created strong incentives for the opposition to present a single candidate. However, the pro-democracy camp split its support between two leaders of the democracy movement, Kim Young Sam and Kim Dae Jung. In spite of the significance of the elections and the tremendous pressure on the two pro-democracy candidates to form an electoral alliance, neither would yield. In the end, General Roh won the 1987 elections with 36.6% of the vote. Kim Young Sam came in second with 28.0%, and Kim Dae Jung came in third with 27.0%. Kim Jong Pil, a leader in the 1961 military coup and former prime minister during the military dictatorship, came in last with 8.1% of the vote. It is typically assumed that had the pro-democracy forces united behind a single candidate, then they would have won these transitional elections (Oh 1999, 109–10; Han 1997, 52–55; Nam 1989, 317; Dong 1988, 170, 185–86,; Kihl 1988, 15).

One explanation for why the pro-democracy candidates failed to form a pre-electoral coalition in these elections focuses on the uncertainty that surrounded the electoral outcome. Electoral uncertainty tends to be high in new democracies, where polls are often unreliable and voters, as well as candidates, do not have previous election results on which to base their expectations. Thus, one interpretation of the 1987 pre-election coordination failure is that Kim Dae Jung thought his prospects were so 'favorable' in a four-party race that he was willing to split from Kim Young Sam and form his own opposition party (Kim 2000*b*). According to one country expert, "It appears that both camps truly believed that their candidates would win the election even with both Kims running" (Kim 1997, 91).

However, others have argued that the opinion polls prior to the election clearly indicated that if both candidates were to remain in the presidential race, then the pro-democracy forces would likely lose (Kihl 1988*b*). Why would the two opposition leaders take this chance? Remember that both Kim Young Sam and Kim Dae Jung considered themselves to be the legitimate leader of a democratic South Korea. In terms of the theoretical model outlined in the previous chapter, it may be the case that the expected payoff from running alone was high enough, given that the election outcome was in doubt that neither candidate was willing to withdraw. Certainly, the cost of reaching an electoral agreement was high for the candidate who would be forced to withdraw from the competition. After all, stepping aside in this foundational election likely meant running the risk of relinquishing all political power in the future. The candidates may not have considered a potential electoral loss from running a separate campaign to be such a terrible thing, especially if they could increase their bargaining power in future elections by polling a significant percentage of the vote.[19] In many respects, this situation mirrors the competition between Jacques Chirac and Valéry Giscard d'Estaing for supremacy over the moderate Right in the 1980s in France. In both situations, party leaders were willing to suffer the loss associated with having the opposition implement policy in order to guarantee their survival as influential political actors.

The Korean political scene has witnessed a whirlwind of party mergers and splits since the transitional elections in 1987. To some extent, this situation has been aided by the fact that there is an unusual absence of policy differentiation among the various parties (Kim 2000*b;* Jaung 2000; Oh 1999; Park 1990). The issue of democracy has been absent from electoral politics since the 1987 elections, and no divisive subject other than geographical affiliation has really emerged to take its place. With no substantive ideological or policy differences, political competition in South Korea has been characterized primarily by personal animosity and long-standing political enmity.

Despite this situation, personal animosities have regularly been put aside in the pursuit of votes and office. For example, Kim Young Sam decided in 1990 to merge his party with those of two former members of the military regime, President Roh and Kim Jong Pil. Kim Jong Pil became the party leader, and Kim Young Sam was rewarded with becoming the party's next presidential candidate. This coalition emerged despite the fact that Kim Young Sam had been imprisoned, placed under house arrest, and expelled from the National Assembly during the military regime's rule. Similarly, despite having nearly been executed by the military regime in 1971 (before being put under house arrest, imprisoned, and sent into exile), Kim Dae Jung later formed an electoral alliance with Kim Jong Pil for the 1996 legislative elections and 1997 presidential elections (Oberdorfer 2001). These examples represent just a few of the cases in which personal enemies put aside their differences to form electoral coalitions. The history of these coalitions in Korea represents as compelling a case as can be made against those who would explain pre-electoral coordination failures purely in terms of personal animosities between party leaders.

Unlike France, pre-electoral coalitions in presidential elections are common in South Korea. This fact raises the question as to how party leaders in Korea have been able to overcome the distributional issues that lie at the heart of presidential coalition formation, whereas their French counterparts have not. Part of the explanation for this empirical difference might lie in the absence of ideological divisions between Korean parties. While there is presumably some truth to this statement, it is important to remember that a lack of ideological conflict also characterized several instances of coordination failure within the French mainstream Right. Perhaps a more compelling explanatory factor is the fact that according to the Korean constitution, the president is permitted to serve only a single five-year term (Kihl 1988*a*).

Consider the 1990 coalition between President Roh, Kim Jong Pil, and Kim Young Sam. Although the presidency is by far the most important position in Korea, the legislature does have the ability to hold up legislation if it is controlled by the opposition (Morriss 1996).[20] It was because he did not enjoy a majority following the 1988 legislative elections that President Roh eventually suggested merging his party with those of Kim Young Sam and Kim Jong Pil. The new party that emerged in 1990 controlled a majority of the seats in the National Assembly. The point here is that Kim Young Sam and Kim Jong Pil were probably more willing to enter into this sort of electoral arrangement because they knew that President Roh could not run again for office and would retire from politics at the end of his term. It is precisely because a president can stay in office for only a single term that the promise of stepping down in favor of one's coalition partner becomes somewhat credible. In this case, President Roh had promised to step down and support Kim Young Sam as the new party's official presidential candidate in the 1992 elections. It seems fairly clear that Kim Young Sam would have been less willing to merge his party with that of President Roh without the institutional feature of term limits.

In fact, pre-electoral agreements of this sort are quite common. Kim Jong Pil had formed his own party in 1992 but was able to command only about 10% of the vote. While this result was certainly not enough to win an election on his own, it was sufficiently large to be useful in an electoral coalition. Kim Jong Pil eventually formed an electoral alliance with another former enemy, Kim Dae Jung. Kim Dae Jung had finished second to Kim Young Sam in the 1992 presidential elections. His problem was that although he typically won almost all of the votes in his native Cholla region, he was unsuccessful elsewhere.[21] As a result, Kim Dae Jung was unlikely to ever win a national election on his own. The pre-electoral coalition bargain reached between these two men involved Kim Dae Jung becoming the presidential candidate for the 1997 elections and Kim Jong Pil becoming the prime minister, with the right to choose his own cabinet.[22]

President Kim Young Sam was unable to run for reelection in 1997, and his party was unable to field a unique candidate against the Kim Dae Jung-Kim Jong Pil electoral alliance. Instead, two candidates, Lee Hoi Chang and Rhee In-je, competed for the votes of the president's party. Lee Hoi Chang was able to co-opt a fifth candidate, Cho Soon, into an electoral alliance of his own. Cho agreed to merge his party with that of Lee Hoi Chang and withdraw his candidacy from the presidential race. In exchange, Cho became leader of the new party, a position that was 'guaranteed' for two years (Kim 2000*a*). The results of the 1997 presidential election were close: Kim Dae Jung received 39.7% of the votes, Lee Hoi Chang 38.2%, and Rhee In-je 18.9% (Kim 2000*b*, 61). Kim Dae Jung clearly benefited from the alliance with Kim Jong Pil. His support from Kim Jong Pil's Ch'ungch'ong region was 20% higher than in any previous election. Given the slim margin of victory, it seems likely that the support from Kim Jong Pil's region was instrumental in finally getting Kim Dae Jung elected (Kim 2000*b*).

The fact that a coalition partner can be promised a prime ministerial position and support as the official presidential candidate in future elections with some credibility, thanks to the institutional feature of term limits, has clearly facilitated the formation of electoral coalitions during presidential elections in South Korea. Term limits are important because they make the presidential office more divisible across time. They are also influential because they place a constraint on the power of the president. By weakening the power of the office that party leaders are fighting over, term limits make it easier for them to compromise.

It is important to remember, though, that even if term limits make electoral coalition proposals more credible, they do not make them sacrosanct. For example, Kim Young Sam offered the role of prime minister and future presidential candidate to Kim Jong Pil in exchange for his support and that of his electorate in the 1992 elections. However, following his successful election with 42% of the vote, President Kim Young Sam changed his mind about his successor.[23] He announced in the middle of his term that he now supported a general policy of 'generational change.' This declaration enabled him to fill most of the leadership posts with his own supporters and consolidate his grip on his party and on the government (Kim 2000*b*). This experience made Kim Jong Pil very wary of future coalitions, and it was only after "two years of an intense courtship" that Kim Dae Jung was able to get him to agree to his 'power sharing' plan for the 1997 elections outlined above (Kim 2000*b*).

Even if term limits ease the coalition formation process in Korea, they can only go so far in helping party leaders overcome their conflicting preferences concerning the distribution of office benefits. Party leaders still have to agree on who is going to step down in favor of whom. It turns out that South Korean presidential candidates have employed highly imaginative mechanisms to make these types of decisions easier. For example, in the 2002 presidential elections, two presidential candidates used opinion polls to decide which of them would withdraw from the race in an attempt to avoid defeat by a third candidate. Poll results indicated that the opposition leader Lee Hoi Chang would win in a three-way race, but that either Roh Moo Hyun or Chung Mong Joon might beat Lee in a two-way race. The second- and third-placed candidates agreed to form an electoral coalition. The question of who would withdraw from the race was decided by polling a sample of the electorate after a televised debate between Roh and Chung. According to the few thousand people voting in the private poll, Chung came in second, and he promptly withdrew from the presidential campaign. Chung began acting as Roh's campaign manager, and it was widely assumed that Roh had promised him significant spoils if they won the election.[24] It is interesting to note that Chung and Roh used the electorate to take the decision about who was going to run for the presidency out of their hands in a similar way to how the French parties use the electoral vote in the first round of legislative elections to decide who is going to withdraw prior to the second round.

5.2.2 Summary

This brief analysis of South Korea provides further evidence of the important role played by office-seeking preferences in the formation of electoral coalitions. Other than the foundational election of 1987, none of the Korean presidential elections have had a significant policy element to them. Thus, policy did not hinder coalitions from forming. Nor did extreme ideological positions on the part of one party encourage opposing coalitions to form, as occurred in France. Distributional conflict was the only significant issue in the coalition formation process. In 1987, Kim Young Sam and Kim Dae Jung both preferred to fight each other instead of guaranteeing a victory for the pro-democracy forces against the incumbent military dictator. Quite possibly, this preference was because neither wanted to jeopardize his future role in a democratic South Korea. Since that election, various electoral coalitions have formed between former adversaries. One factor that has facilitated electoral coalition formation in presidential elections is the use of term limits that, in practice, enable the benefits of the presidential office to be divided across time.

5.3 Conclusion

The theory presented in the previous chapter suggests that the distribution of office benefits, the ideological location of potential coalition partners, and the ideological location of opposition parties play an important role in the formation of electoral coalitions. It is easier to reach an agreement to form a pre-electoral coalition if the parties that are bargaining have similar policy preferences. Also, a large enough 'pie' of expected office benefits is crucial. This requirement is because each party leader will compare the expected share of office benefits and the utility of the coalition policy if part of an electoral coalition to what he or she could get by competing independently. Though party leaders will trade off the two types of benefits, the bottom line is that they agree to join an electoral coalition only if they expect doing so to make them better off. They will be more willing to sacrifice some office benefits if necessary and join an electoral coalition when they expect that by doing so they will be able to prevent an ideologically 'extreme' opposition group from coming to power. By providing incentives to form electoral coalitions, electoral institutions that favor larger parties will also play an important role here. These hypotheses were supported in this chapter with evidence from France and South Korea.

The French analysis illustrated that parties had to be sufficiently ideologically compatible for coalitions to form. For instance, the Socialists and the Communists were willing to consider forming electoral coalitions only after their ideological positions drew sufficiently close to each other in the 1970s. There was also compelling evidence that coalition formation was facilitated if the policy proposed by the likely opposition was extreme. Right-wing parties and voters in France were able to coordinate much more effectively when the Communist Party was considered the dominant party on the left. Likewise, moderate parties on the left and the right occasionally coordinate their pre-electoral strategies if doing so will help defeat a candidate from the extreme right.

In addition to policy and electoral incentives, the history of electoral coalitions in both France and South Korea clearly show that the divisibility of office benefits matters. The bargaining model suggests that it is easier to form electoral coalitions when the benefits of office can be divided in a manner that makes members of both parties better off than they would have been if competing independently. Evidence in support of this idea comes from the fact that electoral agreements have been much more common in legislative elections in France than in presidential ones. One explanation for this variation across elections has to do with the fact that there are nearly 600 offices and government portfolios to share out in legislative elections compared to a single office in presidential elections. It is simply easier to divide office benefits in legislative elections to the satisfaction of both parties in a coalition.

While forming pre-electoral coalitions is easier in legislative elections, the Korean case illustrates that presidential electoral coalitions can form in certain circumstances. In particular, the use of term limits in South Korea makes electoral coalition formation easier by providing for the temporal divisibility of the presidential office. This example suggests that institutional features that can reduce distributional disputes between potential coalition partners will make electoral coalitions more likely. Evidence from both South Korea and France indicate that party leaders try to avoid conflict over the distribution of office by allowing voters to choose the coalition candidate when they can. The institutional feature of the French two-round electoral system helps in this regard. In general, electoral rules that allow voters to vote for more than one party should be especially conducive to the formation of pre-electoral coalitions. Finally, the evidence from France and South Korea suggests that party leaders' personal animosity and myopia, which receive so much emphasis in the description of campaigns and politics in particular countries, play no systematic role in pre-electoral coalition formation. This argument is particularly striking in the South Korean analysis. Indeed, the old adage that 'politics makes strange bedfellows' is perhaps the more appropriate observation.

CHAPTER SIX

Empirical Implications
Testing the Theoretical Model

As I mentioned in chapter one, single parties are unable to command a majority of support in the legislatures of most democracies. Thus, political parties who wish to exercise executive power are typically forced to enter some form of coalition. They can either form a pre-electoral coalition prior to the election or wait to form a government coalition afterwards. The analysis conducted in chapter three took as its starting point the implicit claim in the coalition literature that pre-electoral coalitions are a simple function of electoral rules. Although the results presented in that chapter showed that the incentives to form electoral coalitions are shaped by the specific electoral rules employed in each country, they also indicated that the size of the party system mattered, as well. Specifically, the results showed that electoral coalitions are more likely to form and be successful only when a country employs disproportional electoral institutions *and* there are a large number of parties. The size of the party system matters because there are simply fewer opportunities or incentives to form electoral coalitions in countries where the number of parties is small. This is the case whether the electoral system is highly disproportional or not.

The problem with this initial analysis was that it took account only of the electoral incentives to form a pre-electoral coalition. It ignored the obvious costs that parties incur when they accept pre-electoral agreements. For example, parties that agree to form an electoral coalition have to make compromises on a coalition policy and a division of office benefits. Party leaders ultimately have to weigh the benefits that accrue from forming an electoral coalition against the associated costs. The costs may be so great that party leaders may well decide that they are unwilling to sign a pre-electoral agreement, even if such a coalition could win them more votes or seats. In chapter four, I presented a bargaining model that described the decision calculus facing two party leaders who are deciding whether to form an electoral coalition. Solving the model for sub-game perfect Nash equilibria revealed equilibria in which party leaders either agreed to form an electoral coalition in the first round or decided to run independent electoral campaigns. The comparative statics generated by the model indicated that the probability of electoral coalition formation increases when:

1. the ideological distance between the potential coalition partners (λ_{AB}) decreases.
2. the probability that the coalition wins ($P_u{}^1$, $P_u{}^2$) increases.
3. the probability that the party wins after running alone (P_{i_d}) decreases.
4. the ideological distance between the party's policy and that of the opposition (λ_{i_opp}) increases as long as the coalition is electorally beneficial ($P_u{}^t > P_{i\_d}$).

In chapter five, I evaluated these implications using detailed analyses of electoral coalition history in France and South Korea. The evidence that I presented indicated that not only were the assumptions and implications of the bargaining game plausible, but that they were also informative for explaining the particular patterns of electoral coalition formation observed in these two countries. My theoretical model provided an explanation as to why electoral coalitions were more common in legislative elections as opposed to presidential elections in France, why they were more common in the second round of French legislative elections than in the first, and why they were more common at some points in time than at others. The model also helped to explain why electoral coalitions were much more common in presidential elections in South Korea compared to presidential elections in France, and why South Korean presidential candidates were willing to form electoral alliances with personal rivals and enemies.

Of course, these are but two countries, and the model that I outlined in chapter four purports to provide a general logic of pre-electoral coalition formation that applies in multiple settings. As a result, I now provide a more systematic test of the implications generated by the bargaining model using data on electoral coalitions from 20 advanced industrialized parliamentary democracies from 1946 to 1998.

6.1 Hypotheses

As I show above, the bargaining model provides clear, testable implications. The problem is that some of the variables in the model are difficult to accurately measure with real-world data. For example, how would one measure the probability of a coalition winning ($P_u{}^t$) when no coalition actually forms, or the probability of a party winning on its own (P_{i_d}) when a coalition does form? While it is theoretically possible to calculate these probabilities through the use of survey data asking individuals how they would vote when faced with a variety of different coalition environments, these data do not exist for the elections in my data set.[1] Because of these difficulties, it is necessary to reformulate the model's implications into hypotheses that can actually be tested with real-world data.

The model's first implication is straightforward and can be tested directly. As is the case with government coalitions, pre-electoral coalitions should form more easily between parties with similar ideological positions (Budge & Laver 1992). This is the case because the utility loss associated with having policy set at the coalition's ideal point rather than one's own ideal point is minimized to the extent that the coalition members are ideologically similar. Moreover, a party's electorate, along with its rank-and-file members, should be more willing to support the pre-electoral coalition if there is no need to make significant policy concessions. Thus, the first hypothesis is:

Hypothesis 1:   Pre-electoral coalitions are less likely to form when the ideological distance between potential coalition members increases.

The second implication from the model is that electoral coalitions are more likely the greater the probability that the electoral coalition is going to win. The probability that the coalition is going to be successful is clearly a function of the seat share that the coalition members eventually obtain: the larger the coalition, the greater its chance of electoral success. However, it is important to note that if the coalition becomes sufficiently large, then at least one of the coalition members may begin to think that it has a realistic chance of entering government by running independently. According to the model's third implication, parties will be less likely to form a coalition if this occurs. This line of reasoning suggests that an increase in the potential electoral coalition size should make coalition formation *more* likely when the coalition is small, but should make coalition formation *less* likely when the coalition size is large. Thus, a combination of the model's second and third implications generates the following hypothesis:

Hypothesis 2:   The probability that an electoral coalition forms is a quadratic function of the size of the potential pre-electoral coalition. It should be increasing in the first term (size) and decreasing in the second term ($size^2$).

This last hypothesis suggests that electoral coalitions will be less likely to form if the coalition becomes too large, because at some point at least one of the coalition parties will start to believe that it can enter government by running independently. It naturally follows that the point at which the electoral coalition becomes 'too large' will depend on the relative size of the coalition parties. For example, imagine two potential two-party coalitions, and that each expects to win 40% of the seats. In the first coalition, each party expects to win the same percentage of seats (20%). In the second coalition, one party expects to win 30% of the seats, while the other expects to win only 10%. It seems obvious that the larger party in this second coalition is more likely to want to compete independently than are either of the *smaller* parties in the first potential coalition. This is the case even though the expected size of the two coalitions is the same. In other words, potential coalitions between parties that are asymmetric in size should be less likely to form when the overall coalition size becomes sufficiently large. Thus, the third hypothesis is:

Hypothesis 3:   If the expected coalition size is sufficiently large, then pre-electoral coalitions are less likely to form if there is an asymmetric distribution of electoral strength among the potential coalition parties.

The fourth implication of the model suggests that when parties are faced with an opposition party or coalition that is ideologically extreme relative to their own ideal point, they will be more likely to form an electoral coalition, so long as the probability of winning is larger as a coalition than running separately. This is because not entering government and being in the opposition means receiving no utility from office benefits and suffering a utility loss from having policy implemented by the government. This loss in utility might be quite significant if the government is ideologically extreme relative to one's own ideal point. Parties will presumably want to do all that they can to keep such an 'extreme' government from coming to power. Parties will be likely to form a pre-electoral coalition in these circumstances if the probability of entering government is larger as a coalition than from running independently. In other words, parties will be more likely to form a pre-electoral coalition if this is the best way of keeping an 'extreme' government from coming to power. As I have argued in chapter three, there is strong empirical evidence to suggest that disproportional electoral institutions provide an electoral bonus to large parties or coalitions through their mechanical effect on the translation of votes into seats (Clark & Golder 2006). Thus, the probability of entering government as an electoral coalition compared to running independently should be larger the more disproportional the electoral system. While it is not possible to know the precise identity of the potential government prior to the election, parties should expect to suffer a greater utility loss from government policy when the party system is ideologically polarized. This line of reasoning generates two related hypotheses:

Hypothesis 4:   Party system polarization increases the likelihood of pre-electoral coalitions when the electoral system is sufficiently disproportional.

Hypothesis 5:   An increase in the disproportionality of the electoral system will increase the probability of forming a pre-electoral coalition. This positive effect should be stronger when the party system is polarized.

Although coalition analysts have suggested for years that government coalitions are more likely to form between parties with similar policy preferences, four of the five hypotheses presented here have not appeared in the government coalition literature. To some extent, this fact should not come as a surprise. After all, the disproportionality of the electoral rules should not affect the government coalition formation process. However, one would think that party leaders who are deciding whether to form a coalition and contemplating possibly being in opposition should take account of the ideological position of other potential governments, regardless of whether this coalition bargaining process is occurring prior to the election or afterward. Nevertheless, it is rare for the government coalition literature to address the ideological positions of other potential governments.

6.2 Empirics

6.2.1 Data and Model

The data set used in the following analysis comprises electoral coalitions in 293 legislative elections in 20 advanced industrialized parliamentary democracies between 1946 and 1998. The countries included are Australia, Austria, Belgium, Canada, Denmark, Finland, France, Germany, Iceland, Ireland, Italy, Japan, Luxembourg, the Netherlands, New Zealand, Norway, Portugal, Spain, Sweden, and the United Kingdom. I do not include Israel, Malta, or Greece as I did in chapter three, because data were not available for the ideological variables. The slightly shorter time frame (1946–98 rather than 1946–2002) compared to that in chapter three is also the result of limited ideological data. The data are organized in dyadic format, both to match the formal model and to reflect the fact that the majority of pre-electoral coalitions in my sample (68%) are between two parties.[2] Therefore, each observation is a potential two-party coalition. Using a dyadic format yields 4,460 potential two-party electoral coalitions.

An example might help illustrate the data structure. In the 1983 Australian election, there were three parties, and thus three dyads: Labor Party-National Party, National Party-Liberal Party, and Liberal Party-Labor Party. If the two parties in a dyad formed a pre-electoral coalition (PEC), then the dependent variable is coded as one; it is zero otherwise. If a coalition forms among more than two parties, each of the relevant dyads can be coded accordingly as part of the coalition. For instance, if a pre-electoral coalition forms among three parties on the French left, then the dyads Communist-Socialist, Communist-Greens, and Socialist-Greens would each be coded as one.

I follow Budge et al. (2001) and include "all the significant parties which are represented in the national assembly" in the data set, where the significance of a party is defined in terms of government coalition or blackmail potential.[3] In effect, no parties with less than 1% of the vote are included. Of the 4,460 potential two-party electoral coalitions in the data set that could have formed, only 245 actually formed; this number is slightly more than 5%. As is often the case with dyadic data, the phenomenon of interest occurs only rarely (King & Zeng 2001). The more substantively interesting figure to note, though, is that pre-electoral coalitions competed in 37% of all the elections in the dyadic data set.

Given the dichotomous nature of the dependent variable, I use a probit model to test my hypotheses. In this model, the latent variable PEC^* measures the underlying propensity of party leaders in a dyad to form a pre-electoral coalition. The propensity to form a pre-electoral coalition, PEC^*, is modeled as a linear function of several independent variables:

$$PEC^* = \beta_0 + \beta_1 \text{Ideological Incompatibility} + \beta_2 \text{Polarization}$$
$$+ \beta_3 \text{Effective Threshold} + \beta_4 \text{Polarization} \times \text{Effective Threshold}$$
$$+ \beta_5 \text{Coalition Size} + \beta_6 \text{Coalition Size}^2 + \beta_7 \text{Asymmetry}$$
$$+ \beta_8 \text{Asymmetry} \times \text{Coalition Size} + \varepsilon$$

where PEC^* is a latent variable that is assumed to be less than zero when we do not observe a pre-electoral coalition and greater than zero when we do.

Ideological Incompatibility measures the absolute ideological distance between the parties in the dyad and is a proxy for the lack of ideological compatibility in the coalition. Data on the ideological position of each party are taken from the Manifesto Research Group, which evaluates each party on a one-dimensional scale that ranges from −100 (extreme Left) to +100 (extreme Right) (Budge et al. 2001). The most ideologically incompatible electoral coalition to form occurred in the Australian elections of 1954 between the Liberal Party and the National Party. Out of a possible 200-unit difference, they were 99.1 units apart.

Polarization is a measure of the ideological dispersion in the party system and is calculated as the absolute ideological distance between the largest left- and right-wing parties in the party system. The most polarized party system in which a pre-electoral coalition formed was in Sweden in 1985 (80.9 units), and the least polarized party system was in Belgium in 1978 (0.79 unit). The data are again taken from the Manifesto Research Group. This particular measure of party system polarization is most appropriate because of the fact that government coalitions are almost always going to contain either the main party on the left or the main party on the right. Thus, parties worried about an 'extreme' government (relative to their own ideological positions) coming to power will be concerned primarily with the ideological positions taken by these parties.

As in chapter three, *Effective Threshold* measures the effective electoral threshold (Lijphart 1994). The effective electoral threshold ranges from a low of 0.7 in the Netherlands since 1956 to a high of 35 in countries with single-member districts such as Canada and the United Kingdom. This variable acts as a proxy for the disproportionality of the electoral system: the higher the effective threshold, the larger the disproportionality. Qualitatively similar results to those presented here are found if the log of average district magnitude is used instead of the effective threshold. The interaction term *Polarization × Effective Threshold* is included to test the conditional nature of Hypotheses 4 and 5.

Coalition Size measures the percentage of the total seats won by the two parties in the dyad in the *previous* election. This variable is a proxy for the expected success of the potential coalition in the current election. The largest pre-electoral coalition to form occurred in the Austrian elections of 1959 between the People's Party and the Socialist Party. Between them, the coalition members controlled 95% of the legislative seats. In order to test the quadratic nature of Hypothesis 2, it is necessary to also include *Coalition Size²*.

Asymmetry measures the asymmetric strength of the two parties in the potential coalition dyad and ranges from 0 to 1, with larger numbers indicating a higher level of asymmetry. It is calculated as the ratio of the seat shares of the two parties in the dyad (Party 1 and Party 2):

$$\text{Asymmetry} = \begin{cases} \dfrac{\text{Seatlag}_1}{\text{Seatlag}_1 + \text{Seatlag}_2} & \text{if} \quad \dfrac{\text{Seatlag}_1}{\text{Seatlag}_1 + \text{Seatlag}_2} \geq 0.5 \\[3ex] 1 - \dfrac{\text{Seatlag}_1}{\text{Seatlag}_1 + \text{Seatlag}_2} & \text{if} \quad \dfrac{\text{Seatlag}_1}{\text{Seatlag}_1 + \text{Seatlag}_2} < 0.5 \end{cases}$$

where *Seatlag$_i$* is the percentage of seats won by party i in the previous election. To make interpretation easier, this variable is then normalized to range from 0 to 1 by subtracting 0.5 and multiplying by two. The interaction term *Asymmetry × Coalition Size* is included to test the conditional nature of Hypothesis 3.

The predictions from the hypotheses are shown in table 6.1. The coefficient on *Ideological Incompatibility* (β_1) should be negative, since the likelihood of electoral coalition formation is expected to decline as the potential coalition partners become more ideologically incompatible. The marginal effect of party system

Table 6.1

Predicted Effect of Row Variables on PEC Formation

Variable	Prediction
Ideological Incompatibility (β_1)	Negative
Effective Threshold (β_3)	Positive
Polarization × *Effective Threshold* (β_4)	Positive
Coalition Size (β_5)	Positive
*Coalition Size*² (β_6)	Negative
Asymmetry × *Coalition Size* (β_8)	Negative
$\beta_3 + \beta_4$*Polarization*	Always positive
$\beta_2 + \beta_4$*Effective Threshold*	Positive when *Effective Threshold* is high
$\beta_7 + \beta_8$*Coalition Size*	Negative when *Coalition Size* is high

polarization is $\beta_2 + \beta_4$*Effective Threshold.* This marginal effect is expected to be positive when the electoral system is sufficiently disproportional, i.e., when *Effective Threshold* is high. Thus, β_4 must be positive. The marginal effect of electoral system disproportionality is $\beta_3 + \beta_4$*Polarization.* This marginal effect should be positive irrespective of the level of *Polarization.* It follows then that β_3 should be positive. The coefficient on *Coalition Size* (β_5) is expected to be positive, whereas the coefficient on *Coalition Size*² (β_6) is expected to be negative. This is because the probability of pre-electoral coalition formation should initially increase with coalition size and then decrease. This should be the case irrespective of the level of *Asymmetry.* The marginal effect of *Asymmetry* is $\beta_7 + \beta_8$*Coalition Size.* This marginal effect should be negative, since *Asymmetry* is expected to reduce the likelihood of pre-electoral coalition formation when the potential coalition size is sufficiently large. Thus, β_8 should be negative.

6.2.2 Results and Interpretation

The results from two models are provided in table 6.2. The first column presents results from a random effects probit model, where observations are clustered by election in order to take account of any unobserved factors specific to each election that might influence pre-electoral coalition formation.[4] The second column reports results from a probit model with robust standard errors. The results across the two models are very similar. However, a likelihood ratio test indicates that the random-effects probit model is superior.[5] As a result, my inferences are based on this model. Note, however, that the standard probit model with robust standard errors shows qualitatively similar results.

Table 6.2
Determinants of the Propensity to Form Pre-Electoral Coalitions

Dependent Variable: Did a Pre-Electoral Coalition Form? 1 Yes, 0 No		
Regressor	PROBIT1 (random effects)	PROBIT2
Ideological Incompatibility	-0.007*** (0.003)	-0.006*** (0.002)
Polarization	-0.003 (0.005)	-0.002 (0.002)
Effective Threshold	0.019* (0.01)	0.02*** (0.005)
Polarization × Effective Threshold	0.0005* (0.0003)	0.0003** (0.0001)
Coalition Size	0.053*** (0.011)	0.044*** (0.008)
Coalition Size ^{2}	-0.0006*** (0.0001)	-0.0005*** (0.0001)
Asymmetry	-0.066 (0.297)	-0.041 (0.218)
Asymmetry × Coalition Size	-0.030*** (0.009)	-0.025*** (0.006)
Constant	-2.40*** (0.31)	-2.08*** (0.18)
Observations	3495	3495
Log Likelihood	-625.8	-681.3

Notes: Standard errors are given in parentheses (robust for PROBIT2). Random effects are clustered on each election. Data: 4,460 dyads, 20 advanced industrialized countries, 1946–98.
$*p < 0.10$; $**p < 0.05$; $***p < 0.01$ (two-tailed).

The results presented in table 6.2 indicate that all of the coefficients have the predicted signs and are statistically significant where expected. However, the interpretation of these coefficients is complicated by the use of multiple interaction terms and the fact that the coefficients relate to the latent propensity to form preelectoral coalitions rather than the actual quantity of interest—the probability of forming a pre-electoral coalition. Much more revealing and substantively meaningful information can be obtained if we explicitly examine the marginal effect of each variable on the probability of pre-electoral coalition formation.

A good way to examine the marginal effects of variables in interaction models is graphically (Brambor, Clark, & Golder 2006). Hypothesis 5 states that an increase in the disproportionality of the electoral system will increase the probability of pre-electoral coalition formation and that this positive effect should be stronger when the party system is more polarized. In figure 6.1, I plot the marginal effect of a one-unit increase (from its mean) in the effective threshold on the probability that an electoral coalition forms across the observed range of party system polarization when all other variables are held at their means. The solid black line indicates how this marginal effect changes with party system polarization. The 95% confidence intervals around this line allow us to determine the conditions under which electoral thresholds have a statistically significant effect on the likeli-

Figure 6.1

Marginal Effect of a One-Unit Increase in *Effective Threshold* (from Its Mean)

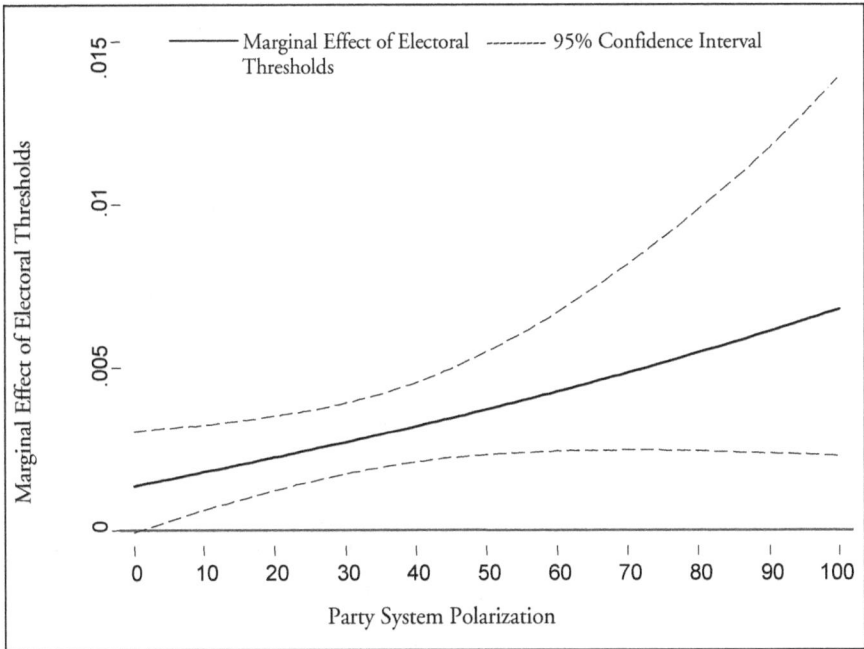

hood of pre-electoral coalition formation.[6] The marginal effect is statistically significant whenever both the upper and lower bounds of the confidence interval are above (or below) the zero line. Figure 6.1 clearly indicates that more disproportional electoral systems increase the probability of electoral coalition formation once the level of party system polarization is above zero. In other words, electoral system disproportionality nearly always makes pre-electoral coalitions more likely. This finding is exactly as predicted. Figure 6.1 also indicates that this positive effect increases with party system polarization. Again, this result is exactly as predicted. Overall, Hypothesis 5 is strongly confirmed by the evidence.

Hypothesis 4 states that party system polarization should increase the likelihood of pre-electoral coalitions only when the electoral system is sufficiently disproportional. In figure 6.2, I plot the marginal effect of a one-unit increase in party system polarization across the observed range of electoral system disproportionality when all other variables are held at their means. Again, the solid black line indicates how this marginal effect changes with the effective threshold when all other variables are set at their means. The dashed lines here represent 90% confidence intervals. Figure 6.2 indicates that party system polarization makes pre-electoral coalitions more likely only when the effective threshold is greater than 17. To get a sense of the substantive significance of this result, it should be noted that

Figure 6.2

Marginal Effect of a One-Unit Increase in Party System *Polarization* (from Its Mean)

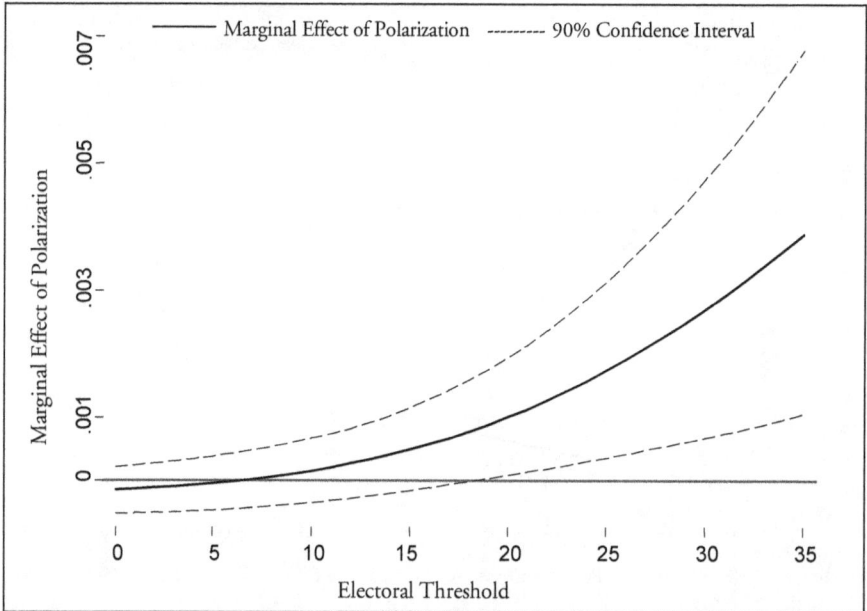

10% of the sample has an effective threshold greater than 17.

Hypothesis 3 states that an increase in the asymmetric distribution of electoral strength among coalition partners should reduce the likelihood of electoral coalition formation when the potential coalition size is sufficiently large. I plot the marginal effect of a 0.01-unit increase in electoral coalition asymmetry across the possible range of coalition size in figure 6.3. Again, all other variables are held at their means. It is easy to see that *Asymmetry* makes electoral coalition formation less likely only when the potential coalition size is greater than 11% of the legislative seats. This finding is exactly as predicted and is substantively significant, since 81% of the sample observations involve potential coalitions that expect to win more than 11% of the seats. Thus, figure 6.3 provides strong support for Hypothesis 3.

Hypothesis 2 states that pre-electoral coalition formation should be a quadratic function of expected coalition size—the likelihood that a pre-electoral coalition forms should initially rise with expected coalition size and then fall. In figure 6.4, I plot the marginal effect of a one-unit increase in expected coalition size at all possible values of coalition size, and at varying levels of *Asymmetry:* when *Asymmetry* is one standard deviation below its mean (figure 6.4a), when *Asymmetry* is at its mean (figure 6.4b), and when *Asymmetry* is one standard deviation above its mean (figure 6.4c).

Consider figure 6.4a first. If the expected size of the coalition is less than 34% of the seats, then an increase in coalition size is expected to make pre-electoral

Figure 6.3

Marginal Effect of a 0.01-Unit Increase in *Asymmetry* (from Its Mean)

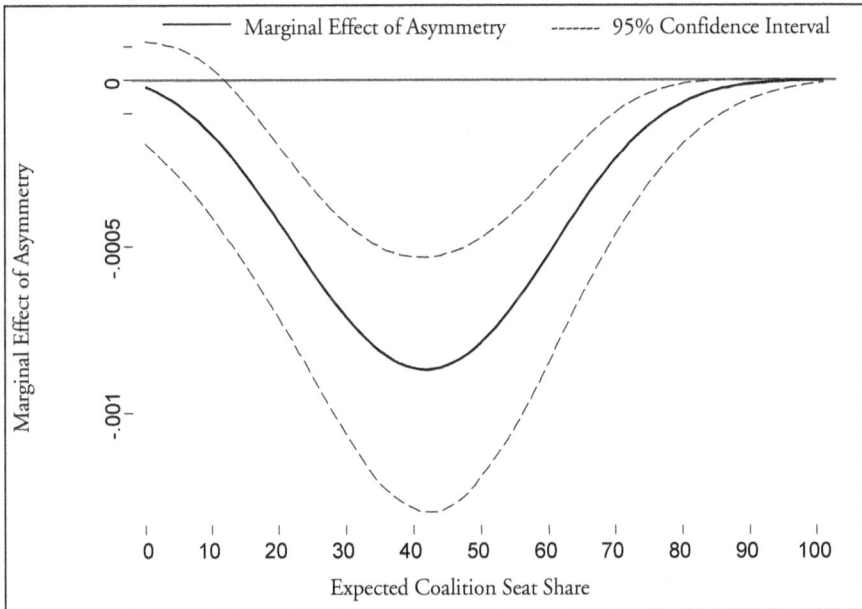

coalition formation more likely. Again, to provide some substantive meaning to this result, it should be noted that nearly 59% of the sample falls into this category. However, if the potential coalition is expected to win more than 43% of the seats, then increasing the coalition size any more is expected to make electoral coalitions less likely. Roughly 29% of the potential coalition dyads expect to win more seats than this percentage. Thus, figure 6.4a provides strong evidence that an increase in coalition size will make electoral coalitions more likely when the expected size of the coalition is small, but less likely when the expected size is large.

While figures 6.4b and 6.4c provide corroborating evidence for this hypothesis, they also allow the reader to see how increasing the asymmetry between coalition parties modifies the effect of an increase in coalition size. The point to note is that as we increase *Asymmetry* (move from 6.4a to 6.4b to 6.4c), the coalition size at which making the coalition any larger would reduce the probability of electoral coalition formation falls. For example, increasing coalition size makes pre-electoral coalitions less likely when the coalition is expected to win more than 43% of the seats if *Asymmetry* is one standard deviation below its mean. However, an increase in coalition size is expected to make electoral coalitions less likely when the coalition is expected to win just 29% of the seats if *Asymmetry* is one standard deviation above its mean. Overall, the evidence presented in figure 6.4 provides strong support for both Hypotheses 2 and 3.

Figure 6.4

Marginal Effect of a One-Unit Increase in Expected Coalition Seatshare

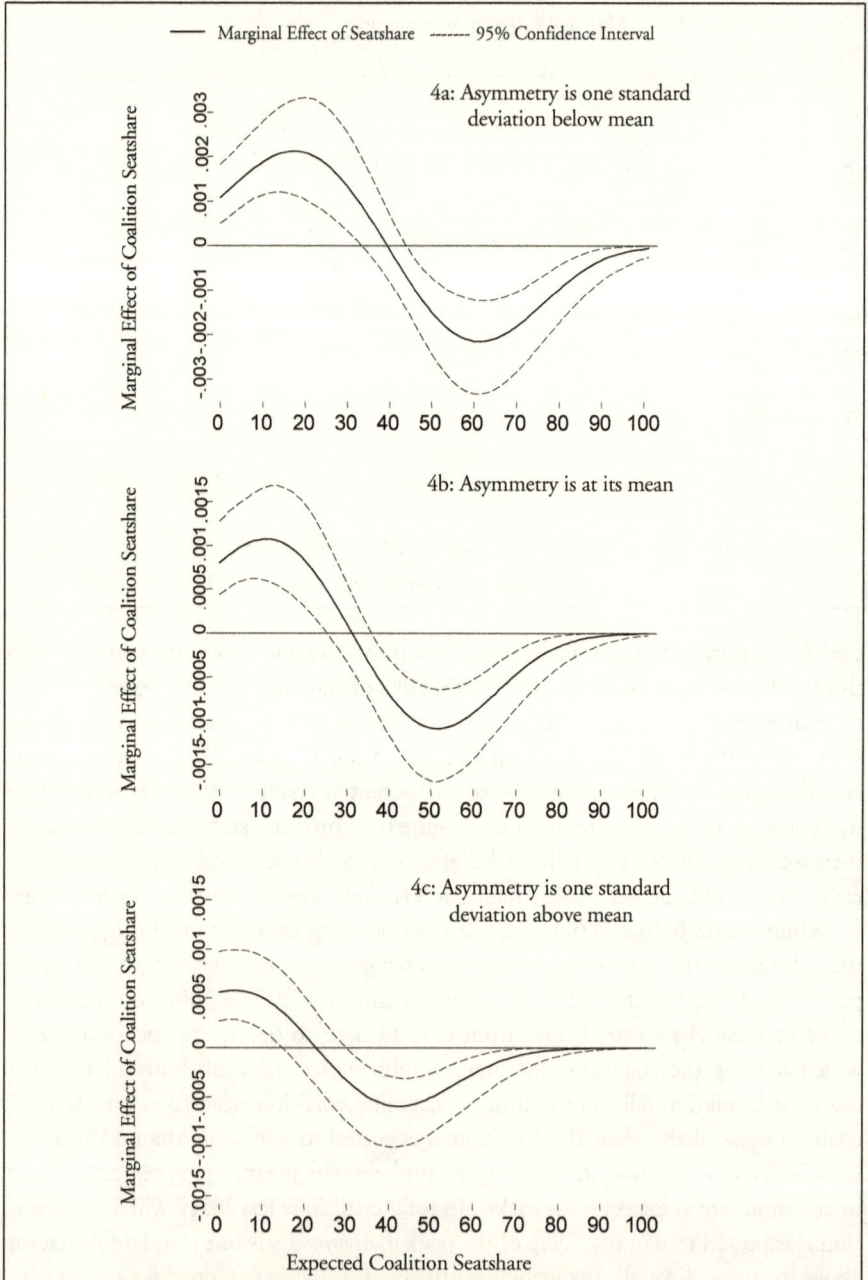

Table 6.3
Substantive Effect of Explanatory Variables on PEC Formation

Variable	Predicted Probability Mean	Plus 1 Std. Dev.	Difference in Probability	Percent Change in Probability	Numerical Significance
Ideological Incompatibility	.034	.024	-.010	-29.1	-44.6
	[.021, .050]	[.013, .039]	[-.017, -.004]	[-45.1, -11.3]	[-75.8, -17.8]
Polarization	.018	.016	-.002	-11.2	-8.9
(Effective Threshold at min)	[.009, .031]	[.007, .031]	[-.010, .007]	[-47.1, 38.0]	[-44.6, 31.2]
Polarization	.180	.267	.087	150.8	+388.0
(Effective Threshold at max)	[.109, .267]	[.165, .384]	[.009, .170]	[104.6, 209.9]	[40.1, 758.2]
Effective Threshold	.032	.048	.016	154.5	+71.3
(Polarization at min)	[.015, .057]	[.023, .086]	[-.001, .039]	[98.4, 233.6]	[-4.5, 173.9]
Effective Threshold	.045	.148	.103	387.3	+459.4
(Polarization at max)	[.011, .110]	[.058, .281]	[.037, .198]	[180.9, 780.9]	[165.0, 883.1]
Asymmetry	.009	.008	-.0004	2.7	-1.8
(Coalition Size at min)	[.003, .019]	[.003, .019]	[-.005, .004]	[-42.2, 52.8]	[-22.3, 17.8]
Asymmetry	.833	.573	-.259	-33.4	-1155.1
(Coalition Size at max)	[.433, .994]	[.167, .921]	[-.425, -.070]	[-64.6, -7.1]	[-1895.5, -312.2]

Notes: The first and second columns present the predicted probability of a pre-electoral coalition forming when the row variable is either at its mean or one standard deviation higher, while all other variables are held at their means (unless otherwise specified). The third and fourth columns present the difference and percentage change in the two predicted probabilities respectively. Given a sample size of 4,460, the final column indicates how many more (or fewer) electoral coalitions are expected to form if the row variable was one standard deviation above its mean. All estimates have 95% confidence intervals in parentheses. Confidence intervals were calculated via simulation.

Thus far, I have shown that each of the explanatory variables affects the probability of electoral coalition formation in the predicted manner. All of the hypotheses were borne out by the results. However, it is natural to ask whether these effects are substantively significant.[7] How much more likely is a pre-electoral coalition to form if I increase one of the variables by a standard deviation? How many more (or fewer) pre-electoral coalitions would be observed in a sample of this size if I increased one of the variables by a standard deviation? This information is presented in table 6.3.

The first column in table 6.3 indicates the predicted probability that a pre-electoral coalition forms when the row variable is at its mean and all of the other variables are held at their means (unless otherwise specified). Thus, the predicted probability that a coalition forms when all the variables are at their means is .034, with a 95% confidence interval [.021, .050]. Similarly, the predicted probability when *Effective Threshold* is at its minimum observed value but all of the other variables are at their means is .018 [.009, .031].[8]

The second column indicates the predicted probability of pre-electoral coalition formation when the row variable increases by one standard deviation above its mean, while all other variables are held at their means (again, unless otherwise specified). For instance, the predicted probability of electoral coalition formation is .024 [.013, .039] when *Ideological Incompatibility* is one standard deviation above its mean and all of the other variables are at their means.

The third column indicates the change in predicted probability between the first and second column. In other words, the third column captures the effect of a one-standard-deviation increase in the named variable on the predicted probability of electoral coalition formation. Thus, an increase of one standard deviation in the effective electoral threshold above its mean increases by .13 [.037, .198] the probability that an electoral coalition forms when *Polarization* is at its maximum observed value and the other variables are at their means.

The fourth and fifth columns provide the most substantively interesting information. The fourth column indicates the percentage change in predicted probability that arises from a one-standard-deviation increase in the named variable. This number is often referred to as the 'relative risk.' Thus, a one-standard-deviation increase in *Ideological Incompatibility* above its mean *reduces* by 29.1% [11.3, 45.1] the probability that a pre-electoral coalition will form when all the other variables are set at their means. It should be noted that although the predicted probabilities associated with the different scenarios presented in table 6.3 appear quite small, it is clearly the case that changes in each explanatory variable can be of significant substantive importance. As King and Zeng (2001, 711) note, "relative risks are typically considered important in rare event studies if they are at least 10–20%" when we increase an explanatory variable from one standard deviation below its mean to one standard deviation above its mean. Note that here I am increasing each variable by only one standard deviation above its mean.

Finally, the fifth column indicates how many more (or fewer) electoral coalitions there would be in a sample of this size (4,460) if the named variable increased by one standard deviation above its mean. This number is calculated as the difference in predicted probability multiplied by the sample size. Thus, a one-standard-deviation increase in *Ideological Incompatibility* above its mean would lead to 45 [17.8, 75.8] fewer electoral coalitions when all of the other variables are held at their means. If the effective threshold were increased by a standard deviation when party system polarization is at its maximum observed value, then we would expect to see an extra 459 [165.0, 883.1] electoral coalitions. Given that there were only 245 pre-electoral coalitions in the data set, the numbers in this column represent quite substantial changes.

Taken together, the results presented in table 6.3 indicate that the explanatory variables not only have a statistically significant effect on pre-electoral coalition formation, but that they have a substantively meaningful effect as well. Even a small change in the effective electoral threshold (all else equal) can have a significant effect on the likelihood of pre-electoral coalition formation. If all of the countries in the sample were to move from a very low threshold of 2% (Denmark in the 1970s) to a slightly higher threshold of 8.9% (Norway in the 1970s) while keeping all other variables at their means, then the percentage increase in the predicted probability of electoral coalition formation would be 175%, and we would expect to see an additional 64 pre-electoral coalitions. More dramatic changes to the electoral threshold would have even larger effects on pre-electoral coalition formation, particularly in countries with smaller or medium-sized parties.

6.3 Conclusion

Given that it is often infeasible for a single party to govern alone in parliamentary democracies, party leaders are faced with a strategic choice. They can either form an electoral coalition prior to the election or participate in government coalition bargaining afterwards. The fact that one regularly observes electoral coalitions across a broad range of countries suggests that they must offer some form of political advantage—at least some of the time. Since electoral coalitions do not always emerge, it must equally be true that there are costs associated with party leaders coordinating their pre-electoral strategies. As a result, I presented a simple bargaining model in chapter four, in which the decision of party leaders to form a pre-electoral coalition depended on the associated costs and benefits. These costs and benefits were modeled in terms of preferences over policy and the division of office benefits. The hypotheses generated by this model were subjected to several tests in this chapter using a data set containing information on potential coalition dyads in 20 industrialized parliamentary democracies from 1946 to 1998. The results indicate that pre-electoral coalitions are more likely to form when the expected coalition size is large, but not too large, and when the potential coalition partners are similar in size. They are also more likely to form if the party system is polarized and the electoral institutions are disproportional.

Chapter one opened with an empirical question: Why did pre-electoral coalitions form in the 2002 French legislative elections but not in the 2002 Dutch elections? The results from the statistical model presented here clearly throw light on this specific question. While France typically had the highest predicted probabilities of coalition formation in the sample, the Netherlands consistently had the lowest. The results presented in table 6.2 indicate that the proportionality of a country's electoral system plays a major role in the likelihood of electoral coalition formation. While the average district magnitude in France is one, the average district magnitude in the Netherlands is the largest in the sample (150). This situation suggests that it should not be surprising to see that pre-electoral coalitions are more likely to form in France compared to the Netherlands. Moreover, the fact that party system polarization is relatively low in the Netherlands compared to France provides a further explanation for the observed variation in coalition formation in these countries.

Appendix: The Disproportionality Hypothesis Revisited

In my initial analysis of electoral coalitions in chapter three, I found evidence in support of what I called the Disproportionality Hypothesis. Specifically, I showed that parties are more likely to be in pre-electoral coalitions, and that these coalitions are more likely to be successful, in countries that have both a disproportional electoral system and a large number of parties. At the time, I indicated that the Disproportionality Hypothesis should also apply to the actual probability of electoral coalition formation—electoral coalition formation should be more likely in countries that have disproportional electoral rules and a large party system. I can now test this hypothesis using the dyadic data set presented in this chapter.

When examining the probability of electoral coalition formation, one might think to treat each election as a single observation and distinguish between elections in which pre-electoral coalitions form and those in which they do not. The problem with this response is that such an approach treats all elections with at least one pre-electoral coalition as the same, regardless of the number of electoral coalitions that form, the electoral significance of these coalitions, and the number of parties involved in these coalitions. This approach is clearly problematic. The dyadic data set described in this chapter avoids these problems and has the advantage of being able to take account of the number of electoral coalition opportunities in a given election.

To test the Disproportionality Hypothesis as it relates to the actual likelihood of electoral coalition formation, I use the same explanatory variables as in chapter three, but I now employ a random-effects probit model, where observations are clustered by election:

$$PEC^* = \beta_0 + \beta_1 \text{Effective Threshold} + \beta_2 \text{Electoral Parties}$$
$$+ \beta_3 \text{Effective Threshold} \times \text{Electoral Parties} + \varepsilon$$

$$(6.1)$$

As before, PEC^* is a latent variable that is assumed to be less than zero when no pre-electoral coalition forms and greater than zero when one does; *Electoral Parties* measures the effective number of electoral parties in each election; and *Effective Threshold* measures the effective electoral threshold. If the Disproportionality Hypothesis is correct, then the coefficient on the interaction term (β_3) should be positive. More importantly, the marginal effect of electoral thresholds should significantly increase the probability of electoral coalition formation once the party system becomes sufficiently large.

The results from my analysis are presented in table 6.4. As predicted, the coefficient on the interaction term is both positive and significant. But does electoral system disproportionality significantly increase the probability of electoral coalition formation when the party system is sufficiently large? To see whether this is the case, I plot the marginal effect of a one-unit increase in the effective threshold

Table 6.4
Disproportionality Hypothesis Revisited

Dependent Variable: Did a Pre -Electoral Coalition Form? 1 Yes, 0 No

Regressor	PROBIT3 (random effects)
Electoral Parties	-0.133***
	(0.047)
Effective Threshold	-0.009
	(0.013)
Effective Threshold × Electoral Parties	0.009***
	(0.003)
Constant	-1.63***
	(0.24)
Observations	4395
Log Likelihood	-816.47

Notes: Standard errors are given in parentheses. Random effects are clustered on each election. Data come from 4,460 dyads in 20 advanced industrialized countries from 1946 to 1998.
$^*p < 0.10$; $^{**}p < 0.05$; $^{***}p < 0.01$ (two-tailed).

across the observed range of party system size in figure 6.5.

As predicted, effective thresholds increase the probability of electoral coalition formation only once the party system is sufficiently large. Specifically, the party system must have more than 2.5 effective electoral parties before an increase in the effective threshold encourages party leaders to form pre-electoral coalitions. Since roughly 90% of the sample has a larger party system than this requirement, this finding indicates that electoral system disproportionality nearly always increases the probability of electoral pacts. As figure 6.5 illustrates, this effect is much stronger when the party system is large.

It is clear that effective thresholds affect the probability of electoral coalition formation in the expected manner. But is the effect substantively meaningful? If I increase the effective threshold from its mean to one standard deviation higher when holding the effective number of electoral parties at its mean, then electoral coalitions are 203.3% [160.8, 253.9] more likely to form. Again, 95% confidence intervals are shown in brackets. In a sample the size of the one analyzed here, an increase in the effective threshold by one standard deviation above its mean would be expected to produce an additional 108.1 [64.4, 164.3] pre-electoral coalitions.

Figure 6.5

Disproportionality Hypothesis Revisited

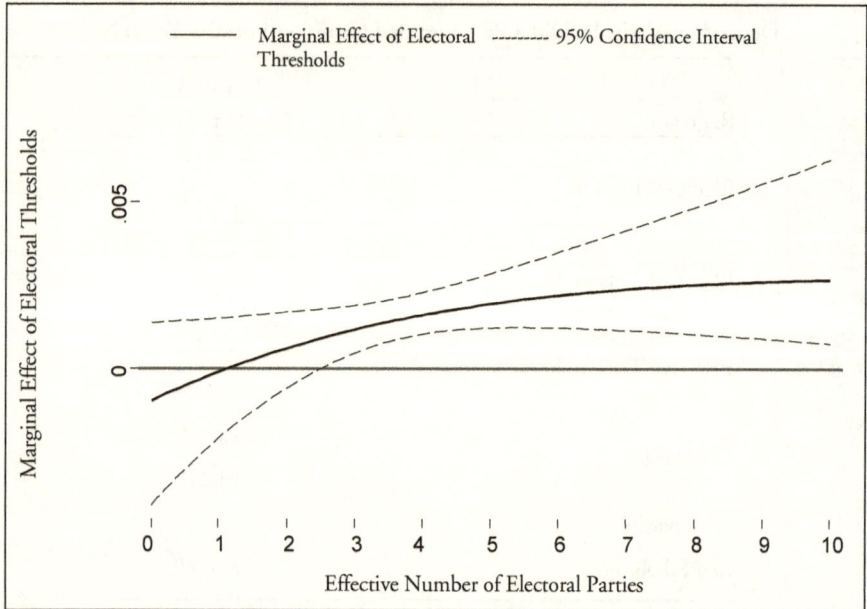

Remember that this is quite a significant number, given that there were only 245 observed coalitions in the data set.

In sum, the analysis conducted here confirms the Disproportionality Hypothesis and produces results remarkably similar to those presented in chapter three. Taken together, the evidence presented here and in chapter three indicates that electoral coalitions are more likely to form and be successful in countries with disproportional electoral rules and a large number of parties.

At this point, the reader might wonder why I did not simply combine the analyses conducted in chapters three and six in a single model. Why, for example, do I not just include *Electoral Parties* and its interaction with *Effective Threshold* in the model (6.1) specified in this chapter? The primary reason is that the Disproportionality Hypothesis was not explicitly generated by the bargaining model outlined in chapter four. Since my goal in this chapter was to specifically test the generalizability of the bargaining model, I did not include the additional variables necessary to test the Disproportionality Hypothesis as well. Moreover, it is arguable that the effective number of parties or party system size is already being taken into account in model (6.1) by the *Coalition Size* variable. While these reasons may not convince all readers that the strategy I followed was correct, I should note that the inclusion of the additional variables would not substantively change any of the inferences drawn from the results in table 6.2.

CHAPTER SEVEN

Pre-Electoral Agreements and Government Coalitions

Thus far, I have developed and tested a theory of pre-electoral coalition formation. I found that factors such as the disproportionality of the electoral system, the ideological compatibility and relative size of potential coalition partners, and the ideological polarization of the party system affect the probability that parties will form pre-electoral coalitions. By focusing solely on electoral coalitions, I have, to some extent, ignored the larger context in which party elites choose pre-electoral strategies. While this is a useful place to start, given our lack of theoretical and empirical knowledge about electoral coalitions, it is important to remember that pre-electoral coalition formation is part of a larger dynamic process, in which party leaders are ultimately interested in government coalition formation. In other words, party elites make choices about their electoral strategies based on how they think that these choices will affect post-electoral outcomes. Indeed, the theory presented in chapter four explicitly recognizes this idea by assuming that party leaders who are deciding whether to coordinate their electoral strategies will consider the impact that forming a pre-electoral coalition would have on their party's chance of entering government following the election. I now begin to investigate in more detail the relationship between pre-electoral agreements and government coalitions.

Although the literature on government coalitions is voluminous and well developed, there are almost no analyses that ever allow for the possibility of pre-electoral coalitions in a systematic manner. In effect, scholars of coalition politics know very little about the relationship between pre-electoral agreements and government coalitions. In this chapter, I begin to remedy this lack of knowledge by addressing four main questions. Are government coalitions based on pre-electoral agreements more likely to form? Do government coalitions based on electoral pacts take less time to form? Are government coalitions based on electoral alliances more ideologically compatible? And are government coalitions based on electoral coalitions more stable and less prone to collapse? The answers to these questions are theoretically, substantively, and normatively important.

The answers are theoretically important, because I have argued that one reason why party elites choose to form pre-electoral coalitions is that these coalitions increase the probability that they get to enter government. In chapter three, I indicated that pre-electoral coalitions will be electorally advantageous in many circumstances, because they can enable parties to overcome electoral thresholds or take advantage of the electoral bonus provided to large parties by disproportional electoral rules (Clark & Golder 2006; Cox 1997; Duverger 1963 [1954]). I also suggested that electoral coalitions can be advantageous in situations where voters are risk averse in regard to the policy positions of potential future governments (Ashworth & Bueno de Mesquita 2006; Snyder & Ting 2002). Ultimately, though, party leaders will typically only be interested in increasing the percentage of seats or votes that they receive to the extent that doing so will help them enter government. As of yet, I have presented no evidence that pre-electoral coalitions actually do increase the probability that parties get to enter government. Clearly, if electoral coalitions do not help parties enter government, then the theory presented in this book might rightfully be called into question.

The answers to the questions posed in this chapter are substantively important as well. Consider the question about how long it takes to form a government coalition. As Martin and Vanberg (2003, 323–24) note:

> delay [in forming government coalitions] has important implications for governance. The caretaker governments that administer the affairs of state while negotiations proceed generally have no authority to take major policy initiatives. In addition, delay in government formation creates uncertainty. The identity of government parties, the allocation of portfolios to particular politicians and the content of policy compromises among coalition partners have yet to be determined. Consequently, the future direction of government policy is uncertain, which may have important implications for domestic and international economic and political actors.

Indeed, there is growing empirical evidence that uncertainty about the identity of government coalitions can have serious consequences on the economy (Bernhard & Leblang 2006). For example, uncertainty over government coalition formation has been found to affect exchange rate markets (Bernhard & Leblang 2002), the likelihood of speculative attacks (Leblang 2002), stock market volatility (Leblang & Mukherjee forthcoming), and the types of assets in which market actors choose to invest (Bernhard & Leblang 2006, chapters 3–4). Given this recent evidence, pre-electoral coalitions could conceivably have a significant substantive effect on the economy, and on governance in general, if they are found to reduce the length of time that it takes a government to form.

Finally, the answers to these questions are also normatively important. As I noted in the introduction, it is reasonable to think that pre-electoral coalitions have significant normative implications for the representative nature of government (Powell 2000), because electoral coalitions increase the identifiability of government alternatives, thereby allowing voters to explicitly register their support for a particular government coalition. Arguably, pre-electoral coalitions also increase the transparency of the government formation process and provide government coalitions with greater legitimacy and stronger mandates. It is worthwhile to investigate whether this added legitimacy and stronger mandate actually translate into more directly observable political outcomes, such as more stable and longer-lived governments. It is also worthwhile to examine whether pre-electoral coalitions have other normative benefits that can be directly observed. For example, are government coalitions that are based on pre-electoral agreements more ideologically compatible? After all, it seems reasonable to consider ideological compatibility as a good quality for government coalitions to have, because it indicates a greater ideological congruence between the electorate of the government and the policy position of the government coalition.

To foreshadow some of the analyses to come, I find that pre-electoral coalitions do increase the probability that parties in these coalitions will enter government. In fact, a government coalition based on pre-electoral agreements is (on average) a staggering 123 times more likely to form than an identical coalition that is not based on a pre-electoral pact. I also find that government coalitions that are based on electoral coalitions are more ideologically compatible than other types of government coalitions. In fact, government coalitions based on pre-electoral coalitions are almost twice as likely to contain parties that are adjacent in the ideological space as governments that are not based on pre-electoral arrangements. In addition, I find that governments that are based on pre-electoral coalitions take much less time to form than other types of government coalitions, so long as the government coalition is sufficiently large. Although pre-electoral coalitions shorten the length of time that it takes to form a government coalition after an election, I find that PECs do not make those government coalitions any more stable or enduring than other types of government coalitions.

7.1 Identity of Government Coalitions

After the voters have gone to the polls and the ballots have been counted, does being part of an electoral coalition make parties more likely to get into government? We know that coordinating an electoral coalition prior to an election can increase the share of votes and seats won by the member parties. But do the benefits of joining a pre-electoral coalition end after the allocation of legislative seats, or do they continue to influence the government coalition formation process?

Elections rarely determine who gets into government in any final sense. While some parties will be seen as winners and others as losers at election time, the precise identity of the government is normally determined only later in negotiations between different political parties (Laver & Shepsle 1996; Cheibub, Przeworski, & Saiegh 2004; Gallagher, Laver, & Mair 2001, 57–66). Once the votes have been tallied and legislative seats have been distributed, there are many government coalitions that could potentially form. In fact, the precise number of potential coalitions in any bargaining situation after an election is $2^p - 1$, where p is the number of legislative parties. The analysis in this section builds on the political science literature examining those factors that influence which of these potential coalitions becomes the government coalition (Martin & Stevenson 2001; Warwick 1996; Franklin & Mackie 1984; Browne 1970).

While it has been hypothesized that various factors (such as whether the potential coalition includes a strong party, whether it is minimal winning or not, and whether it is composed of ideologically compatible parties) affect the identity of the government coalition that ultimately forms, the principal hypothesis of interest here is the following:

Government Coalition Hypothesis: Potential government coalitions that are also electoral coalitions are more likely to be chosen as the government than potential government coalitions that are not based on pre-electoral agreements.

7.1.1 Data and Model

Although there are numerous potential government coalitions that could form after an election, only one is actually 'chosen' to do so. Given this choice situation, it is necessary to model the government formation process "as an unordered discrete choice problem where each formation opportunity (*not* each potential coalition) represents one case and where the set of discrete alternatives is the set of all potential combinations of parties that might form a government" in that formation opportunity (Martin & Stevenson 2001, 38). In the analysis that follows, I employ a conditional logit model to address this unordered discrete choice prob-

lem (McFadden 1973; McFadden 1974).[1] While conditional logit models are perhaps more common in the political science literature addressing questions of voter
choice (Alvarez & Nagler 1995; Alvarez & Nagler 1998; Alvarez & Nagler 2000),
they have recently begun to be used more widely to examine government formation (Bäck 2003; Druckman, Martin, & Thies 2004; Warwick 2005).

According to the conditional logit model, the probability that individual i
chooses outcome m when the dependent variable y has J unordered, discrete outcomes (potential government coalitions) is:

$$P(y_i = m \mid x_i) = \frac{e^{x_{im}\beta}}{\sum_{j=1}^{J} e^{x_{ij}\beta}} \quad \text{for } m = 1 \text{ to } J$$

$$(7.1)$$

where β represents a vector of coefficients and x_{im} represents a row vector of independent variables associated with outcome m for the ith individual (Long 1997).
The model is called 'conditional' because it is specified conditional on the attributes of each outcome (or coalition) as perceived by individual i. Thus, the coefficients for the independent variables are the same for each outcome (β is not
indexed by outcome m), but the values taken by the independent variables for each
individual do differ by outcome (x is indexed by both i and m).

In testing my Government Coalition Hypothesis, I build explicitly on the
work of Martin & Stevenson (2001). They provide perhaps the most comprehensive overview of the government formation literature as it stands at present,
and they test a large number of hypotheses with a variety of model specifications.
I employ the model that they conclude is the best predictor of government formation as a baseline against which to compare the results obtained when I take
account of whether potential government coalitions are based on pre-electoral
agreements. This baseline specification incorporates multiple attributes of potential government coalitions that have been hypothesized over the years to affect
government formation. For example, is the potential coalition a minority coalition, a surplus coalition, or a minimal winning (connected) coalition (Riker
1962; Laver & Shepsle 1996; Axelrod 1970)? How many parties are members of
the coalition, and does it contain the largest legislative party, the median ideological party, the previous prime minister, or the formateur (Leiserson 1968; van
Deemen 1989; Laver & Schofield 1998; Austen-Smith & Banks 1988)? Is the
incumbent coalition (Strøm, Budge, & Laver 1994)? How large are the ideological divisions in the coalition and in the opposition (De Swaan 1973; Warwick
1994; Laver & Schofield 1998)? Is there an anti-system party present in the coalition (Budge & Keman 1990)? Is there a 'Very Strong Party' or a 'Merely Strong

Party' in the coalition (Laver & Shepsle 1996)? And does it matter if the potential government coalition is faced with an investiture vote (Strøm 1990)?

Martin & Stevenson do, in fact, include a variable indicating whether the potential government coalition is based on a pre-electoral agreement. One problem is that their variable is not particularly comprehensive. For example, they find that 19% of elections in their sample have pre-electoral pacts, whereas my own data reveal that 42% of the same elections have electoral coalitions. The correlation between my measure of electoral coalitions and Martin & Stevenson's is less than 0.6. Although I find more than twice the number of electoral coalitions as Martin & Stevenson do in their sample of formation opportunities, my own total actually remains a somewhat conservative estimate. This finding is because some pre-electoral coalitions of two or more parties are included as a single party in the Martin & Stevenson data set owing to the fact that their data on political parties do not list all of the parties separately. For instance, none of the Israeli pre-electoral coalitions is coded as such, since the coalitions themselves are included as though they were single parties.

Using their somewhat limited measure of pre-electoral pacts, Martin & Stevenson conclude that electoral coalitions do increase the probability that member parties will enter government. The question is whether this conclusion will remain valid once the pre-electoral coalition variable is measured more accurately. One reason why this conclusion might be open to question is that Martin & Stevenson's data are based entirely on country studies in Laver & Budge (1992). The electoral pacts listed in these country studies were likely mentioned precisely because many of them had gone on to form government coalitions after the election. This situation obviously has the unfortunate consequence that less successful electoral alliances are systematically omitted from Martin & Stevenson's sample, thereby potentially biasing their results in favor of finding that government coalitions based on pre-electoral pacts are more likely to form. Another problem with Martin & Stevenson's analysis as it relates to pre-electoral pacts is that it examines all government formation opportunities irrespective of whether these formation opportunities occur after an election or in an inter-election period. This is a problem because pre-electoral coalitions should only influence the identity of the government if the government coalition is formed after an election.[2] I do not expect pre-electoral coalitions to play a role in the formation of replacement governments, i.e., those governments that take office following the collapse of the previous government but without a new election being called. In effect, Martin & Stevenson's decision to include all formation opportunities probably results in their underestimating the real effect of pre-electoral coalitions. Thus, there are reasons to believe that Martin & Stevenson overestimate or underestimate the impact of electoral coalition membership on parties entering government. The analysis that follows resolves these problems.

Except where otherwise indicated, I use the Martin & Stevenson (2001) data for the upcoming analysis. The data cover the following countries and years: Austria (1949–86), Belgium (1946–87), Denmark (1945–88), Germany (1961–87), Iceland (1946–87), Ireland (1965–89), Italy (1953–87), Luxembourg (1945–89), the Netherlands (1977–86), Norway (1961–89), and Sweden (1948–88). As with Martin & Stevenson's analysis, I focus only on those formation opportunities in which no single party controls a majority of the legislative seats. This leaves a total of 170 formation opportunities and 24,932 potential government coalitions.

Before presenting the results from my analysis, I should note that the conditional logit model assumes the independence of irrelevant alternatives (IIA) (Alvarez & Nagler 1998). This assumption requires that the relative probability of choosing one alternative (potential government coalition) over another does not depend on any of the other alternatives in the choice set. To evaluate the assumption of IIA, I conducted a test similar to that employed by Martin & Stevenson.[3] The results clearly indicated that I was unable to reject the null hypothesis that IIA holds. As a result, the conditional logit model can be employed to investigate government coalition formation.

7.1.2 Results and Interpretation

The results from four slightly different models are shown in table 7.1. The first model acts as a baseline and corresponds to the model that Martin & Stevenson (2001, 45) find best predicts government formation (Model 10 in their paper). I was able to replicate their results exactly. Arguably, there is reason to believe that this model is misspecified. Although *Single Party* is interacted with both *Very Strong Party* and *Merely Strong Party*, it does not appear as a separate term in their model. This is a problem because it is well established that all constitutive terms should be included in interaction models except in extremely rare circumstances (Friedrich 1982; Braumoeller 2004; Brambor, Clark, & Golder 2006). If the coefficient on an omitted constitutive term is not precisely zero, then all of the parameters of interest will be estimated with bias.[4] Because of this potential for bias in Martin & Stevenson's model, I present results from a model in which *Single Party* is included as a constitutive term (Model 2). As I stated before, Martin & Stevenson analyze all formation opportunities including those that occur in the inter-election period when a government falls but no new election is called. Because of my specific interest in the impact of pre-electoral coalitions on government formation, Model 3 presents results when I focus solely on formation opportunities that occur following an election. Finally, Model 4 presents results when I replace Martin & Stevenson's *Pre-Electoral Coalition* (*M-S*) meas-

Table 7.1

Identity of Government Coalitions

Dependent Variable: Did the Potential Government Coalition Form the Government? 1 Yes, 0 No

Independent Variables	All Formation Opportunities		Post-Election Formation Opportunities	
	Model 1 M-S Replication	Model 2 Add Single Party	Model 3 Post-Election Only	Model 4 PEC (Golder)
Pre-Electoral Coalition (M -S)	3.51***	3.40***	6.54***	
	(0.78)	(0.77)	(1.99)	
Pre-Electoral Coalition (G)				4.81***
				(0.73)
Minority Coalition	0.05	-0.20	-0.42	-0.83
	(0.57)	(0.60)	(0.89)	(0.91)
Minimal Winning Coalition	0.92***	1.32***	2.12***	2.05***
	(0.32)	(0.34)	(0.56)	(0.57)
Number of Parties	-0.26	-0.10	-0.07	-0.10
	(0.17)	(0.17)	(0.26)	(0.26)
Largest Party	0.99***	0.95***	0.96**	1.03***
	(0.30)	(0.30)	(0.38)	(0.39)
Median Party	0.10	0.18	0.46	0.51
	(0.24)	(0.24)	(0.36)	(0.35)
Ideological Divisions	-4.72***	-3.50***	-4.86***	-4.90***
	(1.14)	(1.19)	(1.75)	(1.77)
Ideological Divisions in Majority Opposition	1.04	1.86	2.36	3.12**
	(1.12)	(1.19)	(1.52)	(1.56)
Previous Prime Minister	0.00	0.05	-0.02	0.10
	(0.27)	(0.28)	(0.37)	(0.36)
Incumbent Coalition	1.69***	1.55***	1.81***	1.52***
	(0.24)	(0.24)	(0.35)	(0.37)
Minority Coalition with Investiture	-1.12***	-1.00***	-0.13	-0.12
	(0.38)	(0.38)	(0.55)	(0.55)
Anti-System Presence	-17.05***	-17.43***	-12.15**	-12.31***
	(3.72)	(3.73)	(4.92)	(5.00)
Single Party		1.47***	1.51**	1.80***
		(0.43)	(0.62)	(0.79)
Very Strong Party	1.12**	1.43***	1.78**	1.76**
	(0.48)	(0.51)	(0.79)	(0.62)
Very Strong Party × Single Party	0.93**	0.17	0.20	0.23
	(0.39)	(0.45)	(0.63)	(0.63)
Merely Strong Party	0.34	0.60*	-0.23	-0.30
	(0.33)	(0.35)	(0.50)	(0.48)
Merely Strong Party × Single Party	-1.91*	-2.59**	-2.03	-2.25*
	(1.09)	(1.11)	(1.28)	(1.26)
Log Likelihood	-410	-404	-184	-177
Formation Opportunities	170	170	96	96
Potential Coalitions	24932	24932	11912	11912
Correct Predictions [a]	42.4%	42.9%	47.9%	49%
Average p-value for rejecting IIA [b]	0.75	0.69	0.89	0.74

Notes: 'Model 1' replicates Model 10 from Martin & Stevenson (2001, 45). 'Model 2' adds Single Party as a constitutive term. 'Model 3' drops inter-election formation opportunities and only examines post-election formation opportunities. 'Model 4' uses my measure of pre-electoral coalitions rather than Martin & Stevenson's measure.

[a] indicates the percentage of the time that the coalition with the highest predicted probability actually formed.

[b] A p-value < 0.05 indicates that we can reject IIA.

*$p < 0.10$; **$p < 0.05$; ***$p < 0.01$ (two-tailed). Standard errors are in parentheses.

ure with my own, more comprehensive one, *Pre-Electoral Coalition (G)*. Thus, the four models allow the reader to see how the results change as I first estimate a fully specified version of Martin & Stevenson's model, then focus solely on post-election formation opportunities, and then use my new measure of pre-electoral coalitions. I show these four models to avoid confounding the effect of my new measure of pre-electoral coalitions with the effect of the other adjustments made to Martin & Stevenson's original model.

Before explicitly addressing the effect of pre-electoral arrangements on government formation, it is worth briefly considering how my adjustments to Martin & Stevenson's model affect some of their results more generally. Model 1 indicates that single parties that are very strong are more likely to enter government because the coefficient on the interaction term *Very Strong Party* × *Single Party* is both positive and significant.[5] A Party S is defined as a 'strong party' if it participates in any cabinet preferred by a legislative majority to the cabinet in which Party S holds all of the ministerial portfolios. If there is no alternative cabinet preferred by a majority to the one in which S has all of the portfolios, then S would be considered to be a '*very* strong party' (Laver & Shepsle 1996, 69–71). If a cabinet that includes S in a coalition is preferred by a majority to one in which S makes up the government on its own, then S is a '*merely* strong party.' The results from Model 1 would seem to support the central claim made by Laver & Shepsle in their much-cited model of portfolio allocation that single parties that happen to be very strong parties are likely to be in government. However, it is important to remember that Model 1 omits the constitutive term *Single Party*. As a result, all of the coefficients are potentially biased. It turns out that the inferences that one can draw change quite dramatically once *Single Party* is included as a separate variable.

Consider the following results from Model 2. The coefficient on *Very Strong Party* × *Single Party* shrinks by about 80% and stops being significant.[6] In contrast, the coefficient on the constitutive term *Single Party* is both positive and highly significant. The coefficient on *Merely Strong Party* × *Single Party* remains negative and significant. Together, these three coefficients indicate that being a very strong party or a merely strong party does *not* make it any more likely that a single party will enter government. This conclusion runs directly counter to the received wisdom that single parties have a better chance of forming a government when they are very strong or merely strong (Laver & Shepsle 1996).

In Model 3, I drop all government formation opportunities that do not take place after an election. Doing so reduces the number of formation opportunities from 170 to 96 and the number of potential government coalitions from 24,932 to 11,912. While the focus on post-election formation opportunities appears to leave many of the results unaffected, there are some interesting changes. For example, investiture votes no longer seem to make it harder for minority coalitions to enter government after an election—the coefficient on *Minority Coalition with Investiture* drops in magnitude by nearly 90% and is no longer statistically significant. This result suggests that Strøm's (1984, 1990) widely cited claim that investiture votes make minority governments less likely should be qualified. The evidence presented here indicates that investiture votes pose a hurdle only for minority governments that form in the inter-election period and not those that form after an election. Why this would be the case, however, is unclear. While there are no additional changes in significance among the other variables in Model 3, the size of the coefficients on *Minimal Winning Coalition* and *Pre-Electoral Pact* change quite markedly. These changes indicate that potential coalitions that are minimal winning or based on pre-electoral arrangements are significantly more likely to enter government after an election than they are in the inter-election period.[7] Note that this finding provides support for my earlier claim that Martin & Stevenson underestimate the effect of pre-electoral coalitions by including all government formation opportunities. What these results indicate is that the existing literature on government coalitions may be missing important features of the government formation process by treating post-election and inter-election formation opportunities as identical.

In Model 4, I finally replace Martin & Stevenson's *Pre-Electoral Coalition* measure with my own, more comprehensive one. The results in Model 4 confirm Martin & Stevenson's claim that potential coalitions based on pre-electoral agreements are significantly more likely to enter government than potential coalitions without electoral pacts. More precisely, potential coalitions are 123 [29, 514] times more likely to become the government if they are based on a pre-electoral arrangement than if they are not.[8] Again, 95% confidence intervals are shown in brackets. Clearly, pre-electoral coalitions do help political parties enter government, as I argued in the introduction and in chapter four.

How do my results compare with those of Martin & Stevenson, though? The first thing to note is that my measure of pre-electoral coalitions produces a much more precise estimate of the effect of electoral pacts on government formation than Martin & Stevenson's measure—the standard error associated with the coefficient on *Pre-Electoral Coalition* in Model 4 is about one-third the size of that in Model 3. This finding provides some evidence to suggest that I have measured pre-electoral coalitions more accurately than Martin & Stevenson.

Recall also that there are reasons to think that Martin & Stevenson may have either overestimated or underestimated the impact of a pre-electoral agreement on the government formation process in their original analysis. The results from Model 1, where all formation opportunities are included, indicate that potential coalitions are only 33 [7, 155] times more likely to become the government if they are based on an electoral coalition than if they are not. Thus, Martin & Stevenson's reported results underestimate the positive effect of pre-electoral coalitions by 369%. This finding should not come as a surprise, given that I have already stated that pre-electoral coalitions should only be able to influence government formation after elections. By including inter-election formation opportunities, Martin & Stevenson significantly underestimate the impact of pre-electoral coalitions. What would have happened if Martin & Stevenson had focused solely on post-election formation opportunities, as I do? Although I do not show the results from such a model in table 7.1, they would indicate that potential coalitions are 695 [14, 34,061] times more likely to become the government if they are based on an electoral pact than if they are not. Thus, Martin & Stevenson would now have overestimated the impact of pre-electoral coalitions by 566%. Again, this finding should not come as a surprise, since I have already stated that Martin & Stevenson's data on pre-electoral coalitions is likely to be systematically biased in favor of including only those electoral coalitions that actually entered government owing to the source that they employed (Laver & Budge 1992). In sum, there is evidence that Martin & Stevenson both underestimated and overestimated the effect of pre-electoral agreements on the government formation process.

How well do these models predict the identity of the government that actually emerged in each formation opportunity? To address this issue, I calculated the predicted probability that each potential coalition in a formation opportunity became the government and found the one with the highest predicted probability. In Model 1, the government alternative with the highest predicted probability formed the government in 72 of the 170 formation opportunities. Thus, Model 1 predicts the correct government 42.4% of the time. As Martin & Stevenson (2001, 47) themselves note, this rate "is a real improvement over the usual predictive success of empirical models of government formation." The predictive accuracy of the model increased when I focused solely on post-election formation opportunities. The potential government with the highest predicted probability now formed the government 47.9% of the time (46 out of 96 formation opportunities). This last result indicates that scholars of government coalitions are much better at predicting the identity of government coalitions that form after elections than those that form in inter-election periods. Finally, the predictive accuracy of the model increases even further if I use my more comprehensive measure of pre-electoral pacts. Model 4 now correctly predicts the identity of 47 out of 96 governments (49%). Thus, my preferred model improves by 16% the already high predictive accuracy of Martin & Stevenson's model.

Another way to think about the predictive accuracy of the models in table 7.1 is simply to compare the average predicted probability of those potential coalitions that form the government with those alternatives that do not do so. If the former is higher, then we have some indication that the model performs better than simple chance alone. In Model 4, the average predicted probability for those government alternatives that did form was .38, whereas the average predicted probability for the government alternatives that were not chosen was only .005. Clearly, Model 4 does significantly better than one would expect by chance alone.

To conclude, the results in table 7.1 clearly show that the benefits of forming a pre-electoral coalition do not end on election day. Even after the votes have been counted and the legislative seats have been allocated, being part of an electoral coalition increases the probability that member parties will enter government. Thus, parties have good reasons to join a pre-electoral coalition, even ignoring the mechanical and strategic effect of electoral rules benefiting large parties. Note that the analysis conducted here may help to resolve an issue raised in chapter three. For example, the results in table 7.1 help to explain why parties might form pre-electoral coalitions even in countries such as the Netherlands and Israel that have fairly proportional electoral rules—pre-electoral coalitions help member parties enter government.

7.2 Duration of Government Formation

Once legislative seats have been allocated after an election, the process of bargaining over the next government cabinet begins. The analysis conducted in the previous section indicates that pre-electoral coalitions increase the probability that member parties will enter government. But do they also have an effect on how long it takes for a government to form? The duration of negotiations preceding the formation of a new cabinet is a relatively understudied area of coalition politics. With the exception of studies by Martin & Vanberg (2003) and Diermeier & van Roozendaal (1998), very little is known about the factors that affect the length of time that it takes a government to form. To date, no previous study has examined the effect of electoral pacts on the duration of government formation. This dearth of studies is somewhat surprising, given the growing evidence that ongoing uncertainty over a government's identity has been found to affect various domestic and international economic indicators, such as exchange rate markets (Bernhard & Leblang 2002), stock market volatility (Leblang & Mukherjee 2005), and investment decisions (Bernhard & Leblang 2006).

As table 7.2 indicates, there is considerable cross-national variation in the length of time that it takes to form a government following an election. If one party obtains a majority of the seats, then it is normally understood that this party will form a cabinet on its own, and the only question is who will get which portfolio. This situation explains why it takes only about a week (7.8 days), on average, for a cabinet to form in the United Kingdom. In countries where many parties gain legislative representation, it can take much longer to form a cabinet because it is not always obvious which combination of parties will be able to form the government, how these parties will allocate portfolios amongst themselves, and what the coalition policy will be.[9] For example, the average length of the government formation process in the Netherlands is about three months (85.7 days). In

Table 7.2

Descriptive Data on Duration of Government Formation Process

Country	Min	Max	Mean	N
Austria	23	129	52.1	15
Belgium	2	148	59.7	17
Denmark	0	35	9.5	21
Finland	25	80	54.7	14
France (5th Republic)	1	11	3.5	11
Germany	23	73	36.4	14
Iceland	1	76	30.6	16
Ireland	7	48	18.7	16
Italy	11	126	47.3	14
Luxembourg	19	52	32	9
Netherlands	31	208	85.7	16
Norway	0	16	2.5	13
Portugal	1	45	24	7
Spain	2	58	28.6	7
Sweden	0	25	5.7	17
United Kingdom	1	18	7.8	14
ALL	0	208	31.8	221
*Type of Government**				
No Pre-Electoral Coalition	0	208	47.1	93
Pre-Electoral Coalition	0	129	29.2	46
All Government Coalitions	0	208	41.2	139

Notes: Data come from the Parliamentary Democracy Data Archive (Müller & Strøm 2000a, Strøm, Müller & Bergman 2003) and cover governments that form after an election between 1946 and 1998. Bargaining duration measures the number of days between the election and the day on which the new government is officially inaugurated.
* indicates that data are based only on coalition governments, i.e., single-party governments are omitted.

fact, the longest delay in government formation in this sample of countries occurred in the Netherlands, at almost seven months (208 days) (Timmermans & Andeweg 2000, 370). It is not uncommon for a formateur to fail to form a coalition on the first or even the second attempt in some countries without single-party majorities. For example, it took seven different government coalition proposals over 106 days for a government to finally form after the 1979 Belgian legislative elections (De Winter, Timmermans, & Dumont 2000, 315). Overall, the mean length of time that it takes to form a government after an election is about a month (31.8 days).[10]

There is good reason to think that parties that have already reached a pre-electoral agreement should be able to form governments more quickly than parties that start the bargaining process after an election. Indeed, several of the country experts who contributed to the Müller & Strøm (2000a) volume on coalition governments in Western Europe mention electoral coalitions (or the lack thereof) when discussing the duration of government formation in their country of interest. For example, Nousiainen (2000, 272) states that coalition building in Finland is a "complicated and time-consuming process," owing in part to the fact that there are no party alliances. As table 7.2 illustrates, this observation is reflected in the fact that Finnish governments take about 54.7 days, on average, to form. Thiébault (2000, 506) makes a similar point when he points out that government formation in France tends to be rapid precisely because the parties are so often "linked by an electoral alliance." This situation helps to explain why it takes only about 3.5 days on average for a French government to take office after an election. Likewise Saalfeld (2000, 47) claims in his discussion of German governments that the "phase of orientation and intra-party talks about important policy issues and possible coalition partners . . . can be very short or skipped if there has been a pre-election pact." Thus, there is already considerable anecdotal evidence suggesting that governments based on electoral coalitions should take less time to form than other governments.

Slightly more systematic evidence is shown in the bottom of table 7.2, where I compare the average length of time that it takes a coalition government to form after an election when it is based on a pre-electoral agreement and when it is not. This section of table 7.2 only includes data on coalition governments and, therefore, omits the single-party cabinets found in the United Kingdom and Spain. The data indicate that it takes a government 47.1 days on average to form if it is not based on a pre-electoral coalition, and only 29.2 days if it is. This difference in average bargaining time is statistically significant at the 99% level. This preliminary look at the effect of pre-electoral coalitions on the length of time it takes to form a government suggests that electoral pacts do speed up the process of government formation.

Note, though, that one would expect pre-electoral agreements to have an effect on bargaining delays only if there are a sufficient number of parties bargaining over government formation. For example, if the number of parties in the government is zero (a non-partisan government) or one (a single-party government), then it is impossible for such a government to be based on a pre-electoral pact. Thus, logically it must be the case that the number of parties in the government is two or more for pre-electoral coalitions to have an effect. Note, also, that it probably takes longer to form a government when there are many parties bargaining over government formation (Martin & Vanberg 2003). This longer period is because an increase in the number of parties in a potential government is likely to induce delay by exponentially expanding the number of possible portfolio allocations. It is also because an increase in the size of the potential government is likely to reduce the range of policies acceptable to all of the potential members and create a need for a more detailed coalition agreement; this result, in turn, is likely to cause a further delay in government formation (Tsebelis 2002). It follows that pre-electoral coalitions should have an even stronger reductive effect on the length of time that it takes to form a government if that government contains many parties. Thus, the principal hypothesis to be tested in this section is the following:

Pre-Electoral Coalition Hypothesis: Pre-electoral agreements will reduce the length of time that it takes to form a government so long as there are at least two parties in the government. The size of this reductive effect will increase with the number of parties in the government.

A detailed examination of how pre-electoral agreements affect the delay in government formation should probably control for other factors, such as whether the incumbent government wins the election, the ideological compatibility of the potential government, and the existence of investiture requirements, that might plausibly be thought to affect the length of time that it takes to form a government. For example, it should be the case that governments that were in power prior to an election should form more quickly than governments that include non-incumbent parties. This prediction is because these 'incumbent' governments have presumably already resolved some of their policy differences while in power and may well have already begun negotiations on an allocation of portfolios and coalition policy prior to the election. Governments that are ideologically compatible should also reduce the duration of coalition negotiations compared to those that are not, because party leaders should "be better able to judge which kinds of proposals are acceptable to parties that are ideologically close to their own than for parties that are more ideologically distant" (Martin & Vanberg 2003, 325). Finally, investiture votes are thought to pose a particular hurdle for the formation of minority governments (Strøm 1990, 25). As a result, one might reasonably infer that an investiture requirement slows the formation process for minority governments. One reason is that the formateur has to spend more time gathering information to make sure that the proposed government coalition can actually pass the investiture vote in this situation. In contrast to minority governments, investiture requirements pose no real obstacle to other forms of government because, by definition, they already control majority support in the legislature. Thus, the additional hypotheses to be examined are as follows:

Incumbent Government Hypothesis: Governments that were in power prior to an election should take office more quickly than governments that include non-incumbent parties.

Ideological Compatibility Hypothesis: Governments that are more ideologically incompatible should take longer to form.

Investiture Hypothesis: Investiture requirements should slow the formation of minority governments.

7.2.1 Data and Model

I tested these hypotheses using survival (event history) analysis. The central concept in survival analysis is the hazard function or hazard rate, $h(t)$. This hazard rate is the probability that an 'event' will occur at a particular point in time, given that the 'event' has yet to occur. In terms of the analysis here, the 'event' in question is the formation of a government.[11] One of the issues with employing survival analysis is in choosing a model that appropriately parameterizes this baseline hazard rate (or time dependency). In the analysis that follows, I base my inferences on results from a Weibull model that allows for monotonically increasing or decreasing hazard rates.[12] Although I show the results from a Cox proportional hazards model alongside those from the Weibull model in table 7.3 to indicate their equivalence, I prefer to base my inferences on the Weibull analysis, because I wish to evaluate the effect of pre-electoral coalitions on the *expected duration* of government bargaining delays rather than simply on the hazard ratios (Cleves, Gould, & Gutierrez 2004, 232).

With the exception of the variable *Pre-Electoral Coalition,* indicating whether the government is based on a pre-electoral pact, the data employed in the upcoming analysis come from the Parliamentary Democracy Data Archive (PDDA), unless otherwise stated (Müller & Strøm 2000*a*; Strøm, Müller, & Bergman 2003).[13] *Government Parties* indicates the number of parties in the government. The interaction term *Pre-Electoral Coalition × Government Parties* is required to test the conditional nature of the Pre-Electoral Coalition Hypothesis. *Incumbent Government* indicates whether the government was the incumbent government at election time. *Investiture* indicates whether the government faced an investiture vote, and *Minority Government* specifies whether the government was a minority government. The interaction term *Investiture × Minority Government* is required to test the conditional nature of the Investiture Hypothesis. Finally, *Ideological Range* measures the absolute difference in the ideological positions of the two governmental parties that are furthest apart on the left-right policy dimension according to data from the Manifesto Research Group (Budge et al. 2001). This variable is simply calculated as $|x_R - x_L|$, where x_R is the ideological position of the governmental party furthest to the right and x_L is the ideological position of the governmental party furthest to the left. *Government Formation Duration* is the dependent variable that measures the number of days from the election to the day on which the new government is officially inaugurated. The sample includes data on all cabinets that formed after an election from 1946 to 1998 in the 16 countries listed in table 7.2.

Table 7.3

Determinants of the Duration of Government Formation Process

Independent Variables	Weibull	Cox
Pre-Electoral Coalition	-1.16	-1.38
	(0.92)	(0.99)
Government Parties	-0.35***	-0.40***
	(0.12)	(0.13)
Pre-Electoral Coalition ×	0.60**	0.68**
Government Parties	(0.28)	(0.31)
Incumbent Government	-0.002	0.02
	(0.19)	(0.19)
Ideological Range	-0.002	-0.001
	(0.006)	(0.006)
Investiture	0.06	0.11
	(0.33)	(0.33)
Minority Government	0.67	0.66
	(0.47)	(0.47)
Investiture ×	-0.75	-0.79
Minority Government	(0.50)	(0.51)
Constant	-3.47***	
	(0.89)	
ln ρ (shape parameter)	0.16	
	(0.12)	
Log Likelihood	-261.74	-743.06
Observations	182	182

Notes: Weibull and Cox proportional hazards estimates; robust standard errors clustered by country in parentheses. A test using Schoenfeld residuals indicates that the proportional hazards assumption is not violated. The Efron method is employed for handling ties in the Cox model. Data are based on post-electoral coalition cabinets from the 16 countries shown in table 7.2 between 1946 and 1998. $*p < 0.05$; $**p < 0.01$ (two-tailed).

7.2.2 Results and Interpretation

The results from my analysis are shown in table 7.3. The coefficients in table 7.3 are expressed as proportional hazard estimates. As a result, a positive coefficient indicates that the covariate in question increases the hazard rate or reduces the length of time that it takes to form a government. Conversely, a negative coefficient implies that the covariate reduces the hazard rate or delays the formation of a government. I employ robust standard errors clustered by country to take account of the fact that the observations in each country may not be independent.

The principal hypothesis of interest relates to the effect of pre-electoral coalitions on the duration of government bargaining delays. The fact that the coefficient on *Pre-Electoral Coalition* is indistinguishable from zero indicates that electoral pacts have no effect on the duration of government formation when the number of parties in government is zero (or the government is non-partisan). This finding is exactly as predicted. However, there is strong evidence that pre-electoral

Figure 7.1

Marginal Effect of PECs on Expected Bargaining Duration in Days

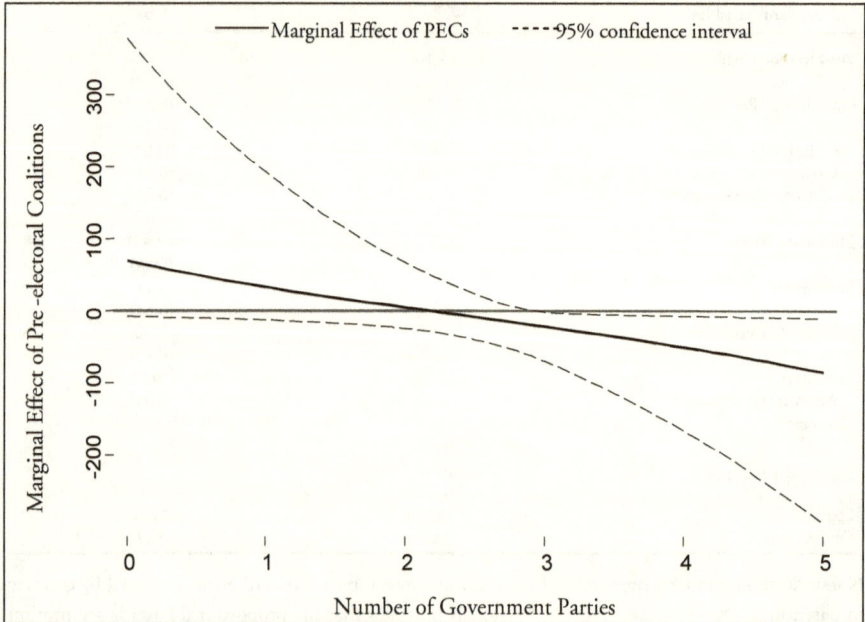

agreements do start to increase the hazard rate or shorten the time it takes to form a government as the number of government parties increases. This finding is because the coefficient on the interaction term *Pre-Electoral Coalition ×* *Government Parties* is positive and significant, as predicted.

To better illustrate the effect of pre-electoral coalitions on government bargaining delays, I plot the marginal effect of electoral pacts on expected bargaining duration, measured in days, across the observed range of the number of government parties in figure 7.1, using the results from the Weibull model.[14] *Ideological Range* is set at its mean value, while *Investiture, Minority Government,* and *Incumbent Government* are all set to zero. The solid line is the marginal effect of pre-electoral arrangements on expected bargaining duration, and the dashed lines are 95% confidence intervals. The marginal effect is significant whenever both the upper and lower bounds are above (or below) the zero line. (Please refer to equation (7.2) in note 14.)

As predicted, pre-electoral coalitions never have a significant reductive effect on expected bargaining delays when the number of parties in government is less than two. This result should come as no surprise, since electoral coalitions require at least two parties. However, electoral pacts do significantly shorten the time that it takes to form a government once there are more than 2.9 governmental parties. This finding is substantively meaningful, since roughly 50% of all coalition cabinets comprise more than two parties. A three-party government not based on a pre-electoral pact would take about 22 additional days to form than an identical cabinet based on an electoral coalition. Thus, in this case one would have about three extra weeks without an operational government. A four-party government not based on a pre-electoral coalition would mean about seven extra weeks (50 days) without an operational government. Clearly, pre-electoral agreements shorten the time that it takes a government to take office after an election.

What about the other hypotheses? First, there is strong evidence that increasing the number of parties in the potential government will increase the length of coalition negotiations so long as there is no pre-electoral pact, because the coefficient on *Government Parties* is negative and significant. In fact, the results from the Weibull model indicate that an extra party in the government when there is no pre-electoral coalition will decrease the hazard rate by 29% [10, 44]. Again, 95% confidence intervals are shown in brackets. At first sight, this result might seem to confirm Martin & Vanberg's (2003, 327) claim that large coalitions have longer government bargaining delays. However, it should be noted that increases in coalition size do not cause additional bargaining delays if the government is based on a pre-electoral coalition, because the marginal effect of *Government Parties* when there is a pre-electoral coalition is now positive rather than negative ($-0.35 + 0.60 = 0.25$). Perhaps this is evidence that pre-electoral pacts resolve the bargaining difficulties that arise with large government coalitions prior to the election, rather than leaving them to be resolved after the election. Thus, coalition size affects government bargaining delays only when there is no pre-electoral agreement.

Second, there is no evidence to support Martin & Vanberg's (2003, 332) claim that "minority governments must endure a longer bargaining process than majority governments." The fact that the coefficient on *Minority* is not significant indicates that minority governments that do not face an investiture vote have no significant effect on government bargaining delays. Although the coefficient on *Investiture × Minority Government* is negative as predicted, it is statistically insignificant. Together, these results clearly indicate that minority governments have no more trouble putting a government together than do majority governments, irrespective of whether they face an investiture vote or not. The results also confirm the findings made by Diermeier & van Roozendaal (1998, 621–22) that investiture votes have no significant effect on government bargaining delays.

Finally, what about the effect of incumbency status and ideological compatibility? Contrary to expectations, experience of being in office together in the immediate past does not seem to shorten the time that it takes to form a cabinet. Also contrary to expectations, ideological divisions within an incoming government have no significant effect on government bargaining delays.[15] This last finding contradicts Martin & Stevenson's (2003, 331) claim that ideological divisions significantly increase government bargaining delays.

To conclude, countries that routinely have government cabinets consisting of more than two parties could significantly reduce the period of time in which no major policies can be implemented while everyone waits for a new government to take office by promoting pre-electoral coalition formation. Given the effect of the extra uncertainty over the identity of the government that bargaining delays are likely to induce, such a reduction may well have significant positive consequences for various political and economic indicators.

7.3 Ideological Compatibility of Government Coalitions

Thus far, I have shown that pre-electoral coalitions affect the likelihood that member parties will enter government and how long those governments take to form. But do they also affect the ideological compatibility of the government coalition that forms? In chapter six, I showed that ideological compatibility between potential coalition partners makes it more likely that these parties will reach a pre-electoral agreement. A similar result holds in the existing coalition literature regarding government coalitions—strong evidence indicates that government coalitions are more likely to form between ideologically similar parties. The question addressed in this section is whether governments based on pre-electoral agreements are *more* ideologically compatible than government coalitions that are not based on electoral pacts.

In chapter four, I speculated that governments based on pre-electoral agreements would be more ideologically compatible. This speculation rested on the belief that the ideological compatibility constraint facing potential coalitions will be stronger prior to elections than afterward, because voters might be unwilling to vote for electoral coalitions comprising parties with incompatible or incoherent policy preferences. At the very least, parties with wildly different policy agendas are unlikely to form an appealing coalition in the eyes of their electorates, with regular voters probably hesitating to support such an electoral pact. This concern with how the ideological divisions within a potential electoral coalition might affect its electoral success is often reflected in the decision of party elites to invest considerable resources to explicitly measure the coalition's expected electoral consequences (Kaminski 2002). For example, there is evidence that party leaders sometimes employ private polling companies to carry out surveys asking voters whether they would support particular coalition arrangements (Kaminski 2001).

Note that I am not claiming that government coalitions do not face ideological compatibility constraints; of course, they do (Warwick 2005). It is entirely reasonable to think that parties feel constrained in their coalition choices even after an election, owing to the fact that voters could potentially punish ideologically incompatible governments at subsequent elections. However, if party leaders think that a particular 'incompatible' coalition is likely to be successful in office, then they may gamble that voters will not punish them in the next election. Party leaders might also be willing to form incompatible government coalitions after an election if they have a high discount rate. In other words, party leaders might prefer to get the benefits of office and the ability to make policy today, even though they know that they will be punished in the future. Indeed, we know empirically that ideologically incompatible coalitions do sometimes form after elections (Brams, Jones, & Kilgour 2002). All I am claiming is that one might expect that parties have additional leeway to form more ideologically incompatible coalitions after an election, because voters are no longer such an immediate constraint on their actions. Of course, whether this is the case is an empirical question and one that, to my knowledge, has never been addressed before. Thus, the principal hypothesis tested in this section is the following:

Ideological Compatibility Hypothesis: Governments based on pre-electoral arrangements should be more ideologically compatible, *on average*, than governments that are not.

7.3.1 Data and Results

I employ a variety of different measures of ideological compatibility to test this hypothesis. I use data from the Manifesto Research Group detailing the positions of parties on the traditional left-right policy dimension to construct measures of the range and spread of ideological diversity in coalition governments for 17 parliamentary democracies from 1946 to 1998 (Budge et al. 2001). The left-right policy dimension ranges from -100 on the left to $+100$ on the right. The countries covered are Australia, Austria, Belgium, Denmark, Finland, France (both the Fourth and Fifth Republics), Germany, Iceland, Ireland, Italy, Japan, Luxembourg, the Netherlands, New Zealand, Norway, Portugal, and Sweden. Canada, Spain, and the United Kingdom are excluded, since the data indicate that these countries have never experienced coalition governments.[16] As in the previous section, the range of ideological diversity is calculated as $|x_R - x_L|$, where x_R is the ideological position of the governmental party furthest to the right and x_L is the ideological position of the governmental party furthest to the left. The spread of ideological diversity is calculated as $\sqrt{\sum_{i=1}^{n} p_i(x_i - \bar{x})^2}$, where p_i is party i's proportion of government-controlled seats in the legislature, x_i is party i's ideological position on the left-right policy scale, $\bar{x}$ is the weighted mean policy position of the government $(\sum_{i=1}^{n} p_i x_i)^2$, and n refers to the number of parties in the government (Warwick 1994, 154).

Some descriptive statistics are shown in table 7.4. The most incompatible government coalition in terms of its ideological range (90.5) is a Finnish government coalition in 1946 that includes the Swedish People's Party, Center Party, Conservatives, and Liberals (the parties are listed from furthest left to furthest right). This government is not based on a pre-electoral agreement. In contrast, the three government coalitions with the lowest range of ideological diversity are all based on pre-electoral agreements. The data in table 7.4 clearly indicate that the average range of ideological diversity for governments that are not based on an electoral agreement (29.0) is higher than that for governments that are based on pre-electoral coalitions (22.3). A difference in means test indicates that we can be 98% confident that governments that are not based on electoral pacts are more incompatible in terms of their ideological range than governments that are based on electoral pacts. The data also indicate that governments that are not based on pre-electoral agreements have greater ideological spread (11.4) on average than governments that are based on pre-electoral agreements (9.2). A difference in means test confirms that we can be 95% confident of this result. Thus, governments that are based on pre-electoral coalitions are more ideologically compatible in terms of both their range and their spread than those that are unconstrained by electoral alliances.

While these data are informative and support my Ideological Compatibility Hypothesis, one might reasonably question whether it is meaningful to compare the ideological compatibility of government coalitions across countries in this way. The data from the Manifesto Research Group may indicate that Party A and Party B in country 1 are ideologically further apart than, say, Party C and Party D in country 2. But is it meaningful to compare these two distances? For example, it might be the case that the party system in country 1 is simply more ideologically diverse than the party system in country 2. If this were the case, then voters in country 1 might very well have a different view of what constitutes an ideologically incompatible coalition than voters in country 2. Even if one ignores the difficulties that arise if one party system is more ideologically diverse than the other, it might also be the case that Parties A and B in country 1 are actually adjacent to each other in the ideological space, while Parties C and D in country 2 are separated by some other party or parties. Again, this type of scenario would probably affect voters' perceptions of the ideological compatibility of a particular coalition.

An alternative measure of ideological compatibility that sidesteps these potential problems focuses on whether or not the government coalition is a 'connected'

Table 7.4

PECs and Ideological Compatibility

Measure	Min	Max	All Governments		No Pre-Electoral Pact		Pre-Electoral Pact	
			Mean	N	Mean	N	Mean	N
Range	0	90.5	26.0	159	29.0	99	22.3	60
Spread	0	36.2	10.6	159	11.4	99	9.2	60

Notes: Data come from the Manifesto Research Group (Budge et al. 2001) and cover 159 governments that formed after an election in 17 parliamentary democracies from 1946 to 1998.

coalition. Since a connected coalition is one in which the coalition members are all adjacent to each other in the ideological space, they are more ideologically compatible than unconnected coalitions (Riker 1962). I constructed two different measures of whether a government coalition is connected or not. The first measure is based on data from Müller & Strøm (2000*a*) and Indriðason (2004) and covers Austria, Belgium, Denmark, Finland, France (Fifth Republic only), Germany, Iceland, Ireland, Italy, Luxembourg, the Netherlands, Norway, Portugal, and Sweden from 1946 to 1998. Using this measure, I found that 82.6% of governments based on pre-electoral coalitions have members who are adjacent in the ideological space; only 46.4% of governments that are not based on electoral coalitions have connected members. A difference in proportions test indicated that we can be over 99% confident that this difference is statistically significant. The second measure is based on data from the Manifesto Research Group (Budge et al. 2001). This second measure includes all of the countries just mentioned, as well as Australia, the French Fourth Republic, Japan, and New Zealand. Using this measure, I found that 61.7% of governments based on pre-electoral coalitions have members who are adjacent in the ideological space; only 42.4% of governments that are not based on electoral coalitions have connected members. A difference in proportions test indicated that we can be 95% confident that this difference is statistically significant. Thus, both measures of connected coalitions provide support for my Ideological Compatibility Hypothesis.

To conclude, there is strong evidence that governments based on pre-electoral coalitions are more ideologically compatible than those that are not. I have illustrated this idea with several different measures of ideological compatibility and a variety of data sources. It seems clear that governments that have no electoral alliances to take into account are less constrained by ideological compatibility concerns than are governments based on electoral alliances. As I argued earlier, this result should not come as a surprise, since voters are likely to be put off by a pre-electoral coalition that they judge to be ideologically incompatible. One of the implications of this analysis is that the policy position of a government based on an electoral pact is likely to be more congruent with that of its electorate than the policy position of governments that are not constrained by a pre-electoral agreement. This is another normatively appealing feature of pre-electoral coalitions.

7.4 Stability of Government Coalitions

I have shown that pre-electoral coalitions improve the chances that a party will enter government, they shorten the time that is needed to form a government, and they make governments more ideologically compatible. Few government scholars would deny that these consequences of electoral coalitions are positive from a normative standpoint. In the introduction, I also argued that pre-electoral coalitions offer significant normative advantages, owing to their effect on the representative nature of government (Powell 2000). Electoral pacts increase the identifiability of government alternatives and allow voters to make a meaningful choice between them. By making the government formation process more transparent, it is arguable that pre-electoral agreements also provide the incoming government with increased legitimacy and a stronger mandate. It seems reasonable to think that this added legitimacy and stronger mandate might translate into the more directly observable effect of more stable and longer-lived governments. The fact that cabinets based on pre-electoral agreements also tend to be more ideologically compatible provides another reason to suspect that they would survive longer than governments that have not reached an electoral pact. This expectation is because ideological compatibility should reduce the occurrence of policy conflicts and, hence, the likelihood of government breakdown (Warwick 1994; Laver & Schofield 1998). In addition, one might also think that pre-electoral coalitions improve government stability by increasing the speed with which governments actually take office, because a speedy government formation probably indicates a less complex bargaining environment and, hence, a more stable political situation (King et al. 1990). Given these claims, the principal hypothesis to be tested in this section is:

Government Survival Hypothesis: Governments based on pre-electoral agreements should last longer than governments that are not.

In order to test this hypothesis, one might want to control for other factors that are hypothesized to affect government survival. Over the past few decades, there have been numerous studies of government duration (Warwick 1979; Cioffi-Revilla 1984; Browne, Frendreis, & Gleiber 1986; King et al. 1990; Warwick & Easton 1992; Warwick 1994; Alt & King 1994; Lupia & Strøm 1995; Grofman

& van Roozendaal 1997; Diermeier & Stevenson 1999; Druckman & Thies 2002). Although few would deny that this literature has significantly improved our understanding of government survival, it is arguable that the accumulation of knowledge in this area is often overstated. One reason for being critical of the existing literature is its disproportionate focus on empirical analysis in the absence of a coherent theoretical model (Laver 2003).[17] This situation often results in one set of scholars providing a plausible, but ad hoc, theoretical argument why the effect of a particular variable should come out one way, and a different set of scholars providing an equally plausible and ad hoc theory suggesting that it should come out another way.[18] While this criticism is obviously of some concern, a bigger problem revealed by my own investigatory analyses is that many of the results reported in the literature are not robust to the sample of countries examined; the precise specification of the survival model; the variables that are included; how those variables are constructed; and whether one focuses only on those governments that form after an election, or whether one also includes governments that form in the inter-election period.

A logical approach to examining the effect of pre-electoral coalitions on government duration would be to start with a sound baseline model that is well accepted in the literature. However, such a model does not really exist; Laver (2003) is correct when he complains that it is not entirely clear at this point which independent variables ought to be included in a model of government duration. Part of the problem is that the existing literature often shows more interest in the specific methodology employed to examine government duration than in the substantive results themselves.[19] While this focus on methodological issues has clearly been fruitful, it appears to have had the consequence that some scholars have adopted pre-existing models without explicitly addressing whether the included variables are suitable or constructed appropriately to test their theories. For example, some recent studies have adopted a model by Warwick as their starting point (Diermeier & Stevenson 1999; Druckman & Thies 2002). These studies do not mention the problems that arise from the fact that this baseline model was generated using "a backward-elimination stepwise procedure" (Warwick 1994, 41).[20] Depending on one's theoretical question, the appropriateness of this baseline model may also be called into question by Warwick's decision throughout most of his book to define the government as including parties in the cabinet, as well as formal or declared support parties in the legislature (Warwick 1994, 30–32).[21] Given my interest in the effect of pre-electoral coalitions on government duration, this definition is clearly inappropriate for testing the Government Survival Hypothesis—theoretically, I am interested only in the parties that are formally in the cabinet. I should be very clear here that my purpose is not to criticize Warwick's model in particular, but simply to illustrate that there is no baseline model of government duration that is well accepted in the literature.

Regardless of the absence of a solid and widely accepted baseline model, it is still necessary to control for other factors when testing my Government Survival Hypothesis. In the upcoming analysis, I control for various attributes of the government, the legislature, and the country. In terms of government attributes, one would expect governments that control a majority of seats to survive longer than minority governments, because they are less likely to be defeated in the legislature (King et al. 1990; Warwick 1994; Laver & Schofield 1998). One would also expect single-party governments to survive longer than coalition governments, because they should be able to reach agreements more easily (Warwick 1994). It is also plausible that ideological compatibility should help governments stay in office longer. Again, this expectation is because the government should have fewer policy conflicts and be able to reach agreements more easily (Warwick 1994; Laver & Schofield 1998). Caretaker governments should not last as long as other forms of government, because the very nature of a 'caretaker' government is that it should be in power for only an interim period while a proper government is formed (King et al. 1990; Warwick 1994). There is some dispute as to whether governments that form after multiple formation attempts should be less likely to survive than those that form more quickly. On the one hand, King et al. (1990, 859) and Laver & Schofield (1998, 162) claim that a higher number of foiled attempts will reduce government duration, because a higher number of attempts indicate a difficult bargaining environment and a higher number of potential governments. On the other hand, Warwick (1994, 37) suggests that the very difficulty experienced in forming the government might oblige parties to stick with the existing coalition.

In terms of legislature attributes, one would expect legislative fragmentation to reduce government duration, because it indicates a more complex bargaining environment and a larger number of potential governments (King et al. 1990; Warwick 1994; Laver & Schofield 1998). In terms of country attributes, several scholars have argued that investiture votes should diminish average government duration by causing some governments to fail very quickly (King et al. 1990; Warwick 1994; Diermeier & Stevenson 1999; Druckman & Thies 2002). For this reason, investiture requirements are included in nearly all models of government duration. Note, though, that the underlying logic of this causal claim is deeply problematic and depends crucially on how one measures government duration, because a 'proposed' government that faces an investiture requirement does not formally take office unless it passes the investiture vote. Thus, 'proposed' governments that fail investiture votes are not actually governments and have no duration—they never enter office. If one measures government duration accordingly, there is no reason to believe that investiture votes should affect government duration; if anything, one might expect governments that face investiture votes to survive longer, because they had to enjoy enough legislative support to pass this additional formal hurdle.

7.4.1 Data and Model

I test my government survival hypothesis using a Cox survival model. Just as with many parametric survival models such as the Weibull, the hazard rate in the Cox model can be expressed in terms of a baseline hazard and a set of covariates:

$$h(t \mid x) = h_0(t) e^{x\beta}$$

(7.3)

where $h_0(t)$ is the baseline hazard. In contrast to the analyst using the parametric models, though, the analyst employing a Cox model has the advantage that she does not have to choose a particular parameterization of the baseline hazard function.[22] Because the Cox model analyzes the order in which observations 'fail' (or governments collapse), it may be the case that more than one observation would fail at the same time. I employed the Efron method to handle these ties in the data (Box-Steffensmeier & Jones 2004, 55). A global test of the Schoenfeld residuals indicated that the assumption of proportional hazards underlying the Cox model is not violated.

One issue that did not arise in my earlier analysis of government bargaining delays was that of censoring and truncation.[23] In line with the literature, I avoided problems with left-truncation by only including observations that began on or after the first day of my data set, and there were no right-censoring issues, because I observed the completion of the government formation process in all cases. My current analysis of government survival does not face any left-truncation issues, because I again only included cases that began on or after the first day of my data set. However, it does face right-censoring issues, because some governments are still in power when my sample period ends. For these governments, all I know is that they have survived up until the last period in my data set; I do not know how long they will survive. Although one might think of dropping these censored observations, doing so potentially introduces selection bias because it typically means omitting stable governments. Fortunately, it is possible to include censored observations and take account of the information that such governments provide, so long as the censoring point is known, as is the case here (Box-Steffensmeier & Jones 2004, 16–19). Other issues with right-censoring also occur because each country has a constitutionally mandated length of time after which new elections must be held. For instance, the constitutional inter-election period (CIEP) is five years in the United Kingdom and three years in Sweden. Thus, any cabinet in power prior to a regularly scheduled election is forced to 'fail,' even though some of them might have continued for years if new elections had not been mandated. Ever since King et al. (1990, 853–55), analysts have addressed this complicating feature of the data by treating all failures in the 12 months prior to the end of the CIEP as censored. I followed this practice here as well.

With the exception of the *Pre-Electoral Coalition* variable, I employ two different sources of data to test the Government Survival Hypothesis. The first is Warwick (1994). These data cover Austria, Belgium, Denmark, Finland, France (Fourth), Germany, Iceland, Ireland, Italy, Luxembourg, the Netherlands, Norway, Portugal, Spain, Sweden, and the United Kingdom from 1946 to 1988.[24] Warwick's data are the most widely employed data in the government survival literature. The second data source is the Parliamentary Democracy Data Archive (Müller & Strøm 2000; Strøm, Müller, & Bergman 2003).[25] These data are brand new and cover the same set of countries (except France Fifth instead of France Fourth) from 1946 to 1998. The Parliamentary Democracy Data Archive (PDDA) does not contain information on the ideological characteristics of governments. Instead, I obtained the required ideological data from the Manifesto Research Group (Budge et al. 2001).

Although the dependent variable (*Government Duration*) is measured in days, these two sources of data actually calculate government duration differently. Both sources of data treat government termination in the same way. They measure the end of a government as being when (i) parliamentary elections are held, (ii) the head of government changes, (iii) the party composition of the government changes, or (iv) the government tenders its resignation. However, they differ on when a new government starts. On the one hand, Warwick follows King et al. (1990) in measuring the start of a government as the time at which it is announced by the head of state. A consequence of this practice is that government duration may start prior to any investiture vote and, hence, prior to the government formally taking office. On the other hand, the Parliamentary Democracy Data Archive measures the start of a government as the time at which the cabinet is installed or inaugurated. In other words, it does not measure government duration prior to an investiture vote. As I have already suggested, this difference in how the dependent variable is calculated is likely to show itself in different estimated effects of investiture requirements across the two data sets.

7.4.2 Results and Interpretation

The results from my analysis are shown in table 7.5. Because of my interest in pre-electoral coalitions, I consider only governments that form after an election. As

Table 7.5

Determinants of Government Survival

Dependent Variable: Duration of Government Survival in Days for Governments Forming after Elections (Cox Model)

Independent Variables	Pooled		Dissolution		Replacement	
	Warwick	PDDA	Warwick	PDDA	Warwick	PDDA
Government Attributes:						
Pre-Electoral Coalition	0.38	0.44	1.00**	1.06*	-0.16	0.29
	(0.29)	(0.27)	(0.43)	(0.62)	(0.45)	(0.38)
Majority Government	-0.94***	-0.90***	-0.87**	-1.54***	-0.59	-0.71***
	(0.34)	(0.30)	(0.36)	(0.52)	(0.48)	(0.24)
Single Party Government	0.06	0.11	1.75***	0.68	-0.001	0.10
	(0.54)	(0.33)	(0.65)	(0.67)	(0.44)	(0.38)
Ideological Range	0.20	0.001	0.57	-0.001	0.10	0.01
	(0.16)	(0.01)	(0.44)	(0.01)	(0.24)	(0.01)
Caretaker Government	1.90***	2.53***	—	—	2.27***	2.33***
	(0.56)	(0.52)			(0.65)	(0.65)
Formation Attempts	0.22***	0.09	0.26***	0.10	0.16**	0.10
	(0.07)	(0.09)	(0.08)	(0.16)	(0.08)	(0.06)
Legislature Attributes:						
Legislative Fragmentation	0.12	0.14	0.28**	0.15	0.06	0.19*
	(0.13)	(0.11)	(0.11)	(0.14)	(0.12)	(0.11)
Country Attributes:						
Investiture	0.75***	0.16	0.80**	0.15	0.63*	0.04
	(0.22)	(0.20)	(0.34)	(0.43)	(0.37)	(0.30)
Log Likelihood	-347.94	-629.62	-189.83	-217.75	-290.89	-599.66
Observations	138	208	138	208	138	208

Notes: Results are Cox proportional hazards estimates where the Efron method was employed for handling ties; robust standard errors clustered by country in parentheses. A test using Schoenfeld residuals indicates that the proportional hazards assumption is not violated. **Dissolution:** The government ended in dissolution and new elections. **Replacement:** The government ended in a replacement government without new elections. **Pooled:** The government ended in dissolution or replacement. **Warwick:** Data come from Warwick (1994) and cover 16 countries from 1946 to 1988. **PDDA:** Data come from the Parliamentary Democracy Data Archive (Müller & Strøm 2000a, Strøm, Müller & Bergman 2003) and the Manifesto Research Group (Budge et al. 2001) and cover 16 countries from 1946 to 1998.
$*p < 0.10; **p < 0.05; ***p < 0.01$ (two-tailed).

before, the coefficients in table 7.5 are expressed as proportional hazard estimates. As a result, a positive coefficient indicates that the covariate in question increases the hazard rate for governments or reduces government duration. Conversely, a negative coefficient implies that the covariate reduces the hazard rate or increases government survival. Once again, I employ robust standard errors clustered by country to take account of the fact that the observations in each country may not be independent.

Note that government failure can lead to either the dissolution of the legislature and new elections, or simply to a replacement government. Recent research suggests that it is important to distinguish between these different termination modes, because the processes leading to dissolution and replacement are different (Diermeier & Stevenson 1999). It is possible to distinguish between these modes of termination using a competing risks version of the Cox model.[26] The first two columns (Pooled) in table 7.5 indicate how the covariates affect government duration without distinguishing between whether one observes dissolution or replacement for the two sources of data. The next two columns (Dissolution) indicate how the covariates affect the duration of governments that end in dissolution. Finally, the last two columns (Replacement) indicate the effect of the covariates on government survival for those governments that terminate with replacement.

Remember that the principal hypothesis of interest relates to the effect of pre-electoral coalitions on government duration. My expectation is that governments based on electoral pacts should last longer than other governments and, hence, that the coefficient on *Pre-Electoral Coalition* will be negative. The results from the pooled and replacement models indicate that pre-electoral coalitions never have any significant effect on government survival. In fact, it is only in the replacement model, with data from Warwick, that the coefficient on *Pre-Electoral Coalition* is ever negative (though insignificant). The results from the dissolution model indicate that far from improving government survival, pre-electoral coalitions actually significantly increase the risk of dissolution.

To be precise, a government based on an electoral agreement is 2.7 [1.2, 6.4] times more likely to fail in dissolution than an identical government that is not based on a pre-electoral coalition, according to the Warwick data, and 2.9 [1, 7.9] times more likely to end in dissolution, according to the PDDA data. Confidence intervals (95% and 90%, respectively) are shown in brackets. Note, though, that the cases for which pre-electoral agreements significantly shorten the lives of governments end in dissolution; in other words, the electorate does get to have its say in the formation of the new government. In sum, and contrary to my expectations, electoral coalitions never increase government survival.[27] They either have no effect on governments that end in replacement, or they actually shorten the lives of governments that end in dissolution.

What about the effect of other government attributes on government duration? First, there is strong evidence to support the standard claim that majority governments survive longer than minority governments—the coefficient on *Majority Government* is always negative and is highly significant in five of the six models. Another common claim in the coalition literature that receives support in this analysis is that caretaker governments collapse more quickly than other governments—the coefficient on *Caretaker Government* is always positive and significant.[28]

However, the results regarding the role of government attributes in table 7.5 do not confirm other findings in the government duration literature. For example, there is little evidence that single-party governments improve the stability of governments, as previous studies have found (Warwick 1994). In fact, there is some evidence that single-party governments actually increase the risk of dissolution when I employ the Warwick data. Similarly, there is no evidence that the ideological diversity of a government makes the government more unstable, as some scholars have reported (Warwick 1994; Diermeier & Stevenson 1999; Druckman & Thies 2002). Substituting other measures of ideological diversity, such as *Ideological Spread* and whether the government coalition is ideologically connected for *Ideological Range,* does not alter this conclusion. There is simply no compelling evidence that ideological compatibility ever affects the survival of governments that form after elections. Finally, evidence is mixed, at best, for the claim that the number of foiled attempts at government formation reduces government survival. The Warwick data consistently provide support for this claim, whereas the PDDA data consistently do not.[29] The inconsistent results in table 7.5 are just one illustration of my earlier point that the findings in the government duration literature are not particularly robust to different data sources or slight variations in how variables are measured.

Having examined the attributes of the government, what about the attributes of the legislature? The results in table 7.5 provide little consistent evidence that legislative fragmentation, as measured by the effective number of legislative parties, ever reduces the duration of governments that form after elections. As predicted, the coefficient on *Legislative Fragmentation* is positive and significant in the dissolution model, but only for the Warwick data and not the PDDA data. The coefficient is also positive and significant in the replacement model, but now only for the PDDA data and not the Warwick data. Again, one can see that the results are not robust across the different sources of data.

As for country attributes, the results are mixed. Table 7.5 indicates that investiture requirements significantly reduce government duration, but only with the Warwick data. As I suggested earlier, this inconsistency is potentially a result of how the two data sources measure government duration. By including announced (but not formal) governments that collapse very quickly because they fail to pass an investiture vote, the Warwick data is likely to overestimate any negative effect of investiture requirements on government duration. In contrast, the PDDA data only measure the duration of formal governments that have taken office. The result that investiture votes do not significantly affect government survival using the PDDA data contradicts virtually all of the claims in the coalition literature regarding the effect of investiture votes on government survival.

I should remind the reader that the analyses conducted here focus only on those governments that form after an election. In contrast, the previous literature on government survival examines governments that form in inter-election periods as well. By including these additional governments, coalition scholars have implicitly assumed that the factors affecting the survival of post-election governments are the same as those affecting inter-election period governments. I examined whether this assumption is valid by estimating the same models as shown in table 7.5 on a sample including inter-election period governments. Although most of my inferences are unaffected, there are a couple of substantive changes. First, there is now strong evidence that legislative fragmentation reduces the duration of governments. Second, it appears that the ideological diversity of the government does significantly reduce government survival based on the Warwick data (though ideology still has no significant effect with the PDDA data). Along with the findings from previous sections, these different results provide further evidence that analysts should begin to distinguish between governments that form after elections and those that form in inter-election periods.

To conclude, pre-electoral coalitions do not increase government survival. In fact, pre-electoral coalitions reduce the duration of governments that collapse in dissolution. The one positive point here, from a normative perspective, is that in those cases where pre-electoral coalitions significantly reduce government stability, the electorate is typically consulted about the identity of the next government. Thus, in some sense, electoral agreements could be said to have a 'bad' effect on government survival, but at least they end in a 'good' way.

7.5 Conclusion

In previous chapters, I have shown that pre-electoral coalitions are not rare and that their formation can be explained in terms of the office- and policy-seeking preferences of political actors. As my bargaining model in chapter four recognizes, the decision to form a pre-electoral coalition is largely determined by whether such a pact is going to increase the probability of entering government. In this chapter, I provide strong evidence that pre-electoral coalitions do indeed make it more likely that member parties will enter government. Although Martin & Stevenson (2001) have reported such a result before, their analysis is based on a small subsample of the electoral coalitions that actually form prior to elections. As I indicate, there are reasons to think that their analysis overestimates and underestimates the effect of pre-electoral coalitions on the identity of the government—I show that this is indeed the case. Overall, though, the evidence clearly indicates that preelectoral coalitions help parties enter government. Moreover, the effect is quite substantial—a potential government is 123 times more likely to enter government if it is based on a pre-electoral agreement than if it is not. For critics of proportional representation and multiparty parliamentary systems, this ought to be an encouraging result, because it implies that voters may often have a more direct say in the identity of the future government than is typically supposed (Pinto-Duschinsky 1999).

The analyses in this chapter also indicate that government coalitions based on pre-electoral agreements are more ideologically compatible than governments that are not constrained by electoral pacts. This result was consistently obtained using several different measures of ideological compatibility. Coalition governments are typically thought to face more difficulties than single-party governments because of the potential for inter-party disagreements over policy. These difficulties are likely to be exacerbated when the coalition partners have disparate policy goals. Being able to agree on and enact policy is an important requisite for a successful government, and ideological compatibility should make this capability more likely to occur. Pre-electoral coalitions help achieve this goal. This result suggests that party leaders are more worried about being punished for forming an ideologically incompatible coalition if the coalition must face the electorate before taking office than if the coalition is negotiated after the election.

After an election has been held, there is wide variation in the amount of time that it takes to form a government. Some governments form immediately after the votes have been counted and the distribution of seats in the legislature has been determined. Others can take several weeks or months to form, with power left in the hands of some sort of caretaker cabinet with no real mandate to make policy in the interim. In these latter cases, this situation means that important, and possibly urgent, legislation is delayed. Moreover, the uncertainty that surrounds the government formation process is likely to have negative economic consequences, with market actors unsure how to make their investments. Anything that can shorten the length of time that it takes to form a government should be welcomed by all political actors. In this chapter, I showed that governments based on pre-electoral coalitions suffer fewer delays in taking office and that this is particularly the case when there are many parties in the cabinet. For example, pre-electoral agreements can reduce the time that it takes to form a three-party government by roughly three weeks. This reduction is quite significant, given that the average time that it takes to form a government in my sample of 16 Western European countries from 1946 to 1998 is 32 days.

Although one might expect pre-electoral coalitions to enhance government stability and increase government duration, I find no evidence for this case. In fact, governments that end in dissolution are likely to be *more* unstable if they are based on pre-electoral coalitions than if they are not. The one saving grace about this situation is that whenever pre-electoral agreements increase the risk of government collapse, the end result is a new election and a chance for the electorate to again influence the government formation process. My analysis indicates that pre-electoral coalitions have no effect on the risk of collapse for governments that end in replacement.

Aside from the normatively pleasing aspects of pre-electoral coalitions (such as giving voters a chance to express their preferences over government alternatives, endowing the government with a stronger mandate, and generally creating a stronger connection between the electorate and the government that eventually forms following an election), the analysis in this chapter shows that pre-electoral coalitions have concrete effects on various aspects of government coalitions as well. They affect who gets into government, how long it takes to form a government, and how ideologically compatible the government is. While pre-electoral agreements do have a negative effect on government survival in some circumstances, they at least result in elections rather than in replacement. Thus, electoral coalitions have a real impact on how coalition governments work in parliamentary democracies—their impact does not end when the votes have been counted and the seats have been allocated.

CHAPTER 8

Conclusion

Coalitions are a fundamental part of democratic politics because democracies generally rely on legislative majorities to determine policy. Since single parties do not form such a majority in most countries, those parties who wish to exercise executive power are typically forced to form some kind of coalition. In effect, political parties have two choices. They can either form a coalition prior to elections, or they can compete independently at election time and try to form a government coalition afterwards. Most scholars have ignored the possibility of pre-electoral coalitions. Instead, they employ a simple dichotomy between single-party governments that appear in the ideal 'Westminster' or 'majoritarian' democracies and coalition governments that appear in the ideal 'proportional representation' or 'consensus' democracies (Lijphart 1999; Powell 2000). The unstated assumption that these analysts make is that electoral coordination among political actors occurs *prior* to elections and *within* parties in majoritarian systems, but *after* elections and *between* parties in proportional representation systems (Bawn & Rosenbluth 2003).[1] Although it captures certain aspects of political reality, it should be obvious to the reader by now that this simple dichotomy is limited in its usefulness, because it overlooks the fact that political parties can, and often do, form multi-party coalitions prior to elections in both majoritarian and proportional representation democracies. For example, I presented evidence in chapter two illustrating that multi-party electoral coalitions routinely form in a wide variety of democracies such as France, Germany, Australia, and Israel. In fact, I found evidence of 240 pre-electoral coalitions competing in the 364 legislative elections held between 1946 and 2002 in the 23 advanced industrialized countries studied in this book; only in Canada and Malta did I fail to find any evidence of national-level electoral coalitions.

Much has been written comparing the relative advantages and disadvantages of the majoritarian and proportional representation visions of democracy. In contrast to the single-party governments typically found in majoritarian democracies, it is common for coalition governments in proportional representation democracies to be criticized for producing a disconnect between the electorate and the government. The basic criticism is that voters in these democracies are largely unaware as to how their votes are ultimately translated into an actual government. The end result is a low level of government accountability and identifiability, as well as an absence of government mandates. Government accountability is low because voters cannot use their votes to reward or punish the government for its policy choices, since they do not know how (or, in some cases, even if) their votes will influence the government formation process. Government identifiability is low because voters have difficulty in identifying the probable government alternatives when casting their ballots. As a consequence, it is not always clear whether government coalitions actually have the support of the electorate in any meaningful sense. As a result of this last point, it is, therefore, difficult for governments to legitimately claim a popular mandate for their policies in proportional representation democracies.

Although these criticisms are often made of coalition governments and the proportional representation vision of democracy more broadly, it should be noted that their strength rests largely on the mistaken belief that coalition governments only form *after* elections have taken place. As I have illustrated in this book, this is far from the case. The presence of pre-electoral coalitions in many countries means that voters in proportional representation democracies are often able to identify the different government alternatives at election time and express their support for one of them. By providing a direct link between the voters and the government that proposes and implements policy, electoral pacts undermine the common criticism that coalition governments lack a convincing mandate from the voters and that the quality of representative democracy is thereby diminished (Pinto-Duschinsky 1999). In fact, one could argue that pre-electoral coalitions provide a unique opportunity to combine the best elements of the majoritarian vision of democracy (increased accountability, government identifiability, strong mandates) with the best elements of the proportional representation vision of democracy (wide choice, more accurate reflection of voter preferences in the legislature). Given these potential normative benefits, electoral coalitions are perhaps something that should be encouraged. This book indicates some of the ways that policy makers might achieve this goal. For example, policy makers could encourage pre-electoral coalition formation by manipulating the electoral rules. Of course, as the analyses conducted in chapters three and six indicate, the actual effect of this manipulation will ultimately depend on the size of the party system and the ideological nature of political competition in each country.

Not only do the pre-electoral strategies of political elites have significant normative consequences, but they also routinely affect the identity of the government that forms in many countries across the world. Fully one-fifth of all the governments that formed after the 364 legislative elections studied in this book were based on pre-electoral pacts. It is worth pointing out that this percentage would be even higher if I restricted my sample to purely coalition governments and if I also counted those governments that contained parties in addition to those participating in an electoral coalition. As the qualitative analysis of electoral coalition history in France and South Korea illustrated, the presence or absence of pre-electoral coalitions can have a quite dramatic effect on election outcomes. For example, it was the failure on the part of left-wing elites to coordinate their electoral strategies that enabled the leader of the extreme-right National Front to progress against all odds to the second round of the French presidential elections in 2002, and it was a similar coordination failure on the part of pro-democracy candidates that gifted electoral victory to the official candidate of the military regime in the first democratic presidential elections in South Korea in 1987. Other examples illustrating the profound effects that pre-electoral agreements can have on election outcomes can be found in numerous other countries. For instance, I briefly described in chapter three how pre-electoral agreements were instrumental in defeating once-dominant parties in Sweden, Ireland, and India.

Given the relative frequency with which electoral coalitions form, the significant normative benefits that they offer, and the tremendous effect that they can have on election outcomes, it is somewhat surprising that so little attention has been paid to them in the existing coalition literature. Although some scholars with knowledge of countries such as Germany or Ireland do mention electoral agreements with some regularity when explaining why certain government coalitions form, this book represents the first systematic cross-national study of pre-electoral coalition formation. I hope that at some point in the future scholars will go further and develop a fully integrated model of coalition formation that incorporates both pre-electoral and government coalitions within a unified framework. Just as existing models of government coalitions ignore the possibility of pre-electoral agreements, the bargaining model that I presented in chapter four does not explicitly take account of any post-election bargaining phase that might occur. Given the state of the coalition literature and the fact that we do not yet have a very satisfying model of government coalition formation, a fully integrated model is probably some way off in the future. As a result, I have undertaken a slightly narrower project in this book by analyzing just the determinants of pre-electoral coalition formation. While such a partial equilibrium approach offers the possibility of important insights into this stage of the coalition formation process, it also holds out the possibility that it could be combined with a model of government coalition formation at a later date. The approach that I take explicitly recognizes that the accumulation of knowledge in the scientific process typically occurs in small steps (Kuhn 1962).

The central question that I address in this book is why some parties choose to coordinate their electoral strategies as part of a pre-electoral coalition, whereas others choose to compete independently at election time. For the purposes of this book, an electoral coalition was defined as a publicly stated coordination of electoral strategies by party leaders at the national level. Rather than address the variety of different forms that electoral agreements can take (nomination agreements, joint lists, dual ballot and vote transfer instructions, public commitments to govern together), I focused simply on whether parties publicly coordinated their electoral strategies in some way at the national level or not. While the dearth of studies on pre-electoral coalitions indicates that this simple dichotomy is a useful starting point, future researchers might well want to disaggregate the different types of electoral agreements. The new data set on pre-electoral coalitions accompanying this book should provide a good foundation on which scholars interested in such an endeavor can build.

Before presenting my theoretical model of pre-electoral coalition formation, I tested two implicit hypotheses regarding electoral coalitions that can be found in the existing government coalition literature. The first hypothesis was that electoral coalitions are more likely to form in countries with disproportional electoral systems because such systems benefit larger parties. The problem with this hypothesis as it stands is that it ignores the fact that the incentives to form electoral coalitions in disproportional systems really exist only when there are a sufficiently large number of parties. For example, one would not expect a pre-electoral coalition to form if there were only two parties. As a result, I tested the Disproportionality Hypothesis that electoral coalitions were more likely to form and be successful in disproportional systems so long as the party system was sufficiently large.

The second hypothesis was that party leaders form pre-electoral coalitions in order to signal the identity of future governments to the electorate. There are several reasons why party elites might want to send such a signal. First, they might want to signal that member parties can form an effective government and thereby convince voters that they would not be wasting their votes by supporting the coalition parties. Second, they might want to signal the identity of a potential future government as clearly as possible out of a desire to give voters a more direct role in choosing the government. Third, they might simply want to signal the identity of the government clearly so as to increase the efficiency of the post-election government coalition bargaining process. I tested the Signaling Hypothesis that electoral coalitions are more likely to form and be successful when government identifiability is low (or when the effective number of parties is high).

While the statistical analyses conducted in chapter three provided considerable support for the Disproportionality Hypothesis, there was no such support for the Signaling Hypothesis—at least, there was no evidence that increasing the effective number of parties makes it more likely that electoral coalitions will form and be successful. As I noted when I discussed these results earlier, one should be wary of rejecting the Signaling Hypothesis outright on the basis of this single analysis for two reasons. First, the effective number of parties is not a particularly good proxy for the identifiability of government alternatives. Second, we do observe pre-electoral coalitions forming in countries, such as Israel and the Netherlands, with highly proportional electoral systems. These two points suggest that the Signaling Hypothesis should be exposed to further scrutiny before it is completely rejected.

The implicit claim in much of the coalition literature is that pre-electoral coalition formation is a simple function of electoral rules. While the analyses conducted in chapter three do indeed confirm that electoral institutions play an important role, this cannot be the full story, because it ignores the fact that pre-electoral agreements can involve significant distributional and ideological costs. Before party leaders can benefit from any increased probability of winning office that might result from forming a coalition, they have to reach an agreement on a coalition policy and a distribution of expected office benefits. It may well be the case that party leaders fail to reach an agreement on these divisive issues even if the potential electoral coalition offers significant electoral benefits. In chapter four, I presented a bargaining model in which party leaders who care about office and policy must weigh the electoral benefits of forming an electoral coalition against the associated distributional and ideological costs.

The implications of the model are quite straightforward. For example, increasing the expected office benefits from running as a coalition makes it more likely that party leaders will reach a pre-electoral agreement. If the likely opposition party is ideologically extreme, then party leaders will be more likely to form a pre-electoral coalition *so long as* the coalition is electorally beneficial. In other words, party leaders want to keep extreme opposition parties or coalitions from coming to power. If this goal is best achieved by forming a coalition, this is what they do. If not, they prefer to run separately. Parties that are ideologically close are more likely to form an electoral coalition than parties with incompatible policy platforms. Finally, party leaders are less likely to form a coalition as the probability of winning office after running separately increases.

The plausibility of the model's assumptions and implications are explored in chapter five using in-depth analyses of electoral coalition history in Fifth Republic France and post-1987 South Korea. These histories are particularly interesting because they highlight that the underlying logic of pre-electoral coalition formation that I present is quite general and not country- or region-specific. Despite significant differences in terms of geography, culture, democratic history, institutions, and ideological divisions, the history of electoral coalitions in both countries provides significant support for my model. In two very different settings, we see that having a disproportional electoral system, in which forming an electoral coalition could reasonably be expected to provide electoral advantages, is not sufficient for pre-electoral agreements to be reached.[2] This situation is perhaps most clearly seen in the first presidential elections after the transition to democracy in South Korea. Both leaders of the democratic opposition preferred to compete separately (and lose) rather than form a pre-electoral agreement, even though opinion polls convincingly indicated that a single democratic candidate would defeat the military incumbent.

The history of pre-electoral coalitions in France indicates that potential coalition partners must be sufficiently ideologically compatible for coalitions to form. For example, the Socialists and the Communists were willing to consider electoral coalitions only after their ideological positions drew sufficiently close to each other in the 1970s. There is also compelling evidence from the French case that coalition formation is facilitated if the policies proposed by the likely opposition are extreme. For instance, right-wing parties and voters were able to coordinate much more effectively when the Communist Party was considered the dominant party on the left. In addition to policy and electoral incentives, both countries also indicated that the divisibility of office benefits matters for the likelihood of pre-electoral coalition formation. The bargaining model presented in chapter four suggested that it is easier to form electoral coalitions when the benefits of office can be divided in a manner that makes both parties better off. Evidence in support of this idea comes from the fact that electoral agreements have been much more common in French legislative elections, where there are nearly 600 offices to share out among coalition partners, than in French presidential elections, where there is only one office at stake. While the Korean analysis illustrates that presidential electoral coalitions can form in certain circumstances, I argued that they are made possible, or more likely, by the use of term limits. The existence of term limits in South Korea is important, because they provide for the temporal divisibility of the presidential office, and because they make it easier for party leaders to compromise by weakening the power of the presidential office. Finally, the evidence from both countries suggests that personal animosity and myopia on the part of party leaders, which receive so much attention in the description of campaigns and party politics in particular countries, play no systematic role in pre-electoral coalition formation. This finding is especially striking in South Korea.

The qualitative analysis of electoral coalitions in France and South Korea suggested that the assumptions and implications of my bargaining model are plausible and informative in these two countries. However, I claimed throughout this book that the logic of pre-electoral coalition formation that I set out in chapter four is more general and applies in multiple settings. To examine whether this is the case, in chapter six I subjected my model's hypotheses to a series of statistical tests using data from 20 advanced industrialized countries. The results strongly supported all of my model's predictions. For example, two parties are more likely to form an electoral coalition when they share similar ideological preferences. They are also more likely to form a coalition if the party system is ideologically polarized and the coalition offers an electoral bonus. Coalitions are also more likely to form when the potential coalition size is large, but not too large. In other words, party leaders prefer to join a coalition if it increases their chances of winning office. On the whole, it is reasonable to think that a coalition's chance of winning office will increase with its size. However, if the coalition becomes too large, such that one of the parties starts to think that it can win office on its own, then the likelihood of coalition formation begins to decline. The more asymmetric the strength of the two parties in the potential coalition, the more quickly this cut-point will be reached. This last point indicates that pre-electoral coalitions are more likely to form between parties of similar size. The cross-national statistical analyses conducted in this chapter clearly support the model of pre-electoral coalition formation that is the centerpiece of this book.

To a large extent, party leaders who decide to form a pre-electoral coalition are ultimately interested in government coalition formation. As I indicated in chapter two, this is particularly the case regarding the national-level electoral pacts that are the focus of the empirical analyses in this book. Therefore, I investigated how pre-electoral agreements affect various aspects of the government formation process in chapter seven. Throughout the book, I had suggested that the primary benefit from forming a pre-electoral coalition is that it improves the probability that member parties will enter government. The statistical analyses conducted in chapter seven confirm this claim—a potential government is 123 times more likely to enter government if it is based on a pre-electoral agreement than if it is not.

The statistical analyses also indicate that governments based on pre-electoral agreements are more ideologically compatible than governments that are not based on such pacts. We already know that both pre-electoral and government coalitions are more likely to form between ideologically compatible parties than incompatible ones. What the results in chapter seven indicate in addition to this fact is that the ideological compatibility constraint facing party leaders thinking about forming a coalition may well be stronger prior to an election than afterwards. One reason is that any proposed pre-electoral coalition, unlike a proposed government coalition, must be immediately put before the voters. It is worth noting that the increased ideological compatibility of governments based on pre-electoral agreements is quite appealing, because it means a greater ideological congruence between the electorate of the government and the policy position of that government.

Finally, the empirical analyses conducted in chapter seven indicate that governments based on pre-electoral coalitions take office more quickly than equivalent governments that are not based on electoral pacts. This is particularly the case when the government consists of many parties. This result suggests that pre-electoral agreements help to resolve some of the bargaining difficulties that arise with large government coalitions prior to the election rather than leaving them to be resolved after the election. By shortening the time that it takes a government to take office, pre-electoral coalitions have the beneficial consequence of reducing the amount of time a country must live under a caretaker government that has no real mandate to make policy. By reducing the period of uncertainty that characterizes the government formation process, electoral coalitions are also likely to have a positive effect on economic actors who would otherwise be uncertain as to how to make their investment decisions. This idea is particularly important given the growing empirical evidence that political uncertainty can have a significant negative impact on a country's economy.

This book represents just a first step toward understanding pre-electoral coalitions, and my hope is that it will generate a wider scholarly debate about their causes and consequences. I believe that the study of electoral coalitions provides a fertile terrain for the opportunistic researcher. Let me briefly describe one avenue of future research that would be worth examining. In chapter two, I argued that one could think of electoral coordination as a continuum, with completely separate and independent parties competing in elections at one end of the spectrum, and party mergers at the other end. Pre-electoral coalitions represent some intermediary position on this continuum of electoral coordination— indeed, the various types of electoral pacts described in chapter two represent different intermediary positions on this continuum. Although I only considered snapshots of party systems prior to elections in this book and asked whether or not a pre-electoral coalition is likely to form, it is worth thinking about what types of electoral coalitions are 'stable' and what types are just a step on the way to a full party merger.

Duverger (1963 [1954], 224) pointed out a long time ago that electoral alliances are frequently "the prelude to the extreme form, total fusion, which is the normal term of the development and is often attended by schism. . . ." For example, the three Christian Democratic parties in the Netherlands originally ran as separate parties prior to competing in elections as a pre-electoral coalition before eventually merging into a single party. By describing "total fusion" as the "normal term of development," Duverger implies that electoral coalitions are somehow ephemeral, simple intermediary steps on the way to party fusion, or failed experiments that ultimately collapse back to complete party independence. I think that this implication is somewhat mistaken and that there are circumstances in which party leaders will prefer to permanently retain their separate identities yet coordinate their electoral campaigns with other parties. What these circumstances are has never really been examined and is beyond the scope of this book.

Nevertheless, I can offer one or two speculations. For example, if two parties have separate electoral bases of support, then they might be less likely to merge. If the electorates are geographically separate, as is the case with the Christian Democratic Union and the Christian Social Union in Germany, or the National Party and the Liberal Party in Australia, then the parties in question can easily form an electoral coalition instead of giving up their separate identities by merging into a single party. It is striking that these two cases—the only two in my sample that can be considered 'permanent' pre-electoral coalitions—have unusually separate geographic bases of support.

Certain electoral institutions should also encourage pre-electoral coalitions as a permanent feature of electoral politics. Consider the situation where a country employs different electoral formulas in national and sub-national elections. In such a country, it is often the case that sub-national elections employing proportional representation give parties and voters incentives to maintain a higher number of parties than would otherwise be the case. For example, France uses a majoritarian formula in single-member districts for its legislative elections, but a proportional representation formula in multi-member districts for its regional (and some local) elections. Small parties in France that might otherwise have disappeared can benefit from the proportional representation elections to win regional and local offices, thereby making them more viable coalition partners on the national political scene. Electoral rules that allow voters to indicate coalition preferences are also likely to make electoral alliances a permanent feature of the political landscape, because they make reaching a pre-electoral agreement so costless that party leaders are simply unwilling to give up their independence by merging into a larger party. For example, the alternative vote in Australia, the single transferable vote in Ireland, and the two-vote system in Germany all allow voters to show their support for more than one party in a given election. As a result, party elites do not need to broker politically costly nomination agreements that force some of their own candidates to withdraw from competition. These are obviously just a few speculations, and further research is required to better evaluate the 'stability' or 'permanence' of pre-electoral coalitions.

Like all good comparative political scientists, I end with an appeal for more (and better) data concerning pre-electoral coalitions. The country-specific material used to build the data set employed in this book varied widely in the amount of useful information that it provided concerning electoral coalitions. It is my opinion that there is a vast amount still to be discovered. With more detailed case studies of electoral coalition formation in various countries, it would be possible to disaggregate the different types of pre-electoral coalitions in terms of the nature of the electoral coordination chosen, or in terms of their purpose—that is, was the coalition formed to get parties over an electoral threshold in order to win legislative seats or in order to enter government? Such distinctions will prove invaluable as scholars develop more precise theories of pre-electoral coalition formation than that presented here.

APPENDIX

In this appendix, I provide detailed information by country on the 240 national-level electoral coalitions that formed prior to the 364 legislative elections held between 1946 and 2002 in the 23 advanced industrialized countries studied in this book. I do not provide tables containing information on Canada (17 elections from 1949–2000) or Malta (8 elections from 1966–98) because I found no national-level electoral coalitions in these countries. Those interested in the coding rules for identifying national-level electoral pacts should examine chapter two. Given that there is sometimes conflicting information regarding the presence or absence of electoral coalitions, I cite all sources consulted in detail so that the interested reader can evaluate my coding decisions. The tables that follow contain the following data:

- **Election Year:** This is the year in which the legislative election was held. Note that if the election was held near the end of the year, it is possible that the government that eventually forms does not enter office until the next year.
- **% Vote for Coalition:** This is the percentage of votes cast for the parties in the electoral coalition. These percentages are taken mainly from Mackie & Rose (1991), the *European Journal of Political Research* (various years), Caramani (2000), or the website www.electionworld.org.
- **PEC:** This is a list of the parties in the pre-electoral coalition. The abbreviations of the party names are explained below each table.
- **In Govt?:** This indicates whether or not the pre-electoral coalition entered government following the election. Unless otherwise indicated, the parties in the pre-electoral coalition form the government without additional parties.
- **MRG:** This indicates whether the electoral coalition members are included as separate parties in the Comparative Manifesto Research Group (MRG) data set (Budge et al. 2001). This data set provides information on the ideological position of the parties from 1946 to 1998. Certain parties or coalitions listed in the appendix are not included in the empirical analyses conducted in chapters six and seven, because the MRG data set does not include all of the parties or because it includes an electoral coalition as a single party.

Table A.1
Electoral Coalitions in Australia, 1946–2002

Election Year	% Vote for Coalition	PEC	In Govt?	MRG
1946	43.9	Lib+Nat	No	Yes
1949	50.3	Lib+Nat	Yes	Yes
1951	50.3	Lib+Nat	Yes	Yes
1954	47	Lib+Nat	Yes	Yes
1955	47.6	Lib+Nat	Yes	Yes
1958	46.5	Lib+Nat	Yes	Yes
	9.4	DLP+QLP	No	No
1961	42.1	Lib+Nat	Yes	Yes
	8.7	DLP+QLP	No	No
1963	46.0	Lib+Nat	Yes	Yes
1966	49.9	Lib+Nat	Yes	Yes
1969	43.4	Lib+Nat	Yes	Yes
1972	41.4	Lib+Nat	No	Yes
1974	44.9	Lib+Nat	No	Yes
1975	53.1	Lib+Nat	Yes	Yes
1977	48.1	Lib+Nat	Yes	Yes
1980	46.3	Lib+Nat	Yes	Yes
1983	43.6	Lib+Nat	No	Yes
1984	45.0	Lib+Nat	No	Yes
1987	45.9	Lib+Nat	No	Yes
1990	43.2	Lib+Nat	No	Yes
1993	44.27	Lib+Nat	No	Yes
1996	47.2	Lib+Nat	Yes	Yes
1998	39.18	Lib+Nat	Yes	Yes
2001	42.7	Lib+Nat	Yes	No

PARTIES: Lib: Liberal Party of Australia, **Nat:** National Party (formerly Country Party); **DLP:** Democratic Labor Party; **QLP:** Queensland Labor Party. The DLP and QLP merged into a single party in 1962.
COMMENTS: All elections: For Lib+Nat coalition, see Klingemann, Hofferbert & Budge (1994, 81), Butler (1999), Powell (2000, 71–72), and McAllister (2003, 381). **1958, 1961:** For the DLP+QLP electoral coalition, see Mackie & Rose, Table 1.1 (1991).

Table A.2
Electoral Coalitions in Austria, 1946–2002

Election Year	% Vote for Coalition	PEC	In Govt?	MRG
1949	82.74	ÖVP+SPÖ	Yes	Yes
1953	83.37	ÖVP+SPÖ	Yes	Yes
1956	89.01	ÖVP+SPÖ	Yes	Yes
1959	88.98	ÖVP+SPÖ	Yes	Yes
1962	89.43	ÖVP+SPÖ	Yes	Yes
1966	90.91	ÖVP+SPÖ	ÖVP only	Yes
1970		No		
1971		No		
1975		No		
1979		No		
1983		No		
1986	(84.41)	ÖVP+SPÖ*	Yes	Yes
	4.82	Green Alternative	No	No
1990	74.84	ÖVP+SPÖ	Yes	Yes
1994	62.59	ÖVP+SPÖ	Yes	Yes
1995	(66.35)	ÖVP+SPÖ*	Yes	Yes
	10.32	Greens+LF	No	Yes
1999		No		
2002		No		

*SPÖ announced intention to govern with ÖVP but ÖVP did not reciprocate.

COALITIONS: Green Alternative: Alternative List of Austria and United Greens of Austria.

PARTIES: SPÖ: Socialist Party. ÖVP: People's Party. LF: Liberal Forum.

COMMENTS: 1949–62: See Müller (2000, 91–92). 1966: See Müller (2000, 91–92) and Dreijmanis (1982, 256). 1986: SPÖ announced an intention to govern with ÖVP. Although the ÖVP did not reciprocate, it did not repudiate the offer (Müller 2000, 92). The Alternative List of Austria and the United Greens (VGÖ) ran joint lists—see Müller (1996, 62) and the Library of Congress Country Studies (http://lcweb2.loc.gov/frd/cs/attoc.htm). 1990: SPÖ announced it would not govern with FPÖ but would govern with ÖVP (Müller 2000, 92). Powell refers to a pre-election coalition victory (2000, 141) but later says that the grand coalition was "only vaguely identified as a pre-electoral coalition" (2000, 213). 1994: Continuation of grand coalition (Müller 2000, 92). 1995: SPÖ announced an intention to govern with ÖVP. Although the ÖVP did not reciprocate, it did not repudiate the offer (Lauber 1996, 256–57).

Table A.3
Electoral Coalitions in Belgium, 1946–2002

Election Year	% Vote for Coalition	PEC	In Govt?	MRG
1946		No		
1949		No		
1950		No		
1954		No		
1958		No		
1961		No		
1965		No		
1968	5.90	FDF+RW	No	Yes
1971	11.23	FDF+RW	No	Yes
1974	10.94	FDF+PLDP+RW	No	Yes
1977	4.7	FDF+RW	No	Yes
1978	7.04	FDF+RW	No	Yes
	1.40	VVP+VNP	No	No
1981	4.21	FDF+RW	No	Yes
	4.92	Eco+Agalev	No	Yes
1985	50.20	CVP+PSC+VLD+PRL	Yes	Yes
1987	17.40	PSC+PRL	Yes*	Yes
1991	1.5	FDF+PPW	No	No
1995	10.30	PRL+FDF	No	Yes
1999	10.14	PRL+FDF	Yes*	No
	5.6	VU+ID21	No	No

*Pre-electoral coalition did not enter government alone.

PARTIES: FDF: Democratic Front of French Speakers. PLDP: French-speaking Liberal Party. CVP: Christian People's Party (Flemish). PSC: Christian People's Party (Walloon). VLD: Liberals (Flemish). PRL: Liberals (Walloon). RW: Walloon Rally. VVP: Flemish People's Party. VNP: Flemish National Party (merged 1979). Eco: Ecologist Confederation for the Organization of New Struggles. Agalev: Live Differently, Greens. PPW: Parti pour la Wallonie. VU: People's Union. ID21: Social-Liberal Party.

COMMENTS: 1968, 1971: See Caramani (2000). 1974: See Caramani (2000) and Dewachter (1987, 295). Note that Mackie & Rose (1991) only mention FDF+PLDP as being in the electoral coalition. 1977: See Caramani (2000). 1978: For the FDF+RW coalition, see Caramani (2000). For the VVP+VNP coalition, see Mackie & Rose (1991). 1981: See Caramani (2000, 158, 185) and Mackie & Rose (1991). Note that with the exception of Louvain, the two Green parties competed in different districts. 1985: See Powell (2000, 73). 1987: See Downs (1998, 190). 1991: See the 1992 *European Journal of Political Research* (22) election report. 1995: See De Winter, Timmermans, and Dumont (2000, 303), the 1996 *European Journal of Political Research* (30) election report, and http://elections.fgov.be/Resultats/electionshtml/710.html. 1999: See http://elections.fgov.be/Resultats/electionshtml/5130.html, http://electionworld.org/belgium.htm, and http://polling2003.belgium.be/electionshome/uk/result/chamber/table_top.html.

Table A.4
Electoral Coalitions in Denmark, 1946–2002

Election Year	% Vote for Coalition	PEC	In Govt?	MRG
1947		No		
1950		No		
1953 (April)		No		
1953 (Sept.)		No		
1957		No		
1960		No		
1964		No		
1966		No		
1968	53.89	RL+Con+Lib	Yes	Yes
1971		No		
1973	7.80	CD+SLE	No	No
1975	2.20	CD+SLE	No	No
1977	6.40	CD+SLE	No	No
1979		No		
1981		No		
1984		No		
1987		No		
1988		No		
1990	1.67	CP+LSP	No	No
1994	3.15	CP+LSP	No	No
1998	2.70	CP+LSP	No	No
2001	2.40	CP+LSP	No	No

PARTIES: **Lib:** Liberals. **Con:** Conservatives. **SD:** Social Democrats. **RL:** Radical Liberals. **CP:** Communist Party. **LSP:** Left Socialist Party. **CD:** Center Democrats (1973 splinter of Social Democrats). **SLE:** Schleswig Party (German-speaking minority).

COMMENTS: **1968:** See Pesonen & Thomas (1983, 71–72), Fitzmaurice (1986, 266), Schou & Hearl (1992, 155), Arter (1999, 210), and Damgaard (2000, 245). **1973, 1975, 1977:** See Mackie & Rose (1991), Table 5.1. See also Elklit (2002, 63). **1979–84:** Powell (2000, 76) implies that a pre-electoral non-bourgeois coalition formed prior to these elections. However, he does not specify the parties that are involved, and other literature on Denmark makes no reference to these electoral coalitions. **1990–2001:** See Esaiasson & Heider (2000, 445–46), Elklit (2002, 64), updates to Mackie & Rose (1991) in the *European Journal of Political Research,* the Danish election update in *Electoral Studies* (1994), and http://electionworld.org.

Table A.5
Electoral Coalitions in Finland, 1946–2002

Election Year	% Vote for Coalition	PEC	In Govt?	MRG
1948		No		
1951		No		
1954		No		
1958		No		
1962		No		
1966		No		
1970	18.22	CE+CHR	No	Yes
1972		No		
1975		No		
1979		No		
1983	17.63	Lib+CE	Yes*	Yes
1987		No		
1991		No		
1995		No		
1999	67.2	Purple Coalition	Yes	No

*Pre-electoral coalition did not enter government alone.

COALITION: Purple Coalition: Conservative Party, Left-Wing League, Swedish People's Party, Social Democratic Party, and Greens.

PARTIES: Lib: Liberals. **CE:** Center Party (formerly Agrarians). **CHR:** Christian League of Finland.

COMMENTS: 1970: The CHR, with only 1.1% of the vote, broke into parliament and, profiting from an electoral alliance with the CE, had 1 MP (Arter 1999, 110). **1983:** According to Appendix 2 in Esaiasson & Heidar (2000, 447–48), the Liberals ran with the Center Party from 1982–86. See also Sundberg (2002, 98) and Caramani (2000, 286). **1999:** Personal communication with Mark Hallerberg: the 'Purple coalition,' which had formed a government coalition following the 1995 election, campaigned asking to be re-elected to form the government again.

Table A.6
Electoral Coalitions in France, 1946–2002

Election Year	% Vote for Coalition *	PEC	In Govt?	MRG
1946		No		
1951		No		
1956		No		
1958		No		
1962	34.39	UNR+UDT+RI (2)	Yes	UNR+UDT = 1 Party
	39.25	PCF+SFIO+PRG (2)	No	Yes
1967	45.7	UNR+UDT+RI (1)	Yes	UNR+UDT = 1 Party
	56.18	UNR+UDT+RI+CD (2)	Yes	UNR+UDT = 1 Party
	16.54	FGDS:SFIO+PRG+CIR (1)	No	SFIO+PRG only
	40.45	FGDS+PCF+PSU (2)	No	SFIO+PRG+PCF only
1968	36.87	UNR+RI (1)	Yes	Yes
	50.96	UNR+RI+PDM (2)	Yes	No PDM
	41.41	FGDS+PCF (2)	No	Yes
1973	34.07	UDR+RI+UC (1)	Yes	Yes
	47.32	UDR+RI+UC+REF (2)	Yes	Yes
	19.10	UGDS:PS+PRG (1)	No	PS only
	42.46	UGDS+PCF+PSU (2)	No	PS+PCF only
1978	20.21	UDF:CDS+PR+RI (1)	Yes	UDF = 1 Party
	42.75	UDF+RPR (2)	Yes	Yes
	24.95	PS+PRG (1)	No	PS only
	45.56	PS+PRG+PCF (2)	No	PS+PCF only
1981	41.16	RPR+UDF (1)	No	Yes
	37.53	PS+PRG (1)	Yes	PS only
	53.66	PS+PRG+PCF (2)	Yes	PS+PCF only
1986 (PR)	42.1	RPR+UDF†	Yes	Yes
	23.8	PS+PRG	No	PS only
1988	37.67	RPR+UDF (1)	No	Yes
	35.90	PS+PRG (1)	Yes*	PS only
	47.22	PS+PRG+PCF (2)	No	Yes
1993	39.47	RPR+UDF (1)	Yes	Yes
	18.49	PS+PRG (1)	No	PS only
	27.67	PS+PRG+PCF (2)	No	PS+PCF only
	7.64	Greens+GE (1)	No	Greens+GE = 1 Party
1997	31.5	RPR+UDF (1)	Yes	Yes
	29.1	PS+PRG+Greens (1)	No	Yes
	39.0	PS+PRG+Greens+PCF (2)	No	Yes
2002	33.7	UMP:RPR+UDF+DL (1)	Yes	No
	30.1	PS+PRG+Greens (1)	No	No
	34.9	PS+PRG+Greens+ PCF (2)	No	No

*Pre-electoral coalition did not enter government alone.

(1) and (2) indicate the round of the two-ballot system in which the pre-electoral coalition formed.

♦The vote percentages are taken from Portelli (1994) for 1958–93. Figures for 1997 are from the election results report in the 1998 *European Journal of Political Research* (34), and the figures for 2002 are from www.electionworld.org.

†The UDF and RPR ran joint lists in 61 districts and separate ones in 35 districts. The joint list won 21.0%, while the separate lists won an additional 9.6% and 11.5% of the vote respectively.

COALITIONS: FGDS: Federation of the Democratic and Socialist Left, SFIO+PRG+CIR (1967, 1968). UGDS: Democratic and Socialist Union, PS+PRG (1973). UDF: Union for French Democracy, CDS+PR+RI (1978). UMP: Union for a Presidential (Popular) Majority, RPR+UDF+DL (2002).

PARTIES: UNR: Gaullist Party (1958–62). UDT: Left Gaullists (merged with the UNR after 1962 elections and became the UNR-UDT 1962–67 and then the UDVe 1967–68). UDR: Gaullist Party

(cont.)

(1968–76, continuation of UDVe). **RPR:** Gaullist Party (1976–2002, continuation of UDR). **UMP:** Gaullist Party (2002–, continuation of RPR). **UDF:** Union for French Democracy. **SFIO:** Socialist Party (1905–69). **PS:** Socialist Party (1969–, continuation of SFIO). **PCF:** Communist Party. **PRG:** Left Radical Party (PRG 1998–, PRS 1996–98, MRG 1973–96, MGRS 1972–73, Radicals 1901–72). **REF:** Reformateurs (split from Radicals in 1972). **PSU:** Unified Socialist Party. **Greens:** Green Party. **GE:** Generation Ecology. **RI:** Independent Republicans. **PR:** Republicans. **UC:** Center Union. **CD:** Democratic Center. **PDM:** Progress and Modern Democracy.

COMMENTS: 1962: See Bell & Criddle (1984, 26) and Cole & Campbell (1989, 97). **1967:** See Bell & Criddle (1984, 47, 76), Cole & Campbell (1989, 100), and Alexandre (1977, 146). **1968:** See Bell & Criddle (1984, 49) and Cole & Campbell (1989, 104). **1973:** See Bell & Criddle (1984, 75), Martin (1993, 53), Lavau & Mossuz-Lavau (1980, 110), and Portelli (1994, 225). **1978:** See Charlot (1980, 82, 108), Martin (1993, 53), Jaffré (1980, 46, 72), Portelli (1994, 236–37), and Bell & Criddle (1984, 101). **1981:** See Ysmal (1989, 129), Martin (1993, 53), Portelli (1994, 304), and Schlesinger & Schlesinger (2000, 136). **1986:** See Bréchon (1995), Martin (1993, 53), Portelli (1994,, 366–37, 371), and Ysmal (1989, 146). **1988:** See Martin (1993, 53), Portelli (1994, 402), and Schlesinger & Schlesinger (2000, 136–38). **1993:** See Charlot (1994, 37), Ysmal (1993), Backman & Birenbaum (1993), Martin (1993, 53), Portelli (1994, 445–47), Thiébault (2000, 502), and http://www.les-verts.org/histoire.html. **1997:** See Schlesinger & Schlesinger (2000, 136–38, 149), Thiébault (2000, 501, 511–12), and http://www.les-verts.org/histoire.html. **2002:** Le Monde, various.

Table A.7

Electoral Coalitions in Germany, 1949–2002

Election Year	% Vote for Coalition	PEC	In Govt?	MRG†
1949		No		
1953	48.38	CDU+CSU+DP	Yes*	CD
1957	53.55	CDU+CSU+DP	Yes	CD
1961	45.31	CDU+CSU	Yes*	CD
1965	47.59	CDU+CSU	Yes*	CD
1969	46.09	CDU+CSU	No	CD
1972	44.86	CDU+CSU	No	CD
	54.21	SPD+FDP	Yes	Yes
1976	48.64	CDU+CSU	No	CD
	50.48	SPD+FDP	Yes	Yes
1980	44.54	CDU+CSU	No	CD
	53.48	SPD+FDP	Yes	Yes
1983	55.73	CDU+CSU+FDP	Yes	CD
1987	53.35	CDU+CSU+FDP	Yes	CD
1990	54.85	CDU+CSU+FDP	Yes	CD
	1.20	B'90+Greens	No	No
1994	41.44	CDU+CSU	Yes*	CD
1998	39.58	CDU+CSU	No	CD
2002	38.5	CDU+CSU	No	No
	47.1	SPD+Greens	Yes	No

*Pre-electoral coalition did not enter government alone.

†CDU/CSU treated as a single party—the Christian Democrats (CD).

PARTIES: CSU: Christian Socialist Union. **CDU:** Christian Democratic Union. **FDP:** Free Democrats. **SPD:** Social Democrats. **DP:** German Party. **B'90:** Alliance '90. **Greens:** Green Party.

COMMENTS: 1953: See Saalfeld (2000, 39). **1957:** See Saalfeld (2000, 39), Mackie & Rose (1991), Table 8.1. **1965:** See Pulzer (1983, 102). **1969:** See Mackie & Rose (1991), Table 8.1. **1972:** See Pulzer (1983, 102), Powell (2000, 141), Schoen (1999, 488), and Conradt (1978, 34). **1976:** See Pulzer (1983, 102), Powell (2000, 72), and Conradt (1978, 45). **1980:** See Pulzer (1983, 102), Powell (2000, 72), and Gunlicks (1990, 3). **1983:** See Powell (2000, 72), Conradt (1990, 45) and Martin & Stevenson (2001). **1987:** See Powell (2000, 72) and Martin & Stevenson (2001). **1990:** See Powell (2000, 72, 210) and Martin & Stevenson (2001). **2002:** *New York Times* (various).

Table A.8
Electoral Coalitions in Greece, 1946–66, 1974–2002

Election Year	% Vote for Coalition	PEC	In Govt?	MRG
1946	55.1	UCNM	Yes	No
	19.3	NPU	No	No
	2.9	UNM	No	No
1950	2.6	FWR+NAPP	No	No
	16.4	EPEK	Yes	No
	9.7	DC	No	No
	8.2	PIC	No	No
	5.3	NRF	No	No
1951		No		
1952	34.2	UP	No	No
1956	48.2	DU	No	No
1958	2.9	UPP	No	No
	10.6	PADU	No	No
1961	33.7	CU+PP	No	No
	14.6	UDL+NAPP	No	No
1963		No		
1964	35.3	NRU+PP	No	No
1974	9.5	UL	No	No
	20.4	CU+NF	No	No
1977	2.7	PLWF	No	No
1981	48.1	UDL+PASOK	Yes	No
	1.4	RCPG+CPG-ML	No	No
1985	45.8	UDL+PASOK	Yes	No
	40.8	PDS+ND	No	No
1989 (June)	13.1	PLWF	No	No
1989 (Nov.)	11.0	PLWF	No	No
1990	10.3	PLWF	No	No
1993		No		
1996		No		
2000		No		

COALITIONS: **UCNM:** United Camp of the Nationally Minded: People's Party, Reformist Party, National Liberal Party, Royalist Party, Panhellenic National Party, Patriotic Union Party, Political Group Forward, Party of Reconstruction, Social Radical Union. **NPU:** National Political Union: National Unity Party, Democratic Socialists, Venizelist Liberals. **UNM:** Union of the Nationally Minded: Party of the Nationally Minded, People's Agrarian Party. **DC** Democratic Camp: Union of Democratic Leftists, Socialist Party—Union of Popular Democracy, Party of Leftist Liberals. **PIC:** Politically Independent Camp: Greek Renaissance Party, Party of the Nationally Minded. **NRF:** National Reconstruction Front: National Unity Party, People's Progressive Party, Panhellenic Party. **EPEK:** National Progressive Center Union: Progressive Liberal Center Party, Democratic Progressive Party. **UP:** Union of the Parties: National Progressive Center Union, Liberal Party, Socialist Party – Union of Popular Democracy. **DU:** Democratic Union: United Democratic Left, Liberal Party I, National Progressives Center Union, Farmers' and Workers' Rally, Democratic Party, Liberal Democrats, People's Party. **UPP:** Union of the People's Parties: People's Party, People's Social Party. **PADU:** Progressive Agrarian Democratic Union: National Progressives Center Union, Farmers' and Workers' Rally, Democratic Party, Progressives Party. **UL:** United Left: Communist Party, Communist Party-Interior, United Democratic Left Party. **PLWF:** Alliance of Progress and Left-Wing Forces: Christian Democrats, Communist Party-Interior, Socialist Initiative, Socialist March, U.D. Left.
PARTIES: **FWR:** Farmers' and Workers' Rally. **NAPP:** National Agrarian Progressive Party. **UDL:** United Democratic Left. **PASOK:** Socialists. **PSP:** Popular Social Party. **NRU:** National Radical Union. **PP:** Progressive Party. **NF:** New Forces. **CU:** Center Union. **RCPG:** Revolutionary Communist Party of Greece. **CPG-ML:** Communist Party of Greece—Marxist Leninist. **PDS:** Party for Democratic Socialists. **ND:** New Democracy.
COMMENTS: **1946–85** See mainly Clogg (1987) but also Mackie & Rose (1991), Kohler (1982, 105–33) for 1961, 1974–77, and Papayannakis (1981, 141–53) for 1956 and 1977. **1989–90:** Various issues of the *European Journal of Political Research*—reports on national elections in western nations.

Table A.9
Electoral Coalitions in Iceland, 1946–2002

Election Year	% Vote for Coalition	PEC	In Govt?	MRG
1946		No		
1949		No		
1953		No		
1956	19.2	People's Alliance I	Yes*	Yes
1959 (June)	15.2	People's Alliance I	No	Yes
1959 (Oct.)	16.0	People's Alliance I	No	Yes
1963	16.0	People's Alliance II	No	No NPP
1967	13.9	People's Alliance I	No	Yes
1971		No		
1974	4.60	ULL+PP	No	Yes
1978		No		
1979		No		
1983		No		
1987		No		
1991	1.8	NP+HP	No	No
1995		No		
1999	26.8	PA+WP+SDP+PM	No	No

*Pre-electoral coalition did not enter government alone.

COALITIONS: **People's Alliance I**: United Socialist Party, Social Democratic Party (1956, 1959, 1967). **People's Alliance II**: United Socialist Party, Social Democratic Party, National Preservation Party (1963).

PARTIES: **IP**: Independence Party. **PP**: Progressive Party. **ULL**: Union of Liberals and Leftists. **NPP**: National Preservation Party. **SP**: United Socialist Party. **PA**: People's Alliance. **WP**: Woman's Party. **SDP**: Social Democratic Party. **PM**: People's Movement. **NP**: National Party. **HP**: Humanist Party.

COMMENTS: **1956–67**: This electoral coalition included the left wing of the SPD only. The coalition eventually merged into a single party (PA) in 1968. See Grimsson (1982, 146), Kristjánsson (1998, 175), Arter (1999, 84–85), Esaiasson & Heidar (2000, 448, 450), Hardarson (2002, 109, 144), Kristjánsson (2002, 126), and Indriðason (2004). **1974**: Includes only a splinter of the PP and not the entire party (Grimsson 1982, 148). **1991**: See the *European Journal of Political Research* 1992 (22)—reports on national elections in western nations. **1999**: See Hardarson (2002, 107).

Table A.10

Electoral Coalitions in Ireland, 1946–2002

Election Year	% Vote for Coalition	PEC	In Govt?	MRG
1948		No		
1951	53.11	FG+L+CnT+CnP	No	Yes
1954	44.28	FG+L+CnT	Yes	Yes
1957		No		
1961		No		
1965		No		
1969		No		
1973	48.75	FG+L	Yes	Yes
1977	42.12	FG+L	No	Yes
1981	46.40	FG+L	Yes	Yes
1982 (Feb.)	46.42	FG+L	No	Yes
1982 (Nov.)	48.6	FG+L	Yes	Yes
1987		No		
1989		No		
1992		No		
1997	40.8	FG+L+DL	No	Yes
	44.0	FF+PD	Yes	Yes
2002		No		

PARTIES: **CnP:** Clann na Poblachta (Party of the Republic). **CnT:** Clann na Talmhan (Party of the Land). **DL:** Democratic Left. **FF:** Fianna Fáil (Soldiers of Ireland). **FG:** Fine Gael (Irish Race). **L:** Labour. **PD:** Progressive Democrats.

COMMENTS: **1951:** See Farrell (1987, 138). **1954:** See Farrell (1987, 138). **1973:** See Sinnott (1987, 93), Mair (1987, 114), Farrell (1987, 138), and Gallagher (1982, 118,190–96). **1977:** See Gallagher (1982, 216–32). **1981:** See Laver (1992). **1982** (February and November): See Gallagher (1982, 249) and Sinnott (1987, 93). **1997:** See Murphy (2003, 4), Collins (2003, 25), and Gallagher (2003, 93).

Table A.11
Electoral Coalitions in Israel, 1948–2002

Election Year	% Vote for Coalition	PEC	In Govt?	MRG†
1949	12.2	URF	Yes*	No
1951		No		
1955	4.7	Torah Front	No	No
1959	4.7	Torah Front	No	No
1961		No		
1965	21.3	Gahal	No	No
1969	21.7	Gahal	Yes*	No
	46.2	Maarakh	Yes*	No
1973	30.2	Likud Bloc	No	No
	39.6	Maarakh	Yes*	No
	1.4	Moked	No	No
	3.8	Torah Front	No	No
1977	33.4	Likud Bloc	Yes*	No
	24.6	Maarakh	No	No
	11.6	DMC	No	No
1981	37.1	Likud Bloc	Yes*	No
	36.6	Maarakh	No	No
1984	31.9	Likud Bloc	Yes*	No
	34.9	Maarakh	Yes*	No
	4.0	HaTehiya+Tsomet	Yes*	No
1988	31.1	Likud Bloc	Yes*	No
1992	24.9	Likud Bloc	No	No
	9.6	Meretz	Yes*	No
1996*	25.8	LGT	Yes*	No
1999*	14.1	Likud Bloc	No	No
	20.2	One Israel	Yes*	No
	3.0	National Union	No	No
	3.7	Yahadut HaTorah	No	No

*Pre-electoral coalition did not enter government alone.
†The MRG data set includes these coalitions as single parties.
◆The Prime Minister was directly elected by the voters in 1996 and 1999.
COALITIONS: **URF** (United Religious Front): Mizrahi, HaPoel HaMizrahi, Agudat Israel and Poalei Agudat Israel. **Torah Religious Front:** Agudat Israel and Poalei Agudat Israel. **Gahal:** Liberal Party and Herut. **Likud Bloc:** Liberal Party, Herut, Free Center, Laam, Movement for a Greater Israel, State List. **Maarakh** (Alignment): Labor Party and Mapam. **Moked:** Maki and Rakah – The Communist Party of Israel was founded in 1949, and in 1965 broke into two factions, Maki and Rakah. They formed an electoral list together in 1973. **DMC** (Democratic Movement for Change): Shinui and Free Center. **Meretz:** Shinui, Mapam and Ratz. **One Israel:** Labor, Gesher and Meimad. **LGT:** Likud Bloc, Gesher and Tsomet. **Yahadut HaTorah:** Agudat Israel and Degel HaTorah. **National Union:** Moledet, Herut and Tekuma.
COMMENTS: See official Knesset website, www.knesset.gov.il. See also the Library of Congress (http://lcweb2.loc.gov/frd/cs/israel/il_appnb.html), Laver & Schofield (1998, 230), Penniman (ed.) (1979), Aronoff (1978).

Table A.12
Electoral Coalitions in Italy, 1946–2002

Election Year	% Vote for Coalition	PEC	In Govt?	MRG
1948	31.0	PCI+PSI	No	Yes
1953	35.3	PCI+PSI	No	Yes
1958		No		
1963		No		
1968		No		
1972		No		
1976		No		
1979		No		
1983		No		
1987		No		
1992		No		
1994	34.3	Progressive Allia nce	Yes*	(1)
	15.7	Pact for Italy	Yes*	Yes
	46.4	Pole of Good Government	No	(2)
1996	43.4	Olive Tree I + RC	Yes†	(3)
	42.1	Freedom Pole	No	(4)
2001	35.0	Olive Tree II	No	No
	45.4	House of Freedom	Yes	No

* Pre-electoral coalition did not enter government alone.

† Although the RC was a member of the electoral alliance, it did not enter government. The RC did support the Olive Tree I government in the legislature, though.

(1) MRG data set does not include the Socialist Party, Social Christians, or Socialist Renewal; (2) MRG data set does not include the Christian Democratic Center, Democratic Union of the Left, Liberal Democratic Pole; (3) MRG data set does not include the Prodi Group or the Sardinian Action Party; 4) MRG data set treats the Christian Democrats as a single party.

COALITIONS: **Progressive Alliance:** Party of the Democratic Left, Communist Refoundation, Greens, Network, Democratic Alliance, Socialist Party, Social Christians, Socialist Renewal. **Pact for Italy:** Popular Party, Segui Pact. **Pole of Good Government:** Forza Italia, National Alliance, Northern League, Panella List-Reformers, Christian Democratic Center, Democratic Union of the Left, Liberal Democratic Pole. **Freedom Pole:** Forza Italia, National Alliance, Christian Democratic Center, United Christian Democrats. **Olive Tree I:** Party of the Democratic Left, Prodi Group, Dini List-Renewed Italy, Green Federation. **House of Freedom:** Forza Italia, National Alliance, Northern League, Union of Christian and Center Democrats (formerly the Christian Democratic Center and the United Christian Democrats), New Italian Socialist Party. **Olive Tree II:** Party of Democratic Left, Italian People's Party, Democrats, Dini-List-Renewed Italy, Democratic Union for Europe, Green Federation, Italian Democratic Socialist Party, Party of Italian Communists.

PARTIES: RC: Communist Refoundation. PCI: Communist Party. PSI: Socialist Party.

COMMENTS: **1948:** See Mackie & Rose (1991), Marradi (1982, 39), and Mastropaolo & Slater (1992, 313). **1953:** See Mastropaolo & Slater (1992, 313). **1994:** See Newell (2000, 32), Mershon (2002), Rhodes (1995, 128–29), Daniels (1999, 82–84), and Verzichelli & Cotta (2000). **1996:** See Mershon (2002), Newell (2000, 38–39), Daniels (1999, 85–89), and Verzichelli & Cotta (2000). **2001:** See Mershon (2002) and www.electionworld.org.

Table A.13
Electoral Coalitions in Japan, 1946–2002

Election Year	% Vote for Coalition	PEC	In Govt?	MRG
1947		No		
1949		No		
1952		No		
1953		No		
1955		No		
1958		No		
1960		No		
1963		No		
1967		No		
1969		No		
1972		No		
1976		No		
1979		No		
1980		No		
1983		No		
1986		No		
1990		No		
1993	37.18	JRP+JSP+CGP+DSP+SDF	Yes*	No SDF
	10.69	NP+JNP	Yes*	Yes
1996		No		
2000		No		

*The government was formed from the two pre-electoral coalitions in 1993.
PARTIES: CGP: Clean Government Party. **DSP:** Democratic Socialist Party. **JNP:** Japan New Party.
JRP: Japan Renewal Party (Shinsei-to). **JSP:** Japan Socialist Party. **NP:** New Party (Sakigake). **SDF:**
Socialist Democratic Federation.
COMMENTS: 1993: See Kohno (1997, 139–41, 149).

Table A.14

Electoral Coalitions in Luxembourg, 1946–2002

Election Year †	% Vote for Coalition	PEC	In Govt?	MRG
1954		No		
1959		No		
1964		No		
1968	68.45	LSAP+CSV	No*▲	Yes
1974		No		
1979	6.64	EF+SI	No	No
1984		No		
1989		No		
1994	9.91	GAP+GLEI	No	1 Party
1999		No		

†The elections of 1949 and 1951 were partial legislative elections and were, thus, not included.

*After the election, the LSAP was prevented from entering the government coalition by its trade union—the CSV did want to form the government coalition based on the electoral pact (Dumont & De Winter 2000, 405).

PARTIES: CSV: Christian Democrats. **LSAP:** Socialists. **GAP:** Alternative Green Party. **GLEI:** Green Left Ecological Initiative. **EF:** Forcibly Enrolled. **SI:** Independent Socialists.

COMMENTS: 1968: See Dumont & De Winter (2000, 405). **1979:** See Mackie & Rose (1991), Table 15.1. **1994:** See Dumont & De Winter (2000, 403).

Table A.15

Electoral Coalitions in the Netherlands, 1946–2002

Election Year	% Vote for Coalition	PEC	In Govt?	MRG
1946		No		
1948		No		
1952		No		
1956		No		
1959		No		
1963		No		
1967		No		
1971	33.70	PvdA+D66+PPR	No	Yes
1972	36.29	PvdA+D66+PPR	Yes*	Yes
1977	31.89	ARP+CHU+KVP	Yes*	1 Party
	35.90	PvdA+PPR	No	Yes
1981		No		
1982		No		
1986	52.00	CDA+VVD	Yes	Yes
1989	67.19	PvdA+CDA	Yes	Yes
	4.10	CPN+PPR+EVP	No	No
1994		No		
1998	62.7	D66+PvdA+VVD	Yes	Yes
2002		No		

*Pre-electoral coalition did not enter government alone.

PARTIES: PvdA: Social Democrats. **D66:** Liberal Democrats. **PPR:** Radical Party. **CHU:** Christian Historical Union. **ARP:** Anti-Revolutionary Party. **KVP:** Catholic People's Party – ARP, CHU and KVP merged to form the Christian Democrat Appeal (**CDA**) in 1979. **VVD:** Liberals. **CPN:** Communist Party. **EVP:** Evangelical People's Party.

COMMENTS: 1971: See Timmermans & Andeweg (2000, 367), Tops & Dittrich (1992, 279), and Daalder (1987, 254). **1972:** See Timmermans & Andeweg (2000, 367), Tops & Dittrich (1992, 279), Daalder (1987, 254), and De Swaan (1982, 223, 230). **1977:** See Koole (1994, 280), Daalder (1987, 217), de Jong & Pijnenburg (1986, 148), De Swaan (1982, 223, 230), and Keesing's. **1986:** See Powell (2000, 141) and Napel (1999, 177). **1989:** See Powell (2000, 55). **1998:** See Irwin (1999).

Table A.16

Electoral Coalitions in New Zealand, 1946–2002

Election Year	% Vote for Coalition	PEC	In Govt?	MRG
1946		No		
1949		No		
1951		No		
1954		No		
1957		No		
1960		No		
1963		No		
1966		No		
1969		No		
1972		No		
1975		No		
1978		No		
1981		No		
1984		No		
1987		No		
1990	5.2	MM+NLP	No	No
1993		No		
1996		No		
1999	46.4	AL+LAB	Yes	No
2002		No		

PARTIES: MM: Mana Motuhake. **NLP:** New Labor Party. **AL:** Alliance Party. **LAB:** New Zealand Labour Party.
COMMENTS: 1990: See Alliance website, http://www.alliance.org.nz. The NLP stood in the general seats, and Mana Motuhake stood in the Maori seats. In 1991, the two parties merged into the Alliance. **1999:** See Vowles (2002) and Alliance website http://www.alliance.org.nz.

Table A.17
Electoral Coalitions in Norway, 1946–2002

Election Year	% Vote for Coalition	PEC	In Govt?	MRG
1949		No		
1953		No		
1957		No		
1961		No		
1965	49.47	SP+H+V+KRF	Yes	Yes
1969	48.88	SP+H+V+KRF	Yes	Yes
1973	11.20	CP+SPP+WIC	No	1 Party
1977	45.78	H+KRF+SP	No	Yes
1981	47.77	H+KRF+SP	No	Yes
1985	45.28	H+KRF+SP	Yes	Yes
1989	37.19	H+KRF+SP	Yes	Yes
1993		No		
1997	26.04	KRF+SP+V	Yes	Yes
2001	22.00	KRF+SP+V	No	No

PARTIES: SP: Center Party. H: Conservative Party. V: Liberal Party. KRF: Christian People's Party. CP: Communist Party. SPP: Socialist People's Party. WIC: Worker's Information Committee.
COMMENTS: 1965: See Groennings (1970, 73–74), Fitzmaurice (1986, 266), Rommetvedt (1992, 59), Hancock (1998, 245), Arter (1999, 210), and Narud & Strøm (2000, 175). 1969: See Fitzmaurice (1986, 266), Strøm & Leipart (1992, 69), and Narud & Strøm (2000, 175). 1973: See Valen & Martinussen (1977, 40–43), Esaiasson & Heidar (2000, 452), and Keesing's. In March 1975 the electoral coalition was transformed into the Socialist Left Party. 1977: See Rommetvedt (1992, 61, 75) and Arter (1999, 210). 1981: See Narud & Strøm (2000, 177), Shaffer (1998, 122) and Rommetvedt (1992, 60, 75). 1985: See Strøm & Leipart (1992, 69) and Narud & Strøm (2000, 175). 1989: See Rommetvedt (1992, 61) and Narud & Strøm (2000, 175). 1997: See Narud & Strøm (2000, 175). 2001: See Valen (2003).

Table A.18

Electoral Coalitions in Portugal, 1976–2002

Election Year	% Vote for Coalition	PEC	In Govt?	MRG
1976		No		
1979	46.30	SD+CDS+PMP	Yes	Yes
	19.51	PCP+MDP	No	Yes
1980	27.80	PS+UEDS+ASDI	No	Yes
	17.32	PCP+MDP	No	Yes
	48.30	SD+CDS+PMP+Ref	Yes	Not Ref
1983	18.69	PCP+MDP+Greens	No	Yes
1985	15.97	PCP+MDP+Greens	No	Yes
1987	12.46	CDU	No	Yes
1991	8.80	CDU	No	1 Party
1995	8.60	CDU	No	1Party
1999	9.02	CDU	No	No
	2.46	UBL	No	No
2002	7.00	CDU	No	No
	2.80	UBL	No	No

COALITIONS: CDU (Unitarian Democratic Coalition): Communist Party and Greens. UBL (United Block of the Left): Worker's Revolutionary Party, Democratic People's Union, and Extreme Left (Politica XXI).

PARTIES: PCP: Communist Party. MDP: Portuguese Democratic Movement. CDS: Center Social Democrats. SD: Social Democrats. DI: Democratic Intervention. Ref: Reformists. PS: Socialist Party. UEDS: Left Social Democratic Union. ASDI: Independent Social Democrats. PRD: Party of Democratic Renovation. PMP: Popular Monarchist Party.

COMMENTS: 1979: See Cunha (1997, 36), Frain (1997, 100–102), Kohler (1982, 196, 209), Bruneau & Macleod (1986, 28–29), Mackie & Rose (1991), Table 20.3a, Magone (2000), and Laver & Schofield (1998, 237). 1980: See Cunha (1997, 37), Frain (1997, 100–102), Bruneau & Macleod (1986, 28–29), Mackie & Rose (1991), Table 20.3a, Magone (2000), and Laver & Schofield (1998, 237). 1983–87: See Cunha (1997, 39–41), Mackie & Rose (1991), Table 20.3a, Magone (2000), and Laver & Schofield (1998, 237). 1991–95: See Cunha (1997, 45–47), Magone (2000, 533). 1999: See Lloyd-Jones (2002) and Keesing's. 2002: See electionworld.org.

Table A.19
Electoral Coalitions in Spain, 1977–2002

Election Year	% Vote for Coalition	PEC	In Govt?	MRG
1977	34.52	UCD	Yes	1 Party
	9.35	PCE+CS	No	Yes
	4.47	PSP+FSP	No	No
1979	5.97	AP+PDP+PL	No	1 Party
	10.82	PCE+CS	No	Yes
1982	23.64	AP+PDP	No	Yes
1986	26.12	AP+PDP+PL	No	Yes
	4.63	PCE+left	No	No
1989	9.13	IU	No	No
1993	9.63	IU	No	No
1996		No		
2000	39.6	PSOE+IU	No	No

COALITIONS: IU (United Left Coalition): Spanish Communist Party, Communist Party of the Peoples of Spain, Catalan Unified Socialist Party, Progressive Federation, Party of Socialist Action, Unitarian Candidature of Workers, Berdak-Les Verds and Republican Left. This was an electoral coalition until 1994, when it became a federation where its members could belong either to the IU itself or to its member parties (Newton 1997, 193, 215). **UCD:** Union of the Democratic Center: an electoral coalition of fourteen center and right-wing parties that merged into a single party in 1978. **AP:** Popular Alliance: an electoral alliance with around seven conservative constituent parties. By 1978, the coalition had split, losing some conservative members and gaining some moderate ones.

PARTIES: PDP: Christian Democrats. **PL:** Liberals. **PCE:** Communists. **CS:** Catalan Unified Socialist Party. **PSOE:** Socialists. **PSP:** Popular Socialist Party. **FSP:** remnant of Federation of Socialist Parties.

COMMENTS: 1977: See Kohler (1982, 17–35), López-Pintor (1985a, 189), Esteban & López Guerra (1985), Mackie & Rose (1991), Heywood (1995, 175), Caramani (2000), and Hopkin (1999, 213). **1979:** See Kohler (1982, 27–28), López-Pintor (1985a, 189), and Esteban & López Guerra (1985). **1982:** See López-Pintor (1985b), Mackie & Rose (1991), and Laver & Schofield (1998, 239–40). **1986:** See Laver & Schofield (1998, 239–40) and Gillespie (1995, 59). **1989:** See Keesings and Newton (1997, 193, 210–11). **1993:** See Keesings, Newton (1997, 193, 210–11), and Budge et al. (2001). **1996:** See Newton (1997, 210–11). **2000:** See Colomer (2001) and www.election-world.org.

Table A.20
Electoral Coalitions in Sweden, 1946–2002

Election Year	% Vote for Coalition	PEC	In Govt?	MRG
1948	47.48	CE+LIB+CON	No	Yes
1952	56.79	SD+CE	Yes	Yes
1956		No		
1958		No		
1960		No		
1964		No		
1968		No		
1970		No		
1973	48.81	CE+LIB+CON	No	Yes
	9.4	SLP+left	No	Yes (SKP)
1976	50.73	CE+LIB+CON	Yes	Yes
1979	49.0	CE+LIB+CON	No	Yes
1982		No		
1985	12.42	CE+CD	No	Yes
1988		No		
1991	31.05	LIB+CON	Yes*	Yes
1994		No		
1998		No		
2002		No		

*Pre-electoral coalition did not enter government alone.
PARTIES: SD: Social Democrats. **SKP:** Left Party. **CE:** Center Party. **LIB:** Liberal Party. **CON:** Conservative Party. **CD:** Christian Democratic Party. **ND:** New Democracy Party.
COMMENTS: 1948: See Särlvik (2002, 243–45, 247). **1952:** See Bergman (2000, 208). **1973:** See Bergman (1995, 74, 84), Särlvik (1977, 75–76), Hadenius (1990, 132–33), Strøm & Bergman (1992, 115) and Powell (2000, 76). **1973:** Keesing's reported an alliance on the left but mentioned only one party by name (SKP). **1976:** See Särlvik (1983, 126), Fitzmaurice (1986, 266), Hadenius (1990, 144), Strøm & Bergman (1992, 115), and Powell (2000, 72, 76, 261). **1979:** See Särlvik (1983, 131), Fitzmaurice (1986, 266), Strøm & Bergman (1992), and Powell (2000, 76, 261). **1985:** See Hadenius (1990, 177), Sannerstedt & Sjölin (1992, 104), Strøm & Bergman (1992, 117), Arter (1999, 111), and Särlvik (2002, 229, 257–58). **1991:** See Bergman (2000, 209).

Table A.21
Electoral Coalitions in the United Kingdom, 1946–2002

Election Year	% Vote for Coalition	PEC	In Govt?	MRG
1950		No		
1951		No		
1955		No		
1959		No		
1964		No		
1966		No		
1970		No		
1974 (Feb.)		No		
1974 (Oct.)		No		
1979		No		
1983	25.37	Lib+SocDem	No	Yes
1987	22.57	Lib+SocDem	No	Yes
1992		No		
1997		No		
2001		No		

PARTIES: **Lib:** Liberals. **SocDem:** Social Democratic Party.

COMMENTS: **1983:** See Boothroyd (2001, 5–8), Kitschelt (1994, 180), Norton (1984, 126–30), and Peele (1995, 202–3). **1987:** See Peele (1995, 202–3) and Boothroyd (2001, 5–8).

NOTES

Notes to Chapter 1

1. I use the terms 'electoral' or 'pre-electoral' interchangeably to characterize coalitions that form prior to elections.

2. Electoral coalitions can also play a role in determining the identity of the government in countries with more proportional electoral rules. For example, the presence of an electoral coalition can affect the choice of government formateur or allow a small party that is a potential government member to surpass an electoral threshold. By affecting the identity of the government, electoral coalitions ultimately influence the types of policy that get implemented. This is the case whether the electoral system is disproportional, as in the stylized example above, or not.

3. Some of these studies do take account of the pre-election environment by incorporating voter choice and candidate entry (Shepsle 1991). For instance, Austen-Smith and Banks (1988) analyze the strategic behavior of voters in their model of government coalition formation. Other more recent work combines voter behavior with post-election elite bargaining (Glasgow & Alvarez 2005; Quinn & Martin 2002). However, none of these analyses ever explicitly allows for pre-electoral coalition formation.

4. I know of only one major cross-national statistical analysis that takes account of pre-electoral coalitions (Martin & Stevenson 2001). However, just as in the rest of the literature, the goal of this study is to better understand government coalitions, not electoral coalitions. Extremely recently, several papers have appeared examining electoral coalitions between particular parties in France (Blais and Indriðason 2004; Spoon 2004; Fauvelle-Aymar & Lewis-Beck 2005).

5. Kaminski (2001) uses a cooperative game-theoretic model to examine pre-electoral coalitions and party mergers in Poland in the 1990s. However, his analysis has not been extended to other cases and does not take account of bargaining or policy issues.

6. I do not claim that pre-electoral coalitions will automatically be electorally advantageous. After all, it may be the case that a coalition is composed of parties that are so ideologically incompatible that their respective electorates refuse to vote for the coalition.

7. Note that this does not have to be the case for a coalition to be advantageous. A coalition that attracts more votes than either party could win on its own, but fewer than the total number of votes they would win running independently, may still be useful if it increases the probability that this coalition enters government or becomes the formateur.

Notes to Chapter 2

1. Powell (2000) has collected data on government majorities that were identifiable

prior to elections. Although he includes some pre-electoral coalitions in his analysis, they are certainly not the main focus of his book. Martin and Stevenson (2001) include a pre-electoral coalition variable in their analysis of government coalitions. However, as I note in chapter seven, they significantly underestimate the presence of electoral coalitions in their sample.

2. Convergencia i Unió is an electoral coalition between the Democratic Convergence of Catalonia and the Democratic Union of Catalonia. Unidade Galega, known as the Socialist Galega Block in 1982 and the Socialist Galega-Left Galega in 1986, is composed of several small Galician parties. The Galician National Popular Block is another Galician electoral coalition in which the Marxist Unión do Pobo Galego is the dominant party. The Basque Left is an electoral coalition of left-wing Basque parties, while Herri Batasuna is an electoral coalition of more extreme left-wing parties in the Basque region.

3. These two electoral coalitions formed in the 1993 legislative elections (Kohno 1997, 139–41, 149). One electoral coalition comprised the Clean Government Party, the Democratic Socialist Party, the Socialist Democratic Federation, the Japan Renewal Party (Shinsei-to) and the Japan Socialist Party. The other comprised the New Party (Sakigake) and the Japan New Party. Both electoral coalitions entered government in 1993.

4. There was a coalition between the Center Party and the Christian League of Finland in 1970 (Arter 1999, 110), a coalition between the Liberals and the Center Party in 1983 (Esaiasson & Heidar 2000, 447–48), and the Purple Coalition in 1999 (personal correspondence with Mark Hallerberg). For more on electoral coalitions in Finland, see Sundberg (2002) and Kuitunen (2002).

5. I do not include Switzerland in this book because my statistical analyses focus on parliamentary, rather than presidential, systems. Were I to do so, though, it would present other ambiguous cases. Parties in Switzerland often form electoral coalitions in particular cantons; however, they are not nation-wide coalitions. The 'magic formula' used after 1959 to determine coalition government composition means that everyone knows in advance which parties will end up in government (Kerr 1987) and that "elections do not have a direct impact on the government composition" (Caramani 1996). I do not consider this agreement over government composition to constitute a pre-electoral coalition, since the parties in question do not coordinate their electoral strategies. Moreover, members of the executive council are elected individually by the parliament and are not "constrained by interparty policy deals" (Church 2004, 20, 117–18). Thus, although Switzerland has pre-electoral coalitions at the local level and the 'magic formula' at the national level, I would code Switzerland as having no national-level pre-electoral coalitions.

6. Prior to the 1960s, the Liberal Party also formed several local electoral coalitions with the Conservative Party. These coalitions took the form of nomination agreements, in which the Liberals agreed "not to contest a particular seat if the Conservatives refrained from offering a candidate in another seat" (Rasmussen 1991, 167).

7. Identifying electoral coalitions in Israel is further complicated by the fact that some parties that form an electoral alliance for certain elections later merge into a single party, where the original constituent parties exist as separate factions. This was the case with Mapai and its electoral alliance partners when they merged to form the Labor Party in 1968. Fortunately the act of officially forming a party does tend to be mentioned in the lit-

erature on elections and parties in Israel.

8. For a more detailed discussion of electoral coordination in mixed and multi-tier electoral systems with dual ballots, see Ferrara & Herron (2005).

9. Because the National and Liberal parties have such a long-standing electoral agreement, most of their pre-electoral bargaining is not actually over the flow of preferences, but rather over the number of districts in which both should compete and the extent to which their policy platforms differ (Sharman, Sayers, & Miragliotta 2002).

Notes to Chapter 3

1. Note that this is equivalent to saying that an increase in the number of parties will only raise the likelihood of pre-electoral coalitions when the electoral system is sufficiently disproportional.

2. However, some commentators analyzing Dutch politics have suggested that electoral coalitions have not been very effective in giving Dutch voters more say over the composition of their governments. For example, De Jong and Pijnenburg (1986, 148) state that "the making of a [government] coalition remains the crucial moment despite the efforts . . . towards more 'political clarity' and pre-electoral agreements . . . Dutch voters will never decide on the composition of their government."

3. A slightly different scenario took place in Italy in 1996, when a number of center-Left parties running under the heading of Olive Tree agreed to go into government together if they were successful at the polls. While the Communist Refoundation (RC) was not part of this coalition and had no intention of going into government with the Olive Tree, it did reach nomination agreements with the member parties of the Olive Tree to avoid splitting the left-wing vote in a number of constituencies (Daniels 1999, 85–86). Following the election, the Olive Tree coalition entered government, and the RC simply supported it from the legislature (Newell 2000, 38). In this case, I do consider that the government was based on an electoral coalition.

4. For another analysis of how electoral system disproportionality and party system size affect the probability of electoral coalition formation, see S. Golder (2005).

5. The effective threshold is the mean of the thresholds of representation and exclusion. It is calculated as

$$\frac{50\%}{M+1} + \frac{50\%}{2M}$$

where M is the district magnitude. If there are legal thresholds and/or upper-tier seats, the calculation is slightly more complicated (Lijphart 1994, 25–30). For more information on electoral thresholds, see Taagepera (1998a, 1998b).

Notes to Chapter 4

1. However, it is important to recognize that actual election results may rule out certain combinations, so that a party may reconsider its alliance strategy afterwards. It may

also be the case that voters do not clearly show their support for a particular electoral coalition. In these circumstances, party leaders can more easily justify not honoring the terms of the electoral coalition. After all, agreements over the division of government spoils do not necessarily specify appropriate behavior if the coalition loses. It is, perhaps, interesting to note that some pre-electoral agreements are sufficiently detailed that they take these possibilities into account and prescribe particular actions. This is an indication that party leaders are clearly aware of the commitment problems associated with electoral coalitions.

2. If the main issue for voters in a particular election was incumbent corruption, then parties at opposing extremes could potentially form an anti-incumbent, anti-corruption electoral coalition that could generate a significant amount of voter support. In fact, this is the story often told of the defeat of the Congress Party in India in 1989 (Andersen 1990).

3. Note that the fact that a coalition may be sub-additive does not necessarily mean that it offers no significant electoral gains. It is possible for a coalition to be sub-additive and yet still be sufficiently large to represent the largest 'party,' thereby winning itself the role of government formateur.

4. This does not rule out the possibility that politicians will overestimate the support they would receive from running separately or from forming an electoral coalition. Estimates of party or coalition support are likely to be uncertain in volatile or new party systems. Although the extent to which these estimates are inaccurate can obviously affect the range in which coalition bargains are feasible, I have not explicitly modeled this source of uncertainty.

5. The core of any bargaining game is that two players are bargaining over a 'pie.' The size of this pie is typically normalized to 1. An agreement is a pair (x_1, x_2), in which x_1 is Player A's share of the pie and x_2 Player B's share. The set of possible agreements is: $X = \{(x_1, x_2) \in \Re^2 : x_1 + x_2 = 1 \text{ and } x_i \geq 0 \text{ for } i = 1, 2\}$.

6. As long as party leaders have single-peaked preferences over the policy space, then the use of a quadratic loss function does not affect any of the model's implications.

7. It is not difficult to see that this feature of presidential elections would make it rather difficult to find a coalition bargain acceptable to both sides. The problems caused by non-divisible presidential offices will be illustrated in the next chapter.

8. Although there are three possible sub-game perfect Nash equilibria, there is always a unique sub-game perfect Nash equilibrium for any given set of values for the model's parameters.

9. However, this assumption is not entirely innocuous, since it does affect the number of possible sub-game perfect Nash equilibria. It turns out that if I allow the players to remain indifferent between making and not making an offer, there would be an additional equilibrium in which Party A makes an offer, B rejects this offer, and B makes no counter-offer. The outcome would be that no electoral coalition forms.

10. If this assumption is not made and the players are allowed to remain indifferent, then there is a fourth sub-game perfect Nash equilibrium. The outcome is that Player A makes an initial offer, which is rejected. The game enters a second period, but Player B does not make a counter offer. The end result is that no electoral coalition forms.

Notes to Chapter 5

1. Le Pen received 16.86% of the vote in the 2002 presidential election compared to 15% in 1995. A rival far-right candidate, Bruno Mégret, won another 2.34% of the vote in 2002. These figures come from the *Election Politique* website at http://www.election -politique.com.

2. The electoral system used for the 1986 elections was different. In an attempt to prevent an expected right-wing legislative majority, President Mitterrand introduced a proportional representation system similar to that used in the Fourth Republic. He hoped that this system would encourage voters to support the extremist National Front and siphon off votes from the moderate right-wing parties. Although a large number of voters did support the National Front, the leader of the moderate right, Jacques Chirac, still managed to become prime minister, albeit with a legislative majority of just two. Chirac immediately restored the traditional two-round electoral system.

3. The early 5% threshold was based on the actual number of votes cast. When the threshold was raised to 10% in 1966, the percentage of votes a party now needed to advance to the second round was 10% of the *registered* voters. This method remained in place when the threshold was raised to 12.5% (Duhamel 1999, 138–39). Given turnout levels, a party often needs around 17% of the actual vote to qualify for the second round.

4. A small number of moderate right-wing deputies regularly call for an electoral coalition with the National Front in certain districts. However, they tend to be isolated very quickly by the party elites (Hecht & Mandonnet 1998). For example, when several mainstream right politicians were elected with the help of the National Front in the cantonal and regional elections of 1998, President Chirac immediately went on national television to denounce all alliances between the moderate and the extreme right. The politicians were then kicked out of their parties (Martin 1999).

5. Cohabitation refers to a time when the presidential and prime ministerial positions are held by people from opposing parties.

6. The origins of this federation can be found in a series of discussions that took place around the presidential candidate of a mysterious 'Monsieur X.' It was only once the idea of a candidate of the center-Left had been 'tested' in the weekly magazine, *L'Express,* that Gaston Deferre came out and announced that he was actually Monsieur X (Chagnollaud & Quermonne 1996).

7. The PCF were opposed to the alliance, because they did not want to be sidelined as they had been in the Fourth Republic. Since the Gaullists opposed the alliance and wanted the centrist voters for themselves, they constantly raised the religious issue to drive a wedge between the Socialists and the MRP.

8. Parties of the right during the Third and Fourth Republics had always suffered from elite fragmentation and the poor organization of their mass electoral following. However, the Gaullists were able to gain control of the local 'notables' and achieve a high degree of parliamentary discipline, centralization, and nationalization (Schain 1991).

9. The other three cases include one with multiple left-wing candidates, and two with multiple right-wing candidates. In the fourth district in the Maine-et-Loire department, the left-wing candidate managed to win with only 36.57% of the vote, because two mainstream-Right candidates split the right-wing vote between them.

10. In the proportional representation elections of 1986, the UDF and the Gaullists ran joint lists in 61 of the 96 electoral districts. They ran separate lists in the remaining 35.

11. Along with a small band of followers, the UDF leader François Bayrou was one of the few who refused to join the new 'Union for a Presidential Majority.' He was worried that the Gaullists would dominate the new coalition and control the bulk of the campaign funding from the government.

12. Socialist voters were much less likely to vote for a Communist candidate in the second round than Communist voters were to support a Socialist candidate. The vast majority of centrist voters simply refused to vote for an electoral union of the Left led by the PCF (Hanley 2002; Bell & Criddle 1984; Johnson 1981; Alexandre 1977).

13. Rivalry among the various leaders of the moderate Left was intense; anecdotes of the personal nature of this rivalry are rife in the descriptive literature (Du Roy & Schneider 1982; Alexandre 1977). It is important to note that this rivalry did not prevent the merger. As a result, one should be wary of the 'personal animosity' story as an explanation for coordination failure.

14. It is important to remember that the 1986 election was held under a proportional representation system. It is worth stating, though, that there is some doubt as to how many of the French voters actually realized this prior to the election. The simulation would certainly be more useful had the poll been taken during an election held under the usual two-round system.

15. Analysts of French politics often refer to the parties on the right using a typology developed by René Rémond (1982), according to which the Right has been divided since Napoleon into Orleanist, Bonapartist, and Monarchist wings. In recent years, references to this typology have diminished. For a further discussion, see Golder (2000).

16. There were seven candidates representing the Right. See http://www.election-politique.com for a complete listing of candidates and results.

17. So far, the National Front has not managed to win seats in the legislature, with the exception of 35 seats in the 1986 proportional representation elections.

18. As one might expect, these electoral agreements are often a source of conflict between the party elites and the local candidates.

19. Both Kim Young Sam and Kim Dae Jung were confident of at least receiving the votes from their own native region (Im 2000; Nam 1989, 196; Dong 1988, 181–82).

20. Although the Korean system is often treated as presidential (Przeworski et al. 2000), it does have a prime minister subject to the approval of parliament. The president is not responsible to parliament and does not have the ability to dissolve it. The government of the prime minister can be brought down, though, by a vote of no confidence. In many ways, this system is similar to that used in France. The main difference is that the South Korean president does not have the power to dissolve the parliament, as the French president does.

21. In the absence of ideological conflict, regional distinctions have become central to much of Korean politics. Regional antagonisms were encouraged during Park Chung Hee's reign (Nam 1989, 279, 316–17). This applies particularly to the split between the Cholla region and the rest of the country. Morriss (1996) argues that regional voting did not develop before the 1970s but has grown rapidly since then. He emphasizes that this pattern is a political construct, since there are no intrinsic regional differences, and that in "the absence

of other socio-economic cleavages, regional attachments provide a way for leaders to differentiate themselves, and a basis on which to appeal to their supporters."

22. Kim Dae Jung also promised to change the institutional setup and create more of a parliamentary regime in which the president would have no more than a ceremonial role (Diamond & Shin 2000; Kim 2000*b*). Since parliament was controlled by Kim Young Sam's party at the time, it would obviously be difficult to get such a measure passed. As a result, this second promise was never entirely credible.

23. Kim Young Sam's long-term rival, Kim Dae Jung, came second with 33.8% of the vote, while Chung Ju Yung came third with 16.3%.

24. Shortly before the election, though, Chung abruptly ended his alliance with Roh. Despite this change, Roh still won the election.

Notes to Chapter 6

1. Kaminski (2001) has used a similar survey approach to the one suggested here to analyze coalition stability in Poland.

2. Dyadic data is also the format of choice in the international relations literature addressing coalition or alliance behavior.

3. 'Government potential' refers to a party that is a former, actual, or (realistically) possible member of government. 'Blackmail potential' refers to a party that is able to affect the tactics of party competition among government-oriented parties (Budge et al. 2001, 216). The Budge et al. criteria are themselves drawn from Sartori (1976).

4. Random effects are similar to fixed effects in that they are both used to model unobserved heterogeneity. However, they measure unobserved heterogeneity in different ways. The fixed effects model introduces dummy variables, essentially modeling unobserved heterogeneity as an intercept shift. In contrast, a random effects estimation models unobserved heterogeneity with an additional disturbance term that is drawn from a normal distribution with mean zero. There are at least two reasons why random effects are preferable here. Theoretically, a random-effects specification is more appropriate when inferences are being made about a population on the basis of a sample as is the case here (Greene 2003; Hsiao 2003). More practically, running a fixed-effects model by election would mean that all elections in which no pre-electoral coalition formed would be dropped. Doing so would leave me with only 37% of the observations and potentially introduces selection bias.

5. The log-likelihood from the model with random effects is -625.79, while the log-likelihood from the model without them is -681.29. This gives a χ^2 statistic of 111.0, i.e., $2(-625.79 + 681.29) = 111.0$. The p-value of obtaining a χ^2 statistic of this magnitude or larger if the random effects are not required is less than .0001, with one degree of freedom. This result strongly suggests that random effects should be retained.

6. Confidence intervals are based on simulations using 10,000 draws from the estimated coefficient vector and variance-covariance matrix.

7. One might also wonder about the predictive power of my analysis. As with all rare event data, the predicted probability of a pre-electoral coalition forming is quite low (King & Zeng 2001). However, the results from my analysis show that the mean predicted prob-

ability of an electoral coalition forming for those dyads that actually did form an electoral coalition (.10) is twice as large as the mean predicted probability for those dyads that did not form a coalition (.05). The fact that simulations show that we can be highly confident (greater than 99%) that these mean predicted probabilities are different provides support for the predictive power of my analysis.

8. I show the effect of a change in *Polarization* by one standard deviation from its mean both when *Effective Threshold* is at its minimum value and when it is at its maximum value. This result shows the effect of a reasonable change in *Polarization* over the whole range of values of *Effective Threshold* in the sample. I do this for the other interacted variables as well.

Notes to Chapter 7

1. See Martin & Stevenson (2001, 38) for a discussion of the reasons why more traditional regression methods are unsuitable for analyzing which parties enter government.

2. Martin & Stevenson do, in fact, code some potential government coalitions as being based on pre-electoral agreements during inter-election periods. They do not discuss the justification for coding these observations in this way.

3. The test essentially involves comparing the estimated parameters produced by a fully specified model (all potential choices are included) with the estimated parameters from a model where the set of choices is restricted (some choices have been dropped). If IIA holds and the dropped choices are irrelevant, then the estimates of the model parameters will be the same. While Martin & Stevenson conducted their test by randomly dropping 20% of the potential government coalitions, I employed a more stringent test and randomly dropped 50% of the potential governments. I then repeated this procedure 50 times to make sure that the randomization procedure did not produce an unusual answer. If the p-value from the test is less than .05, then the null hypothesis of IIA is rejected. The average p-values from the 50 tests for the four models that I estimated in table 7.1 range from .69 to .89. I also conducted more stringent tests, where I dropped more than 50% of the potential government coalitions; I was still unable to reject the IIA assumption.

4. By the same logic, one might also worry about the omission of *Investiture* from the model, since this variable is interacted with *Minority* status. However, *Investiture* does not vary across the choices for a given formation opportunity, and including it along with its interaction with *Minority* status would lead to perfect multi-collinearity. Thus, omitting the constitutive term *Investiture* is appropriate and necessary in this particular case (Brambor, Clark, & Golder 2006).

5. Martin & Stevenson draw this same inference, but in slightly different terms. They state that "[v]ery strong parties do tend to get into government and, even more, to rule alone" (2001, 46).

6. The inclusion of the constitutive term *Single Party* also affects some of the other coefficients. For example, it increases the size of the coefficient on *Minimal Winning Coalitions* by 43% and reduces the size of the coefficient on *Ideological Divisions* by 26%. This is just further evidence of the bias arising from the omission of *Single Party* in Model 1.

7. These two claims cannot be verified by simply looking at the results in Model 3

and comparing them to those in Model 2. However, the results from a model in which I interact all of the variables in table 7.1 with a *Post-Election* dummy variable do support these claims—the coefficients on the interaction terms *Minimal Winning Coalition* × *Post-Election* and *Pre-Electoral Pact* × *Post-Election* are both positive and significant in this model. These results are not shown.

8. The odds that a potential coalition becomes the government if it is based on a pre-electoral coalition compared to the exact same potential coalition that is not based on an electoral pact is calculated as $e^{\beta_{PEC}}$ where β_{PEC} is the coefficient on the *Pre-Electoral Coalition* variable in table 7.1 (Long 1997, 168–70).

9. In addition, non-political factors such as holidays affect the length of time between the election and the date the new government takes office. For instance, forming the German government at the end of the year in 1990 took extra time because of the Christmas holidays (Saalfeld 2000, 48).

10. The data in table 7.2 refer only to governments that formed after an election. Governments also form in inter-election periods after a cabinet falls. The mean length of time that it takes to form a government in an inter-election period is only 13.5 days. A difference in means test indicates that we can be well over 99% confident that governments that form after an election take a much longer time to take office than those that form in an inter-election period.

11. The hazard rate has two components. The first is a set of covariates that are hypothesized to systematically affect the timing of an event. The second is the baseline hazard function that indicates the rate of event occurrence when all the covariates are zero, i.e., the baseline hazard reflects how the rate of event occurrence changes with time only (Martin & Vanberg 2003).

12. The results from a generalized gamma model, as well as an examination of the Cox-Snell residuals, indicate that the Weibull model is appropriate for examining the duration of government formation (Box-Steffensmeier & Jones 2004, 41–43, 124–25, 137–39). The fact that the results from a Cox proportional hazards model are qualitatively similar to those that I obtain from the Weibull model indicates that I can be particularly confident that my results are not dependent on my choice of the Weibull distribution to parameterize the baseline hazard function. This is because the Cox model does not have to specify a particular distribution of the hazard rate. The results from estimating the Cox model also indicate that the proportional hazards assumption underlying both the Weibull and Cox models is not violated—the *p*-value from the global test of the Schoenfeld residuals is .21 (Grambsch & Therneau 1994; Box-Steffensmeier & Jones 2004; Cleves, Gould, & Gutierrez 2004, 178–80).

13. See http://www.pol.umu.se/ccpd/.

14. Figure 7.1 illustrates the change in expected duration as the *Pre-Electoral Coalition* variable goes from 0 to 1 across the range of observed values for *Government Parties*. The change in expected duration in the Weibull model for a given number of *Government Parties* is calculated as:

$$E(T_{PEC=0}|\text{Parties}) - E(T_{PEC=1}|\text{Parties}) =$$
$$\left[\left(\frac{1}{\lambda}\right)^{\frac{1}{p}}\Gamma\left(1+\frac{1}{\rho}\right)\right]_{PEC=0|Parties} - \left[\left(\frac{1}{\lambda}\right)^{\frac{1}{p}}\Gamma\left(1+\frac{1}{\rho}\right)\right]_{PEC=1|Parties} \tag{7.2}$$

where $\lambda = e^{x\beta}$ is a scale parameter, ρ is a shape parameter, and Γ is the gamma function. Confidence intervals around this change in expected duration are based on simulations using 10,000 draws from the estimated coefficient vector and variance-covariance matrix. Change in expected duration and confidence intervals are then calculated for all of the observed values of *Government Parties,* and these values are then plotted in figure 7.1.

15. In addition to using the *Ideological Range* variable, I also examined whether the *Ideological Spread* and *Ideological Connectedness* of the incoming government affected the duration of the government formation process. I found no evidence that they did. These additional variables are described in some detail in the next section.

16. I should note, though, that the 1977 Spanish government was actually based on a 14-party pre-electoral coalition. The problem is that the ideological data from the Manifesto Research Group have this government coded as a single party even though the parties did not merge until 1978.

17. As Laver (2003, 30) notes in a recent review article on government duration and termination, scholars have "tended to assemble a portfolio of independent variables gleaned from previous published work and the author's own ideas, each given a brief ad hoc 'theoretical' justification in its own terms. But the set of independent variables taken as a whole does not amount to the empirical elaboration of a coherent model of government termination."

18. In some cases, both sets of scholars will find a model and sample that support their 'contradictory' theoretical claims. For example, Strøm (1985) argues and finds that the number of days of 'crisis' before a government forms increases cabinet duration, while King et al. (1990) argue and find that the same variable actually decreases cabinet duration.

19. For example, much of the debate over questions of government duration has centered on the advantages of survival analysis as compared to ordinary least squares regression (King et al. 1990), whether the hazard rate is rising or falling and how it should be interpreted (Alt & King 1994; Warwick 1992, 1994; Beck 1998), and whether analysts should be employing a competing risks model or not (Diermeier & Stevenson 1999).

20. While Warwick (1994, 42) seems aware of some these problems, this does not change the fact that this type of procedure is problematic in the presence of multi-collinearity and leads to confidence intervals that are too small and p-values that cannot be interpreted in the usual way (Altman & Andersen 1989). Another problem is that this elimination procedure cannot distinguish between predictors of direct substantive interest and those whose effects one wants to control for (Singer & Willett 2003). Moreover, the end result is a model that tends to be sample specific. This last point may help to explain why the results from government duration models are not always robust across different samples.

21. Warwick does provide measures for different definitions of the government; he just prefers the more inclusive definition stated above.

22. The principal reason for employing the Weibull model earlier was that it made it easier to evaluate the conditional effect of pre-electoral coalitions on government bargaining delays in figure 7.1.

23. Censoring issues occur when the analyst does not observe the end of a duration period (right-censoring), while truncation issues occur when the analyst does not observe the duration of an observation that occurs prior to the start point of the data (left-truncation).

24. Although Warwick's data actually start in 1945, I only have data on pre-electoral coalitions from 1946.

25. Another source of data commonly used in the government duration literature is King et al. (1990). These data measure government duration in months, whereas the two data sources that I employed measure it in days. Since the data provided by King et al. are less accurate, I did not use them in my analysis.

26. Competing risks (or multiple destination) models take account of the fact that observations can terminate in different ways (Box-Steffensmeier & Jones 2004). I employ a latent survivor time approach to the competing risks problem where there are two specific destination states (dissolution or replacement), each of which has a latent failure time associated with it for each observation (Diermeier & Stevenson 1999).

27. I have already shown in previous sections that pre-electoral coalitions increase the ideological compatibility of governments and shorten the length of time that it takes to form a government. As a result, one might reasonably wonder if the effect of pre-electoral coalitions on government survival is being muted by the fact that I include *Ideological Range* and *Formation Attempts* as independent variables in table 7.5. However, analyses where I drop *Ideological Range* and *Formation Attempts* do not change my inferences.

28. The '——' symbol for the risk of dissolution indicates that the coefficient on *Caretaker Government* tends toward infinity, because there are no cases (Warwick data) or only one case (PDDA data) of a caretaker government that forms after an election ending in dissolution (Box-Steffensmeier & Jones 2004, 171). The one case of a caretaker government ending in dissolution in the PDDA data occurs in Iceland in 1959. Since the categorization of this particular government is open to interpretation, I should note that my results do not change if this government is not classified as a caretaker government (Indriðason 2004).

29. A cursory glance at the data reveals that Warwick and PDDA often measure the number of foiled formation attempts for the same governments differently. In fact, the correlation between the Warwick and PDDA variables is only 0.54.

Notes to Chapter 8

1. There are a few exceptions, of course. For example, Powell (2000) makes a point of considering both single parties and pre-electoral coalitions in 'majoritarian' democracies. He does so because he is interested in the identifiability of government alternatives. However, a more typical example is Laver and Schofield (1998, 1). Although they include a nice discussion of pre-electoral coalitions in their book on multi-party government, they still state that the "[t]he special forms of bargaining and negotiation that characterize the politics of coalition can be found *after* nearly every election that does not produce an unassailable 'winner' in the shape of a single party that controls a majority of the seats in the legislature." Emphasis added.

2. This suggests that a cooperative game-theoretic approach where coalitions automatically form whenever they are expected to be super-additive in seats or votes (Kaminski 2001) is less appropriate for modeling electoral coalition formation than the non-cooperative approach that I employ in this book.

REFERENCES

Akzin, Benjamin. 1979. "The Likud." In *Israel at the Polls: The Knesset Elections of 1977*, ed. Howard R. Penniman. United States: American Enterprise Institute for Public Policy Research.

Alexandre, Philippe. 1977. *Le roman de la gauche.* Paris: Librairie Plon.

Alt, James E. & Gary King. 1994. "Transfers of Governmental Power: The Meaning of Time Dependence." *Comparative Political Studies* 2: 190–210.

Altman, D. G. & P. K. Andersen. 1989. "Bootstrap Investigation of the Stability of a Cox Regression Model." *Statistics in Medicine* 8: 771–83.

Alvarez, Michael R. & Jonathan Nagler. 1995. "Economics, Issues, and the Perot Candidacy: Voter Choice in the 1992 Election." *American Journal of Political Science* 39: 714–44.

———. 1998. "When Politics and Models Collide: Estimating Models of Multi-Party Elections." *American Journal of Political Science* 42: 55–96.

———. 2000. "A New Approach for Modeling Strategic Voting in Multiparty Elections." *British Journal of Political Science* 30: 57–75.

Amorim Neto, Octavio & Gary W. Cox. 1997. "Electoral Institutions, Cleavage Structures, and the Number of Parties." *American Journal of Political Science* 41: 149–74.

Andersen, Walter K. 1990. "Election 1989 in India: The Dawn of Coalition Politics?" *Asian Survey* 30: 527–40.

Andeweg, Rudy B. 1989. "Institutional Conservatism in the Netherlands: Proposals for and Resistance to Change." In *Politics in the Netherlands: How Much Change?*, ed. Hans Daalder & Galen. A. Irwin. London: Frank Cass.

Argersinger, Peter H. 1980. "'A Place on the Ballot': Fusion Politics and Antifusion Laws." *American Historical Review* 85: 287–306.

Aronoff, Myron J. 1978. "Political Parties and the Emergence of Israel's Second Republic." In *Faction Politics: Political Parties and Factionalism in Comparative Perspective*, ed. Frank P. Belloni & Dennis C. Beller. California: American Bibliographical Center—Clio Press.

Arter, David. 1999. *Scandinavian Politics Today.* Manchester: Manchester University Press.

Ashworth, Scott & Ethan Bueno de Mesquita. 2006. "Informative Party Labels with Institutional and Electoral Variation." Manuscript.

Austen-Smith, David & Jeffrey Banks. 1988. "Elections, Coalitions, and Legislative Outcomes." *American Political Science Review* 82: 405–22.

———. 1990. "Stable Portfolio Allocations." *American Political Science Review* 84: 891–906.

Axelrod, Robert. 1970. *Conflict of Interest.* Chicago: Markham.

Bäck, Hannah. 2003. "Explaining and Predicting Coalition Outcomes: Conclusions from Studying Data on Local Conditions." *European Journal of Political Research* 42: 441–72.

Backman, François & Guy Birenbaum. 1993. "Heurs et malheurs de la sélections des candidats RPR et UDF." In *Le vote sanction: Les élections législatives des 21 et 28 mars 1993*, ed. Pascal Perrineau & Colette Ysmal. Paris: Département d'Études Politiques du Figaro et Presses de la Fondation Nationale des Sciences Politiques.

Baron, David. 1991. "A Spatial Bargaining Theory of Government Formation in Parliamentary Systems." *American Political Science Review* 85: 137–65.

Baron, David & John Ferejohn. 1989. "Bargaining in Legislatures." *American Political Science Review* 83: 1181–1206.

Bawn, Kathleen & Frances Rosenbluth. 2003. "Coalition Parties versus Coalitions of Parties: How Electoral Agency Shapes the Political Logic of Costs and Benefits." Presented at the American Political Science Association Annual Meeting, Philadelphia.

Beck, Nathaniel. 1998. "Modelling Space and Time: The Event History Approach." In *Research Strategies in the Social Sciences: A Guide to New Approaches*, ed. Elinor Scarbrough & Eric Tanenbaum. New York: Oxford University Press.

Beck, Nathaniel & Jonathan Katz. 1995. "What to Do (and Not to Do) with Time-Series Cross-Section Data." *American Political Science Review* 89: 634–47.

Becker, Jean-Jacques. 1994. *Histoire politique de la France depuis 1945*. Paris: Armand Colin.

Bell, David S. 2000. *Parties and Democracy in France: Parties under Presidentialism*. United States: Ashgate.

Bell, David S. & Byron Criddle. 1984. *The French Socialist Party: Resurgence and Victory*. New York: Oxford University Press.

Bergman, Torbjörn. 1995. "Constitutional Rules and Party Goals in Coalition Formation: An Analysis of Winning Minority Governments in Sweden." Ph.D. Thesis, Department of Political Science, Umea University (Sweden).

———. 2000. "Sweden: When Minority Cabinets Are the Rule and Majority Coalitions the Exception." In *Coalition Governments in Western Europe*, ed. Wolfgang C. Müller & Kaare Strøm. Oxford: Oxford University Press.

Bergounioux, A. & Gerard Grunberg. 1992. *Le long remords du pouvoir: Le parti socialiste français, 1905–1992*. Paris: Fayard.

Bernhard, William & David Leblang. 2002. "Democratic Processes and Political Risk: Evidence from Foreign Exchange Markets." *American Journal of Political Science* 46: 316–33.

———. 2006. *Pricing Politics: Democratic Processes and Financial Markets*. New York: Cambridge University Press.

Blais, André & Indriði Indriðason. 2005. "Making Candidates Count: The Logic of Electoral Alliances in Two-Round Legislative Elections." Manuscript.

Boothroyd, David. 2001. *The History of British Political Parties*. London: Politico's Publishing.

Bourcek, Françoise. 1998. "Electoral and Parliamentary Aspects of Dominant Party Systems." In *Comparing Party System Change*, ed. Paul Pennings & Jan-Erik Lane. United States: Routledge.

Bourlanges, Angéline. 1986. "L'Horizon 86: Les enquêtes Figaro/Sofres." In *SOFRES: Opinion publique 1986*. Paris: Éditions Gallimard.

Box-Steffensmeier, Janet M. & Bradford S. Jones. 2004. *Event History Modeling: A Guide for Social Scientists*. United States: Cambridge University Press.

Boy, Daniel & Bruno Villalba. 1999. "Le dilemme des écologists: Entre stratégie nationale et diversités locales." In *Le vote incertain: Les élections régionales de 1988*, eds. Pascal Perrineau & Dominique Reynié. Paris: Presses de la Fondation Nationale des Sciences Politiques.

Brambor, Thomas, William Roberts Clark, & Matt Golder. 2006. "Understanding Interaction Models: Improving Empirical Analyses." *Political Analysis* 14: 63-82.

Brams, Steven, Michael A. Jones, & D. Marc Kilgour. 2002. "Single-Peakedness, Coalition Formation and Disconnected Coalitions." *Journal of Theoretical Politics* 14: 359–83.

Braumoeller, Bear. 2004. "Hypothesis Testing and Multiplicative Interaction Terms." *International Organization* 58: 807–20.

Bréchon, Pierre. 1995. *La France aux urnes: Cinquante ans d'histoire électorale.* Édition 1995, Notes et études documentaries, No. 5008 (1995–2003). Paris: La Documentation Française.

Browne, Eric C. 1970. "Testing Theories of Coalition Formation in the European Context." *Comparative Political Studies* 3. 391–412.

Browne, Eric C., John P. Frendreis, & Dennis W. Gleiber. 1986. "The Process of Cabinet Dissolution: An Exponential Model of Duration and Stability in Western Democracies." *American Journal of Political Science* 30: 628–50.

Bruneau, Thomas C. & Alex Macleod. 1986. *Politics in Contemporary Portugal: Parties and the Consolidation of Democracy.* Colorado: Lynne Reinner Publishers, Inc.

Budge, Ian et al. 2001. *Mapping Policy Preferences: Estimates for Parties, Electors, and Governments 1945–1998.* United States: Oxford University Press.

Budge, Ian & Hans Keman. 1990. *Parties and Democracy: Coalition Formation and Government Functioning in Twenty States.* United States: Oxford University Press.

Budge, Ian & M. J. Laver. 1992. "Coalition Theory, Government Policy and Party Policy." In *Party Policy and Government Coalitions*, ed. Ian Budge & M. J. Laver. United States: St. Martin's Press, Inc.

Butler, David. 1999. "Australia." *Electoral Studies* 18: 411–13.

Caramani, Daniele. 1996. "The Swiss Parliamentary Election of 1995." *Electoral Studies* 15: 128–37.

———. 2000. *Elections in Western Europe since 1815: Electoral Results by Constituencies.* London: Macmillan Reference, 2000.

Cayrol, Roland. 1971. "Les préparitifs de la gauche." In *Les élections législatives de mars 1967*, ed. Roland Cayrol. Paris: Librairie Armand Colin.

Chagnollaud, D. & Jean-Louis Quermonne. 1996. *Le gouvernement de la France sous la cinquième république.* Paris: Fayard.

Charlot, Jean. 1971. "Les préparitifs de la majorité." In *Les élections législatives de mars 1967*, ed. Roland Cayrol. Paris: Librairie Armand Colin.

———. 1980. "L'opposition à la veille des élections législatives." In *SOFRES: L'état de l'opinion 1993*. Paris: Éditions du Seuil.

———. 1994. *La politique en France.* Le Livre de Poche.

Cheibub, José, Adam Przeworski, & Sebastian Saiegh. 2004. "Government Coalitions and Legislative Success under Presidentialism and Parliamentarism." *British Journal of Political Science* 34: 565–87.

Chhibber, Pradeep K. & Ken Kollman. 2004. *The Formation of National Party Systems:*

Federalism and Party Competition in Canada, Great Britain, India and the United States. New Jersey: Princeton University Press.

Christensen, Ray. 2000. *Ending the LDP Hegemony: Party Cooperation in Japan.* Honolulu: University of Hawaii Press.

Church, Clive H. 2004. *The Politics and Government of Switzerland.* United Kingdom: Palgrave Macmillan.

Cioffi-Revilla, Claudio. 1984. "The Political Reliability of Italian Governments." *American Political Science Review* 78: 318–37.

Clark, William Roberts & Matt Golder. 2006. "Rehabilitating Duverger's Theory: Testing the Mechanical and Strategic Modifying Effects of Electoral Laws." *Comparative Political Studies* 39.

Cleves, Mario A., William W. Gould, & Roberto G. Gutierrez. 2004. *An Introduction to Survival Analysis using STATA: Revised Edition.* College Station: STATA Press.

Clogg, Richard. 1987. *Parties and Elections in Greece: The Search for Legitimacy.* Durham: Duke University Press.

Cole, Alastair. 1990. "The Return of the Orleanist Right: The Union for French Democracy." In *French Parties in Transition,* ed. Alastair Cole. Great Britain: Dartmouth Publishing Company Limited.

Cole, Alastair & Peter Campbell. 1989. *French Electoral Systems and Elections since 1789.* England: Gower Publishing Company Limited.

Collins, Stephen. 2003. "Campaign Strategies." In *How Ireland Voted 2002,* ed. Michael Gallagher, Michael Marsh, & Paul Mitchell. Great Britain: Palgrave Macmillan.

Colomer, Josep. M. 2001. "The 2000 General Election in Spain." *Electoral Studies* 20: 490–95.

Conradt, David P. 1978. "The 1976 Campaign and Election: An Overview." In *Germany at the Polls: The Bundestag Election of 1976,* ed. Karl H. Cerny. Washington, D.C.: American Enterprise Institute for Public Policy Research.

———. 1990. "The Electorate, 1980–83." In *Germany at the Polls: The Bundestag Elections of the 1980s.* ed. Karl H. Cerny. United States: American Enterprise Institute for Public Policy Research.

Cox, Gary W. 1997. *Making Votes Count: Strategic Coordination in the World's Electoral Systems.* New York: Cambridge University Press.

Cunha, Carlos. 1997. "The Portuguese Communist Party." In *Political Parties and Democracy in Portugal: Organizations, Elections and Public Opinion,* ed. Thomas Bruneau. Colorado: Westview Press.

Daalder, Hans. 1987. "The Dutch Party System: From Segmentation to Polarization—And Then?" In *Party Systems in Denmark, Austria, Switzerland, the Netherlands, and Belgium,* ed. Hans Daalder. New York: St. Martin's Press.

Damgaard, Erik. 2000. "Denmark: The Life and Death of Government Coalitions." In *Coalition Governments in Western Europe,* ed. Wolfgang C. Müller & Kaare Strøm. Oxford: Oxford University Press.

Daniels, Philip. 1999. "Italy: Rupture and Regeneration?" In *Changing Party Systems in Western Europe,* ed. David Broughton, & Mark Donovan. London: Pinter.

De Jong, Jan & Bert Pijnenburg. 1986. "The Dutch Christian Democratic Party and Coalitional Behavior in the Netherlands: A Pivotal Party in the Face of Depillarisation."

In *Coalitional Behavior in Theory and Practice: An Inductive Model for Western Europe,* ed. Geoffrey Pridham. Great Britain: Cambridge University Press.

De Swaan, Abram. 1973. *Coalition Theories and Government Formation.* Amsterdam: Elsevier.

———. 1982. "The Netherlands: Coalitions in a Segmented Polity." In *Government Coalitions in Western Democracies,* ed. Eric C. Browne & John Dreijmanis. New York: Longman Inc.

De Winter, Lieven, Arco Timmermans, & Patrick Dumont. 2000. "Belgium: On Government Agreements, Evangelists, Followers and Heretics." In *Coalition Governments in Western Europe,* ed. Wolfgang C. Müller & Kaare Strøm. Oxford: Oxford University Press.

Dewachter, Wilfried. 1987. "Changes in a Particratie: The Belgian Party System from 1944 to 1986." In *Party Systems in Denmark, Austria, Switzerland, the Netherlands, and Belgium,* ed. Hans Daalder. New York: St. Martin's Press.

Diamond, Larry & Doh Chull Shin. 2000. "Institutional Reform and Democratic Consolidation in Korea." In *Institutional Reform and Democratic Consolidation in Korea,* ed. Larry Diamond & Doh Chull Shin. United States: Hoover Institution Press.

Diermeier, Daniel & Antonio Merlo. 2004. "An Empirical Investigation of Government Coalitional Bargaining Procedures." *Journal of Public Economics* 88: 783–97.

Diermeier, Daniel, Hulya Eraslan, & Antonio Merlo. 2003. "Bicameralism and Government Formation." Presented at the Annual Meeting of the Midwest Political Science Association, Chicago.

Diermeier, Daniel & Peter van Roozendahl. 1998. "The Duration of Cabinet Formation Processes in Western Multi-Party Democracies." *British Journal of Political Science* 28: 609–26.

Diermeier, Daniel & Randy T. Stevenson. 1999. "Cabinet Survival and Competing Risks." *American Journal of Political Science* 43: 1051–98.

Donegani, Jean-Marie & Marc Sadoun. 1992. "1958–1992: Le jeu des institutions." In *Histoire des droites en France: Politique (Vol. 1),* ed. Jean-François Sirinelli. Paris: Éditions Gallimard.

Dong, Wonmo. 1988. "Student Activism and the Presidential Politics of 1987 in South Korea." In *Political Change in South Korea,* ed. Ilpyong J. Kim & Young Whan Kihl. United States: Korean PWPA, Inc.

Downs, Anthony. 1957. *An Economic Theory of Democracy.* New York: Harper and Row.

Downs, William. 1998. *Coalition Government, Subnational Style: Multiparty Politics in Europe's Regional Parliaments.* Ohio: The Ohio State University Press.

Dreijmanis, John. 1982. "Austria: The 'Black'–'Red' Coalitions." In *Government Coalitions in Western Democracies,* ed. Eric C. Browne & John Dreijmanis. New York: Longman Inc.

Druckman, James N., Lanny W. Martin, & Michael F. Thies. 2005. "Influence without Confidence: Upper Chambers and Government Formation." *Legislative Studies Quarterly* 30: 529–48.

Druckman, James N. & Michael F. Thies. 2002. "The Importance of Concurrence: The Impact of Bicameralism on Government Formation and Duration." *British Journal of Political Science* 28: 609–26.

Du Roy, Albert & Robert Schneider. 1982. *Le roman de la rose: D'Épinay à l'Élysée, l'aventure des socialistes.* Paris: Éditions du Seuil.

Duhamel, Alain. 2000. "L'image de l'opposition vue par les Français." In *Analyses et résultats d'études: Chronique d'Alain Duhamel,* ed. Sofres. http://www.sofres.fr: Taylor Nelson/Sofres.

Duhamel, Olivier. 1995. "L'Après-élection: Quelle majorité?" In *Le vote de crise: L'Élection présidentielle de 1995,* ed. Pascal Perrineau & Colette Ysmal. Paris: Département d'Études Politiques du Figaro et Presses de la Fondation Nationale des Sciences Politiques.

———. 1999. *Droit constitutionnel: 1. Le pouvoir politique en France,* 4e Édition. Paris: Éditions du Seuil.

Dumont, Patrick & Lieven De Winter. 2000. "Luxembourg: Stable Coalitions in a Pivotal Party System." In *Coalition Government in Western Europe,* ed. Wolfgang C. Müller & Kaare Strøm. Oxford, Oxford University Press.

Duverger, Maurice. 1963 [1954]. *Political Parties: Their Organization and Activity in the Modern State.* 2nd ed. New York: John Wiley & Sons, Inc.

———. 1996. *Le système politique français.* 21st ed. Paris: PUF.

Elazar, Daniel J. 1979. "Israel's Compound Polity." In *Israel at the Polls: The Knesset Elections of 1977,* ed. Howard R. Penniman. United States: American Enterprise Institute for Public Policy Research.

Elklit, Jørgen. 2002. "The Politics of Electoral System Development and Change: The Danish Case." In *The Evolution of Electoral and Party Systems in the Nordic Countries,* ed. Bernard Grofman & Arend Lijphart. United States: Agathon Press.

Enelow, James & Melvin J. Hinich. 1981. "A New Approach to Voter Uncertainty in the Downsian Spatial Model." *American Journal of Political Science* 25: 483–93.

Esaiasson, Peter & Kurt Heidar. 2000. *Beyond Westminster and Congress: The Nordic Experience.* Ohio: The Ohio State University Press.

Esteban, Jorge de & Luis López Guerra. 1985. "Electoral Rules and Candidate Selection." In *Spain at the Polls, 1977, 1979, and 1982,* ed. Howard R. Penniman & Eusebio M. Mujal-León. United States: Duke University Press.

Fabre, Robert. 1978. *Toute vérité est bonne à dire: Histoire de la rupture.* Paris: Fayard.

Farrell, Brian. 1987. "Government Formation and Ministerial Selection." In *Ireland at the Polls 1981, 1982, and 1987: A Study of Four General Elections,* ed. Howard R. Penniman & Brian Farrell. United States: Duke University Press.

Fauvelle-Aymar, Christine & Michael Lewis-Beck. 2005. "Coalition Strategies and the National Front Vote in French Legislative Contests." *French Politics* 3: 164–77.

Ferrara, Frederico & Erik S. Herron. 2005. "Going It Alone? Strategic Entry under Mixed Electoral Rules." *American Journal of Political Science* 49: 16–31.

Fitzmaurice, John. 1986. "Coalitional Theory and Practice in Scandinavia." In *Coalitional Behavior in Theory and Practice: An Inductive Model for Western Europe,* ed. Geoffrey Pridham. Great Britain: Cambridge University Press.

Frain, Maritheresa. 1997. "The Right in Portugal: The PSD and the CDS/PP." In *Political Parties and Democracy in Portugal: Organizations, Elections, and Public Opinion,* ed. Thomas Bruneau. Colorado: Westview Press.

Franklin, Mark N. & Thomas T. Mackie. 1984. "Reassessing the Importance of Size and Ideology for the Formation of Governing Coalitions in Parliamentary Democracies." *American Journal of Political Science* 28: 671–92.

Frears, J. R. & Jean-Luc Parodi. 1979. *War Will Not Take Place: The French Parliamentary Elections of March 1978.* New York: Holmes and Meier Publishers.

Friedrich, Robert. 1982. "In Defense of Multiplicative Terms in Multiple Regression Equations." *American Journal of Political Science* 26: 797–833.

Fysh, Peter. 1996. "Candidates and Parties of the Right." In *Electing the French President: The 1995 Presidential Elections,* ed. Robert Elgie. New York: Macmillan Press Ltd.

Gaffney, John. 1997. "The Mainstream Right: Chirac and Balladur." In *French Presidentialism and the Election of 1995,* ed. John Gaffney & Lorna Milne. Vermont: Ashgate Publishing Company.

Gallagher, Michael. 1982. *The Irish Labour Party in Transition 1957–82.* Manchester: Manchester University Press.

———. 2003. "Stability and Turmoil: Analysis of the Results." In *How Ireland Voted 2002,* ed. Michael Gallagher, Michael Marsh, & Paul Mitchell. Great Britain: Palgrave Macmillan.

Gallager, Michael, Michael Laver, & Peter Mair. 2001. *Representative Government in Modern Europe: Institutions, Parties and Governments.* New York: McGraw-Hill.

Gildea, Robert. 1997. *France since 1945.* Oxford: Oxford University Press.

Gillespie, Richard. 1995. "Factionalism, the Left and the Transition to Democracy in Spain." In *Factional Politics and Democratization,* ed. Richard Gillespie, Michael Waller, & Lourdes López Nieto. London: Frank Cass and Co. Ltd.

Glasgow, Garrett & R. Michael Alvarez. 2005. "Voting Behavior and the Electoral Context of Government Formation." *Electoral Studies* 24: 245–64.

Golder, Matt. 2006. "Presidential Coattails and Legislative Fragmentation." *American Journal of Political Science* 50: 34–48.

———. 2005. "Democratic Electoral Systems around the World, 1946–2000." *Electoral Studies* 24: 103–21.

Golder, Sona N. 2005. "Pre-Electoral Coalitions in Comparative Perspective: A Test of Existing Hypotheses." *Electoral Studies* 24: 643–63.

———. 2000. "A New Theory of the Dynamics of Mainstream Right Parties in France." Presented at the Annual Meeting of the American Political Science Association.

Goldey, David. 1997. "Analysis of Election Results." In *French Presidentialism and the Election of 1995,* ed. John Gaffney & Lorna Milne. Vermont: Ashgate Publishing Company.

———. 1999. "The French Elections of 1997: The Stupidest Right in the World." Talk presented at the Institute of French Studies, New York University.

Grambsch, P. M. & T. M. Therneau. 1994. "Proportional Hazards Tests and Diagnostics Based on Weighted Residuals." *Biometrika* 81: 515–26.

Greene, William H. 2003. *Econometric Analysis.* 5th ed. New Jersey: Prentice-Hall, Inc.

Grimsson, Olafur R. 1982. "Iceland: A Multilevel Coalition System." In *Government Coalitions in Western Democracies,* ed. Eric C. Browne & John Dreijmanis. United States: Longman, Inc.

Groennings, Sven. 1970. "Notes toward Theories of Coalition Behavior in Multiparty Systems: Formation and Maintenance." In *The Study of Coalition Behavior: Theoretical Perspectives and Cases from Four Continents,* ed. Sven Groennings, E. W. Kelley, & Michael Leiserson. United States: Holt, Rinehart and Winston Inc.

Grofman, Bernard & Peter van Roozendaal. 1997. "Review Article: Modelling Cabinet Durability and Termination." *British Journal of Political Science* 27: 419–51.

Gunlicks, Arthur B. 1990. "Between the Elections in West Germany, 1976–90 and 1980–83." In *Germany at the Polls: The Bundestag Elections of the 1980s,* ed. Karl H. Cerny. United States: American Enterprise Institute for Public Policy Research.

Hadenius, Stig. 1990. *Swedish Politics during the 20th Century.* Sweden: The Swedish Institute.

Han, Sung-Joo. 1997. "South Korea: Politics in Transition." In *Democracy in Korea: Its Ideals and Realities,* ed. Sang-Yong Choi. Korea: Seoul Press.

Hancock, M. Donald. 1998. "Sweden's Nonsocialist Parties: What Difference Do They Make?" In *The European Center-Right at the End of the Twentieth Century,* ed. Frank L. Wilson. New York: St. Martin's Press.

Hanley, David. 1999. "Compromise, Party Management and Fair Shares: The Case of the French UDF." *Party Politics* 5: 171–89.

———. 2002. *Party, Society and Government: Republican Democracy in France.* New York: Berghahn Books.

Hardarson, Olafur T. 2002. "The Icelandic Electoral System 1844–1999." In *The Evolution of Electoral and Party Systems in the Nordic Countries,* ed. Bernard Grofman & Arend Lijphart. United States: Agathon Press.

Hayward, Jack. 1993. "The President and the Constitution: Its Spirit, Articles and Practice." In *De Gaulle to Mitterrand: Presidential Power in France,* ed. Jack Hayward. London: Hurst and Company.

Hecht, Emmanuel & Eric Mandonnet. 1987. *Au coeur du RPR: Enquête sur le parti du president.* Paris: Flammarion.

Henderson, Gregory. 1988. Constitutional Changes from the First to the Sixth Republics: 1948–1987. In *Political Change in South Korea,* ed. Ilpyong J. Kim & Young Whan Kihl. United States: Korean PWPA, Inc.

Heywood, Paul. 1995. *The Government and Politics of Spain.* New York: St. Martin's Press.

Hillebrand, Ron & Galen A. Irwin. 1999. "Changing Strategies: The Dilemma of the Dutch Labour Party." In *Policy, Office, or Votes? How Political Parties in Western Europe Make Hard Decisions,* ed. Wolfgang C. Müller & Kaare Strøm. United States: Cambridge University Press.

Hopkin, Jonathan. 1999. "Spain: Political Parties in a Young Democracy." In *Changing Party Systems in Western Europe,* ed. David Broughton & Mark Donovan. London: Pinter.

Hsiao, Cheng. 2003. *Analysis of Panel Data.* 2nd ed. Cambridge: Cambridge University Press.

Huber, John. 1996. *Rationalizing Parliament.* United States: Cambridge University Press.

Im, Hyug Baeg. 2000. "South Korean Democratic Consolidation in Comparative Perspective." In *Consolidating Democracy in South Korea,* ed. Larry Diamond & Byung-Kook Kim. United States: Lynne Rienner Publishers Inc.

Indriðason, Indriði. 2005. "A Theory of Coalitions and Clientelism: Coalition Politics in Iceland 1945–2000." *European Journal of Political Research.*

Irwin, Galen A. 1999. "The Dutch Parliamentary Election of 1998." *Electoral Studies* 18: 271–300.

Jackson, Julian. 1990. *The Popular Front: Defending Democracy, 1934–38.* Cambridge: Cambridge University Press.

Jaffré, Jérome. 1980. "The French Electorate in March 1978." In *The French National Assembly Elections of 1978*, ed. Howard R. Penniman. Washington D.C.: American Enterprise Institute for Public Policy Research.

———. 1986. "Les surprises de la droite." In *SOFRES: Opinion publique 1986*. Paris: Éditions Gallimard.

Jaung, Hoon. 2000. "Electoral Politics and Political Parties." In *Institutional Reform and Democratic Consolidation in Korea*, ed. Larry Diamond & Doh Chull Shin. United States: Hoover Institution Press.

Jenson, Jane. 1991. "The French Left: A Tale of Three Beginnings." In *Searching for the New France*, ed. James Hollifield & George Ross. New York: Routledge.

Johnson, R. W. 1981. *The Long March of the French Left*. Paris: Édition Gallimard.

Johnson, Stephen. 2000. *Opposition Politics in Japan: Strategies under a One-Party Dominant Regime*. London: Routledge.

Judt, Tony. 1986. *Marxism and the French Left: Essays on Labour and Politics in France, 1830–1981*. Oxford: Clarendon Press.

Kaminski, Marek. 2001. "Coalitional Stability of Multi-Party Systems: Evidence from Poland." *American Journal of Political Science* 45: 294–312.

———. 2002. "Do Parties Benefit from Electoral Manipulation? Electoral Laws and Heresthetics in Poland, 1989–1993." *Journal of Theoretical Politics* 14: 325–58.

Keeler, John T. S. & Martin A. Schain. 1996. "Presidents, Premiers, and Models of Democracy in France." In *Chirac's Challenge: Liberalization, Europeanization, and Malaise in France*, ed. John T. S. Keeler & Martin A. Schain. New York: St. Martin's Press.

Kerr, Henry H. 1987. "The Swiss Party System: Steadfast and Changing." In *Party Systems in Denmark, Austria, Switzerland, the Netherlands, and Belgium*, ed. Hans Daalder. New York: St. Martin's Press.

Kihl, Young Whan. 1988a. "Party Politics on the Eve of a Gathering Storm: The Constitutional Revision Politics of 1986." In *Political Change in South Korea*, ed. Ilpyong J. Kim & Young Whan Kihl. United States: Korean PWPA, Inc.

———. 1988b. "South Korea's Search for a New Order: An Overview." In *Political Change in South Korea*, ed. Ilpyong J. Kim & Young Whan Kihl. United States: Korean PWPA, Inc.

Kim, Byung-Kook. 2000a. "Electoral Politics and Electoral Crisis, 1997–1998." In *Consolidating Democracy in South Korea*, ed. Larry Diamond & Byung-Kook Kim. United States: Lynne Rienner Publishers Inc.

———. 2000b. "Party Politics in South Korea's Democracy: The Crisis of Success." In *Consolidating Democracy in South Korea*, ed. Larry Diamond & Byung-Kook Kim. United States: Lynne Rienner Publishers Inc.

Kim, HeeMin. 1997. "Rational Choice Theory and Third World Politics: The 1990 Party Merger in Korea." *Comparative Politics* 30: 83–100.

King, Gary et al. 1990. "A Unified Model of Cabinet Dissolution in Parliamentary Democracies." *American Journal of Political Science* 34: 846–71.

King, Gary, Robert Keohane, & Sidney Verba. 1994. *Designing Social Inquiry: Scientific Inference in Qualitative Research*. New Jersey: Princeton University Press.

King, Gary & Langche Zeng. 2001. "Explaining Rare Events in International Relations." *International Organization* 55: 693–715.

Kitschelt, Herbert. 1994. *The Transformation of European Social Democracy.* United States: Cambridge University Press.

Klingemann, H.-D., R. Hofferbert, & Ian Budge. 1994. *Parties, Policies and Democracy.* Boulder: Westview Press.

Knapp, Andrew. 1999. "What's Left of the French Right: The RPR and the UDF from Conquest to Humiliation, 1993–1998." *West European Politics* 22.

Kohler, Beate. 1982. *Political Forces in Spain, Greece and Portugal.* London: Butterworth & Co (Publishers) Ltd.

Kohno, Masaru. 1997. *Japan's Postwar Party Politics.* New Jersey: Princeton University Press.

Koole, Ruud A. 1994. "The Vulnerability of the Modern Cadre Party in the Netherlands." In *How Parties Organize in Western Democracies,* ed. Richard S. Katz & Peter Mair. London: Sage Publications.

Krisjánsson, Svanur. 1998. "Electoral Politics and Governance: Transformation of the Party System in Iceland." In *Comparing Party System Change,* ed, Paul Pennings & Jan-Erik Lane. London: Routledge.

———. 2002. "Iceland: From Party Rule to Pluralist Political Society." In *Party Sovereignty and Citizen Control: Selecting Candidates for Parliamentary Elections,* ed. Hanne Marthe Narud, Mogens N. Pederesn, & Henry Valen. Denmark: University Press of Southern Denmark.

Kuhn, Thomas. 1962. *The Structure of Scientific Revolutions.* Chicago: University of Chicago Press.

Kuitunen, Soile. 2002. "Finland: Formalized Procedures with Member Predominance." In *Party Sovereignty and Citizen Control: Selecting Candidates for Parliamentary Elections,* ed. Hanne Marthe Narud, Mogens N. Pederesen, & Henry Valen. Denmark: University Press of Southern Denmark.

Laakso, Markku & Rein Taagepera. 1979. "Effective Number of Parties: A Measure with Application to Western Europe." *Comparative Political Studies* 12: 3–27.

Lauber, Volkmar. 1996. "Conclusion and Outlook." In *Contemporary Austrian Politics,* ed. Volkmar Lauber. Colorado: Westview Press Inc.

Lavau, George & Janine Mossuz-Lavau. 1980. "The Union of the Left's Defeat: Suicide or Congenital Weakness." In *The French National Assembly Elections of 1978,* ed. Howard, R. Penniman. Washington D.C.: American Enterprise Institute for Public Policy Research.

Laver, Michael. 1998. "Models of Government Coordination." *Annual Review of Political Science* 1: 1–25.

———. 2003. "Government Termination." *Annual Review of Political Science* 6: 23–40.

Laver, M. J. 1992. "Coalition and Party Policy in Ireland." In *Party Policy and Government Coalitions,* ed. M. J. Laver & Ian Budge. New York: St. Martin's Press.

Laver, M. J. & Ian Budge. 1992. *Party Policy and Government Coalitions.* New York: St. Martin's Press.

Laver, Michael & Kenneth Shepsle. 1990. "Coalitions and Cabinet Government." *American Political Science Review* 84: 873–80.

———. 1996. *Making and Breaking Governments: Cabinets and Legislatures in Parliamentary Democracies.* United States: Cambridge University Press.

Laver, Michael & Norman Schofield. 1998. *Multiparty Government: The Politics of Coalition in Europe*. 2nd ed. United States: University of Michigan Press.

Leblang, David. 2002. "Political Uncertainty and Speculative Attacks." In *Coping with Globalization: Cross-National Patterns in Domestic Governance and Policy Performance*, ed. Steve Chan & James Scarritt. London: Frank Cass.

Leblang, David & Bumba Mukherjee. 2005. "Elections, Partisanship and Stock Market Performance: Theory and Evidence from a Century of American and British Returns." *American Journal of Political Science* 49: 780–802.

Leiserson, Michael. 1968. "Factions and Coalitions in One-Party Japan: An Interpretation Based on the Theory of Games." *American Political Science Review* 62: 70–87.

Lijphart, Arend. 1994. *Electoral Systems and Party Systems: A Study of Twenty-Seven Democracies 1945–1990*. New York: Oxford University Press.

———. 1999. *Patterns of Democracy: Government Forms and Performance in Thirty-Six Countries*. New Haven: Yale University Press.

Lloyd-Jones, Stewart. 2002. "The 1999 Parliamentary Elections and 2001 Presidential Elections in Portugal." *Electoral Studies* 21: 114–22.

Long, J. Scott. 1997. *Regression Models for Categorical and Limited Dependent Variables*. London: Sage Publications.

López-Pintor, Rafael. 1985a. "Francoist Reformers in Democratic Spain: The Popular Alliance and the Democratic Coalition." In *Spain at the Polls, 1977, 1979, and 1982*, ed. Howard R. Penniman & Eusebio M. Mujal-León. United States: Duke University Press.

———. 1985a. "The October 1982 General Election and the Evolution of the Spanish Party System." In *Spain at the Polls, 1977, 1979, and 1982*, ed. Howard R. Penniman & Eusebio M. Mujal-León. United States: Duke University Press.

Lupia, Arthur & Kaare Strøm. 1995. "Coalition Termination and the Strategic Timing of Legislative Elections." *American Political Science Review* 89: 648–65.

Mackie, Thomas & Richard Rose. 1991. *The International Almanac of Electoral History*. London: Macmillan.

Magone, José M. 2000. "Portugal: The Rationale of Democratic Regime Building." In *Coalition Governments in Western Europe*, ed. Wolfgang C. Müller & Kaare Strøm. Oxford: Oxford University Press.

Mair, Peter. 1987. "Party Organization, Vote Management, and Candidate Selection: Toward the Nationalization of Electoral Strategy in Ireland." In *Ireland at the Polls 1981, 1982, and 1987: A Study of Four General Elections*, ed. Howard R. Penniman & Brian Farrell. United States: Duke University Press.

———. 1999. "Party Competition and the Changing Party System." In *Politics in the Republic of Ireland*. 3rd ed. Ed. John Coakley & Michael Gallagher. New York: Routledge.

Marradi, Alberto. 1982. "Italy: From 'Centrism' to Crisis on the Center-Left Coalitions." In *Government Coalitions in Western Democracies*, ed. Eric C. Browne & John Dreijmanis. United States: Longman, Inc.

Martin, Lanny W. & Georg Vanberg. 2003. "Wasting Time? The Impact of Ideology and Size on Delay in Coalition Formation." *British Journal of Political Science* 33: 323–44.

Martin, Lanny W. & Randolph T. Stevenson. 2001. "Government Formation in Parliamentary Democracies." *American Journal of Political Science* 45: 33–50.

Martin, Pierre. 1993. "La désignation des candidats socialistes: Plus de continuité que de changement." In *Le vote sanction: Les élections législatives des 21 et 28 mars 1993*, ed. Pascal Perrineau & Colette Ysmal. Paris: Département d'Études Politiques du Figaro et Presses de la Fondation Nationale des Sciences Politiques.

———. 1999. "Les élections du 15 mars 1998 dans la région Rhône-Alpes." In *Le vote incertain: Les élections régionales de 1998*, ed. Pascal Perrineau & Domonique Renié. Paris: Presses de la Fondation Nationale des Sciences Politiques.

Massart, Alexis. 1999. *L'Union pour la Démocratie Française (UDF)*. Paris: L'Harmattan.

Mastropaolo, Alfio & Martin Slater. 1992. "Party Policy and Coalition Bargaining in Italy, 1948–87: Is There Order behind the Chaos?" In *Party Policy and Government Coalitions*, ed. M. J. Laver & Ian Budge. New York: St. Martin's Press.

Mayhew, David. 1974. *Congress: The Electoral Connection*. New Haven: Yale University Press.

Mazey, Sonia. 1996. "The Issue Agenda in Perspective." In *Electing the French President: The 1995 Presidential Elections*, ed. Robert Elgie. New York: Macmillan Press Ltd.

McAllister, Ian. 2003. "The Federal Election in Australia, November 2001." *Electoral Studies* 22: 381–87.

McFadden, D. 1973. "Conditional Logit Analysis of Qualitative Choice Behavior." In *Frontiers of Economics*, ed. P. Zarembka. New York: Academic Press.

———. 1974. "The Measurement of Urban Travel Demand." *Journal of Public Economics* 3: 303–28.

Melchior, Eric. 1993. *Le PS, du projet au pouvoir: L'impossible concordance*. Paris: L'Atelier.

Mény, Yves. 1996. "France: The Institutionalization of Leadership." In *Political Institutions in Europe*, ed. Josep Colomer. New York: Routledge.

Merlo, Antonio. 1997. "Bargaining over Governments in a Stochastic Environment." *Journal of Political Economy* 105: 101–31.

Mershon, Carol. 2002. *The Costs of Coalition*. United States: Stanford University Press.

Mitchell, Paul. 1999. "Government Formation: A Tale of Two Coalitions." In *How Ireland Voted 1997*, ed. Michael Marsh & Paul Mitchell. Colorado: Westview.

Morriss, Peter. 1996. "Electoral Politics in South Korea." *Electoral Politics* 15: 550–62.

Morrow, James. 1994. *Game Theory for Political Scientists*. New Jersey: Princeton University Press.

Müller, Wolfgang C. 2000. "Austria: Tight Coalitions and Stable Government." In *Coalition Governments in Western Europe*, eds. Wolfgang C. Müller & Kaare Strøm. Oxford: Oxford University Press.

Müller, Wolfgang C. and Kaare Strøm. 1999. "Political Parties and Hard Choices." In *Policy, Office, or Votes? How Political Parties in Western Europe Make Hard Decisions*, eds. Wolfgang C. Müller & Kaare Strøm. United States: Cambridge University Press.

———. 2000a. *Coalition Governments in Western Europe*. Oxford: Oxford University Press.

———. 2000b. "Conclusions: Coalition Government in Western Europe." In *Coalition Governments in Western Europe*, eds. Wolfgang C. Müller & Kaare Strøm. Oxford: Oxford University Press.

Murphy, Gary. 2003. "The Background to the Election." In *How Ireland Voted 2002*, eds. Michael Gallagher, Michael Marsh & Paul Mitchell. Great Britain: Palgrave Macmillan.

Nam, Koon Woo. 1989. *South Korean Politics: The Search for Political Consensus.* United States: University Press of America.

Napel, Hans-Martien Ten. "The Netherlands: Resilience amid Change." In *Changing Party Systems in Western Europe,* ed. David Broughton & Mark Donovan. London: Pinter.

Narud, Hanne Marthe & Kaare Strøm. 2000. "Norway: A Fragile Coalition Order." In *Coalition Governments in Western Europe,* ed. Wolfgang C. Müller & Kaare Strøm. Oxford: Oxford University Press.

Nay, Catherine. 1994. *Le dauphin et le régent.* Paris: Éditions Grasset et Fasquelle.

Newell, James L. 2000. *Parties and Democracy in Italy.* Vermont: Ashgate.

Newton, Michael T. 1997. *Institutions of Modern Spain: A Political and Economic Guide.* New York: Cambridge University Press.

Norpoth, Helmut. 1982. "The German Federal Republic: Coalition Government at the Brink of Majority Rule." In *Government Coalitions in Western Democracies,* ed. Eric C. Browne & John Dreijmanis. United States: Longman, Inc.

Norton, Philip. 1984. *The British Polity.* London: Longman.

Nousiainen, Jaako. 2000. "Finland: The Consolidation of Parliamentary Governance." In *Coalition Governments in Western Europe,* ed. Wolfgang C. Müller & Kaare Strøm. Oxford: Oxford University Press.

Oberdorfer, Don. 2001. *The Two Koreas: A Contemporary History.* United States: Basic Books.

Oh, John Kie-chiang. 1999. *Korean Politics: The Quest for Democratization and Economic Development.* New York: Cornell University Press.

Osborne, Martin & Ariel Rubinstein. 1990. *Bargaining and Markets.* United States: Academic Press.

Papayannakis, Michalis. 1981. "The Crisis on the Greek Left." In *Greece at the Polls: The National Elections of 1974 and 1977,* ed. Howard R. Penniman. Washington D.C.: American Enterprise Institute for Public Policy Research.

Pappi, Franz Urban & Paul W. Thurner. 2002. "Electoral Behavior in a Two-Vote System: Incentives for Ticket Splitting in German Bundestag Elections." *European Journal of Political Research* 41: 207–32.

Park, Jin. 1990. "Political Change in South Korea: The Challenge of the Conservative Alliance." *Asian Survey* 30: 1154–68.

Peele, Gillian. 1995. *Governing the UK.* 3rd ed. Oxford: Blackwell Publishers Ltd.

Penniman, Howard R., ed. 1979. *Israel at the Polls: The Knesset Elections of 1977.* Washington D.C.: American Enterprise Institute for Public Policy Research.

Pesonen, Pertti & Alastair H. Thomas. 1983. "Coalition Formation in Scandinavia." In *Coalition Government in Western Europe,* ed. Vernon Bogdanor. Great Britain: Heinemann Educational Books.

Pierce, Roy. 1980. "French Legislative Elections: The Historical Background." In *The French National Assembly Elections of 1978,* ed. Howard R. Penniman. Washington D.C.: American Enterprise Institute for Public Policy Research.

Pinto-Duschinsky, Michael. 1999. "Send the Rascals Packing: Defects of Proportional Representation and the Virtues of the Westminster Model." *Representation* 36: 117–26.

Portelli, Hughes. 1994. *La politique en France sous la Ve République.* Paris: Grasset.

Powell, G. Bingham. 2000. *Elections as Instruments of Democracy: Majoritarian and Proportional Visions.* New Haven: Yale University Press.

Przeworski, A. et al. 2000. *Democracy and Development: Political Institutions and Material Well-Being in the World, 1950–1990.* New York: Cambridge University Press.

Pulzer, Peter. 1983. "Germany." In *Democracy and Elections: Electoral Systems and Their Political Consequences,* ed. Vernon Bogdanor & David Butler. Cambridge: Cambridge University Press.

Quinn, Kevin M. & Andrew D. Martin. 2002. "An Integrated Computational Model of Multiparty Electoral Competition." *Statistical Science* 17: 405–19.

Rae, Douglas. 1967. *The Political Consequences of Electoral Laws.* New Haven: Yale University Press.

Rasmussen, Jorgen. 1991. "They Also Serve: Small Parties in the British Political System." In *Small Parties in Western Europe: Comparative and National Perspective,* ed. Ferdinand Müller-Rommel & Geoffrey Pridham. London: Sage.

Rémond, René. 1982. *Les droites en France.* Paris: Éditions Auber Montaigne.

Rhodes, Martin. 1995. "Reinventing the Left: The Origins of Italy's Progressive Alliance." In *Italian Politics: Ending the First Republic,* ed. Carol Mershon & Gianfranco Pasquino. United States: Westview Press.

Riker, William. 1962. *The Theory of Political Coalitions.* New Haven: Yale University Press.

Roberts, Geoffrey K. 1988. "The 'Second-Vote' Campaign Strategy of the West Germany Free Democratic Party." *European Journal of Political Research* 16: 317–37.

Rochan, Thomas R. 1999. "Adaptation in the Dutch Party System: Social Change and Party Response." In *Comparative Political Parties and Party Elites: Essays in Honor of Samuel J. Eldersveld,* ed. Birol A. Yeþilada. Ann Arbor: University of Michigan Press.

Rommetvedt, Hilmar. 1992. "Norway: From Consensual Majority Parliamentarism to Dissensual Parliamentarism." In *Parliamentary Change in the Nordic Countries,* ed. Erik Damgaard. Oslo: Scandinavian University Press.

Saalfeld, Thomas. 2000. "Germany: Stable Parties, Chancellor Democracy, and the Art of Informal Settlement." In *Coalition Governments in Western Europe,* ed. Wolfgang C. Müller & Kaare Strøm. Oxford: Oxford University Press.

Sannerstedt, Anders & Mats Sjölin. 1992. "Sweden: Changing Party Relations in a More Active Parliament." In *Parliamentary Change in the Nordic Countries,* ed. Erik Damgaard. Oslo: Scandinavian University Press.

Särlvik, Bo. 1977. "Recent Electoral Trends in Sweden." In *Scandinavia at the Polls: Recent Political Trends in Denmark, Norway, and Sweden,* ed. Karl H. Cerny. Washington D.C.: American Enterprise Institute for Public Policy Research.

———. 1983. "Coalition Politics and Policy Output in Scandinavia: Sweden, Denmark and Norway." In *Coalition Government in Western Europe,* ed. Vernon Bogdanor. Great Britain: Heinemann Educational Books.

———. 2002. "Party and Electoral System in Sweden." In *The Evolution of Electoral and Party Systems in the Nordic Countries,* ed. Bernard Grofman & Arend Lijphart. United States: Agathon Press.

Sartori, Giovanni. 1976. *Parties and Party Systems.* Cambridge: Cambridge University Press.

Schain, Martin. 1991. "Toward a Centrist Democracy? The Fate of the French Right." In *Searching for a New France,* ed. James Hollifield & George Ross. New York: Routledge.

Schlesinger, Joseph & Mildred Schlesinger. 2000. "The Stability of the French Party

System: The Enduring Impact of the Two-Ballot Electoral Rules." In *How France Votes*, ed. Michael S. Lewis-Beck. New York: Chatham House Publishers.

Schmidt, Vivien. 1996. *From State to Market: The Transformation of French Business and Government.* Cambridge: Cambridge University Press.

Schoen, Harald. 1999. "Split-Ticket Voting in German Federal Elections, 1953–90: An Example of Sophisticated Balloting?" *Electoral Studies* 18: 473–96.

Schou, Tove-Lise & Derek John Hearl. 1992. "Party and Coalition Policy in Denmark." In *Party Policy and Government Coalitions*, ed. M. J. Laver & Ian Budge. London: Macmillan.

Shaffer, William R. 1998. *Politics, Parties, and Parliaments: Political Change in Norway.* Ohio: The Ohio State University Press.

Sharman, C., A. M. Sayers, & N. Miragliotta. 2002. "Trading Party Preferences: The Australian Experience of Preferential Voting." *Electoral Studies* 21: 543–60.

Shepsle, Kenneth A. 1991. *Models of Multiparty Electoral Competition.* New York: Harwood Academic Publishers.

Shepsle, Kenneth A. & Mark S. Bonchek. 1997. *Analyzing Politics: Rationality, Behavior, and Institutions.* New York: W. W. Norton and Company, Inc.

Shugart, Matthew Soberg. 2001. "Extreme Electoral Systems and the Appeal of the Mixed-Member Alternative." In *Mixed-Member Electoral Systems: The Best of Both Worlds?*, ed. Matthew Soberg Shugart & Martin P. Wattenberg. United States: Oxford University Press.

Sigelman, Lee & Langche Zeng. 1999. "Analyzing Censored and Sample-Selected Data with Tobit and Heckit Models." *Political Analysis* 8: 167–82.

Singer, Judith D. & John B. Willett. 2003. *Applied Longitudinal Data Analysis: Modeling Change and Event Occurrence.* New York: Oxford University Press.

Sinnott, Richard. 1987. "The Voters, the Issues, and the Party System." In *Ireland at the Polls 1981, 1982, and 1987: A Study of Four General Elections,* ed. Howard R. Penniman & Brian Farrell. United States: Duke University Press.

Smith, Alastair. 2004. *Election Timing.* United States: Cambridge University Press.

Snyder, James M., Jr & Michael M. Ting. 2002. "An Informational Rationale for Political Parties." *American Journal of Political Science* 46: 90–110.

Spoon, Jae-Jae. 2004. "The Evolution of New Parties: From Electoral Outsiders to Downsian Players—Evidence from the French Greens." Presented at the Annual Meeting of the American Political Science Association, Chicago.

Strøm, Kaare. 1984. "Minority Governments in Parliamentary Democracies: The Rationality of Nonwinning Cabinet Solutions." *Comparative Political Studies* 17: 199–227.

———. 1985. "Party Goals and Government Performance in Parliamentary Democracies." *American Political Science Review* 79: 738–54.

———. 1990. *Minority Governments and Majority Rule.* Cambridge: Cambridge University Press.

Strøm, Kaare, Ian Budge, & Michael J. Laver. 1994. "Constraints on Cabinet Formation in Parliamentary Democracies." *American Journal of Political Science* 38: 303–35.

Strøm, Kaare & Jorn Y. Leiphart. 1992. "Norway: Policy Pursuit and Coalition Avoidance." In *Party Policy and Government Coalitions*, ed. Ian Budge & M. L. Laver. United States: St. Martin's Press.

Strøm, Kaare & Torbjörn Bergman. 1992. "Sweden: Social Democratic Dominance in One Dimension." In *Party Policy and Government Coalitions,* ed. Ian Budge & M. L. Laver. United States: St. Martin's Press.

Strøm, Kaare & Wolfgang C. Müller. 2000. "The Keys to Togetherness: Coalition Agreements in Parliamentary Democracies." In *The Uneasy Relationship between Parliamentary Members and Leaders,* ed. Lawrence D. Longley & Reuven Y. Hazen. London: Frank Cass and Company Limited.

Strøm, Kaare, Wolfgang C. Müller, & Torbjörn Bergman, eds. 2003. *Delegation and Accountability in Parliamentary Democracies.* Oxford: Oxford University Press.

Sundberg, Jan. 2002. "The Electoral System of Finland: Old and Working Well." In *The Evolution of Electoral and Party Systems in the Nordic Countries,* ed. Bernard Grofman & Arend Lijphart. United States: Agathon Press.

Taagepera, Rein. 1998a. "Effective Magnitude and Effective Threshold." *Electoral Studies* 17: 393–404.

———. 1998b. "Nationwide Inclusion and Exclusion Thresholds." *Electoral Studies* 17: 405–17.

Taagepera, Rein & Matthew Shugart. 1989. *Seats and Votes: The Effects and Determinants of Electoral Systems.* New Haven: Yale University Press.

Thiébault, Jean-Louis. 2000. "France: Forming and Maintaining Government Coalitions in the Fifth Republic." In *Coalition Governments in Western Europe,* ed. Wolfgang C. Müller & Kaare Strøm. Oxford: Oxford University Press.

Timmermans, Arco & Rudy B. Andeweg. 2000. "The Netherlands: Still the Politics of Accommodation?" In *Coalition Governments in Western Europe,* ed. Wolfgang C. Müller & Kaare Strøm. Oxford: Oxford University Press.

Tops, Pieter & Karl Dittrich. 1992. "The Role of Policy in Dutch Coalition Building, 1946–81." In *Party Policy and Government Coalitions,* ed. M. J. Laver & Ian Budge. New York: St. Martin's Press.

Tsebelis, George. 1990. *Nested Games: Rational Choice in Comparative Politics.* California: University of California Press.

———. 2002. *Veto Players: How Political Institutions Work.* New Jersey: Princeton University Press.

Valen, Henry & Willy Martinussen. 1977. "Electoral Trends and Foreign Politics in Norway: The 1973 Storting Election and the EEC Issue." In *Scandinavia at the Polls: Recent Political Trends in Denmark, Norway and Sweden,* ed. Karl H. Cerny. Washington D.C.: American Enterprise Institute for Public Policy Research.

van Deemen, A. M. A. 1989. "Dominant Players and Minimum Size Coalitions." *European Journal of Political Research* 23: 1–33.

Verzichelli, Luca & Maurizio Cotta. 2000. "Italy: From 'Constrained' Coalitions to Alternating Governments." In *Coalition Governments in Western Europe,* ed. Wolfgang C. Müller & Kaare Strøm. Oxford: Oxford University Press.

Vowles, Jack. 2002. "The General Election in New Zealand, November 1999." *Electoral Studies* 21: 134–39.

Warwick, Paul V. 1979. "The Durability of Coalition Governments in Parliamentary Government." *Comparative Political Studies* 11: 465–98.

———. 1992. "Rising Hazards: An Underlying Dynamic of Parliamentary Government." *American Journal of Political Science* 36: 857–76.

———. 1994. *Government Survival in Parliamentary Democracies.* New York: Cambridge University Press.

———. 1996. "Coalition Government Membership in Western European Parliamentary Democracies." *British Journal of Political Science* 26: 471–99.

———. 1999. "Ministerial Autonomy or Ministerial Accommodation? Contested Bases of Government Survival in Parliamentary Democracies." *British Journal of Political Science* 29: 369–94.

———. 2005. "Do Policy Horizons Structure the Formation of Parliamentary Governments? The Evidence from an Expert Survey." *American Journal of Political Science* 49: 373–87.

Warwick, Paul V. & James N. Druckman. 2001. "Portfolio Salience and the Proportionality of Payoffs on Coalition Governments." *British Journal of Political Science* 31: 627–49.

Warwick, Paul V. & S. T. Easton. 1992. "The Cabinet Stability Controversy: New Perspectives on a Classic Problem." *American Journal of Political Science* 36: 122–46.

Williams, Philip M., David Goldey, & Martin Harrison. 1970. *French Politicians and Elections 1951–1969.* London: Cambridge University Press.

Wilson, Frank L. 1998. "The French Right in Search of Itself." In *The European Center-Right at the End of the Twentieth Century,* ed. Frank L. Wilson. New York: St. Martin's Press.

Wooldridge, Jeffrey M. 2002. *Econometric Analysis of Cross Section and Panel Data.* Cambridge: MIT Press.

Wright, Gordon. 1995. *France in Modern Times: 1760 to the Present.* Chicago: Rand McNally and Company.

Ysmal, Collette. 1989. *Les parties politiques sous la Ve République.* Paris: Éditions Montchestien.

———. 1993. "Les logiques d'un choix sous contraintes: Le second tour." In *Le vote sanction: Les élections législatives des 21 et 28 mars 1993,* ed. Pascal Perrineau & Collete Ysmal. Paris: Département d'Études Politiques du Figaro et Presses de la Fondation Nationale des Sciences Politiques.

AUTHOR INDEX

SUBJECT INDEX

Parliaments and Legislatures

JANET M. BOX-STEFFENSMEIER AND DAVID T. CANON, SERIES EDITORS

Parliaments and Legislatures is a series of books on legislative and parliamentary assemblies across the globe, with a focus on the U.S. Congress. We are actively recruiting new work of high quality and innovation for publication in the series and welcome all methodological approaches.

Challenging Parties, Changing Parliaments: Women and Elected Office in Contemporary Western Europe
Miki Caul Kittilson

Parties, Rules, and the Evolution of Congressional Budgeting
Lance T. LeLoup

The Power of the People: Congressional Competition, Public Attention, and Voter Retribution
Sean M. Theriault

101 Chambers: Congress, State Legislatures, and the Future of Legislative Studies
Peverill Squire and Keith E. Hamm

Doing the Right Thing: Collective Action and Procedural Choice in the New Legislative Process
Lawrence Becker

Authorizing Policy
Thad Hall

Congress Responds to the Twentieth Century
Edited by Sunil Ahuja and Robert Dewhirst

Committees in Post-Communist Democratic Parliaments: Comparative Institutionalization
Edited by David M. Olson and William E. Crowther

U.S. Senate Exceptionalism
Edited by Bruce I. Oppenheimer

www.ingramcontent.com/pod-product-compliance
Lightning Source LLC
Chambersburg PA
CBHW020702270326
41928CB00005B/229